THE SUFI MESSAGE

VOLUME V

Pir-o-Murshid
Hazrat Inayat Khan

HAZRAT INAYAT KHAN

Spiritual Liberty

MOTILAL BANARSIDASS PUBLISHERS
PRIVATE LIMITED • DELHI

Reprint : Delhi, 1995, 2003, 2009
First Indian Edition : Delhi, 1989

Vol. V ISBN : 978-81-208-0609-2 (Cloth)
ISBN : 978-81-208-0610-8 (Paper)
Set ISBN : 978-81-208-0494-4 (Cloth)
ISBN : 978-81-208-0495-1 (Paper)

MOTILAL BANARSIDASS
41 U.A. Bungalow Road, Jawahar Nagar, Delhi 110 007
8 Mahalaxmi Chamber, 22 Bhulabhai Desai Road, Mumbai 400 026
203 Royapettah High Road, Mylapore, Chennai 600 004
236, 9th Main III Block, Jayanagar, Bangalore 560 011
Sanas Plaza, 1302 Baji Rao Road, Pune 411 002
8 Camac Street, Kolkata 700 017
Ashok Rajpath, Patna 800 004
Chowk, Varanasi 221 001

PRINTED IN INDIA
BY JAINENDRA PRAKASH JAIN AT SHRI JAINENDRA PRESS,
A-45, NARAINA, PHASE-I, NEW DELHI 110 028
AND PUBLISHED BY NARENDRA PRAKASH JAIN FOR
MOTILAL BANARSIDASS PUBLISHERS PRIVATE LIMITED,
BUNGALOW ROAD, DELHI 110 007

CONTENTS

PREFACE TO THE SERIES

THE present volume is the first of a series including all the works intended for publication of Hazrat Inayat Khan (Baroda 1882–New Delhi 1927), the great Sufi mystic who came to the Western world in 1910 and lectured and taught there until his passing away in 1927.

A new edition of this series, which was published for the International Headquarters of the Sufi Movement in the West in the '60s, is now made available in the Indian subcontinent and the Middle East. In this way Hazrat Inayat Khan's inspired and universal vision of the Sufi Message returns to his own beloved country, where it originated and where interest in it is growing.

This book and other volumes of this series have not been written down by the author. They contain his lectures, discourses and other teachings as taken down in shorthand and other handwriting. When preparing for publication great care was taken, not only to avoid distortion of their intent and meaning, but also to leave intact, as far as possible, the flow of mystical inspiration and poetical expression which add so much to their spell, and without which a significant part of his message would be lost. Although speaking in a tongue foreign to him, he moulded it into a perfect vehicle for his thought, at times somewhat ungrammatical and unusual, but always as clear and precise as his often difficult and abstruse subjects would allow.

It goes without saying that neither in the present nor in the previous edition anything has been altered which would involve even the slightest deviation from the author's intention and no attempt has been made to transform his highly personal and colourful language into idiomatically unimpeachable English. Already so much is necessarily lost by the transfer of the spoken word to the printed page, that every effort has been made, as it should, to preserve the Master's melodious phrasing, the radiance of his personality, and the subtle sense of humour which never left him.

Hazrat Inayat Khan's teaching was nearly all given during the years 1918–1926. It covers a great many subjects, several of which were grouped in series of lectures and taken up again some years later. Certain subjects may cover nearly the same ground as others; stories and examples which abound in most of his works are met again elsewhere; and much of what he taught one finds repeated in several places. This was intentional, as repetition belonged to Hazrat Inayat Khan's method of teaching; it is for the student to become aware of the subtle differences in each context. For these and other reasons it would be difficult to follow a rigid system in publishing Hazrat Inayat Khan's works; a chronological grouping of his lectures would be very unsatisfactory, and a stringent classification according to subject-matter hardly feasible.

The complete series contains fourteen volumes. The last volume is the Index. This edition is the first one to present an index to the Sufi Message of Hazrat Inayat Khan.

Each volume is complete in itself, and therefore may be read without any necessity to study following or previous ones. However, one may get a spiritual and mental appetite to continue reading. One will find that a meditative way of reading will convey not only the words but also the spiritual power emanating from them, tuning mind, heart and soul to the pitch which is one's own.

W.v.L.

PREFACE TO VOLUME V

"Beloved ones of God, you may belong to any race, caste, creed, or nation, still you are impartially beloved by God" (p. 11). This book is on our divine heritage, the light of the soul, a spark of the Divine Light. The soul longs for freedom. Therefore Hazrat Inayat Khan has termed the Sufi Message the message of spiritual liberty. This refers to the state where one is no longer dependent on outer circumstances and on the fancies of one's mind for inner peace and happiness. Liberty is reached through discipline. Discipline is gained through love and sympathy for both the goal and the way.

This book presents a number of texts on this subject matter. In 1910 Hazrat Inayat Khan set forth from his native India to the West, where he was to bring his Sufi message. In the first four years he travelled extensively in the United States and Europe, and at the outbreak of the First World War he settled down temporarily in London, where he gathered around him a group of pupils to whom he started to teach the fundamentals of Sufi thoughts and ideas. A part of those teachings which were suited for wider distribution were collected in the books contained in this volume, the fifth of the series now in course of publication.

A *Sufi Message for Spiritual Liberty* is the first of these. It appeared in 1914, in 1918 followed by *Aqibat, Life after Death*. The other books, of this volume, *Love, Human and Divine*, *Pearls from the Ocean Unseen*, and *The Phenomenon of the Soul* were published in 1919. *Metaphysics* is also an early set of teachings; its first publication, however, was deferred to until 1939.

The part on *Spiritual Liberty* is a wonderfully concise presentation of the Sufi way, with a stress on enlightened philosophy, which in *Pearls* is supplemented by the psychological side of it, all permeated by the inspired myticism of the Murshid

Aqibat and *The Phenomenon* cover the item of death and life hereafter in chapters like Death, The day of judgment, Heaven and hell, Manifestation, The world of the angels, Heredity and Reincarnation.

Besides, it touches spiritism in Obsession, Haunted places, and Spiritualism. *Metaphysics* supplements this part of Hazrat Inayat Khan's philosophy by offering views on the realtionship with our life on earth, and the soul's relation to one's body and mind, ending with a wonderful chapter on the radiance of the soul.

Love, Human and Divine teaches the essential morals of love, not in terms of do's and don'ts, but of the wonderful essence of it: to forget the self absorbed as one is in the beauty of the Self. It is illustrated by some ancient stories on the subject.

W.v.L.

A SUFI MESSAGE OF SPIRITUAL LIBERTY

GOD

BELOVED ones of God, you may belong to any race, cast, creed, or nation, still you are all impartially beloved by God. You may be a believer or an unbeliever in the supreme Being, but He cares not. His mercy and grace flow through all His powers, without distinction of friend or foe.

> 'Every leaf of tree, Allah's praise displays,
> Only the pious mind can hear their sacred lays.'

The sun, moon, and stars give light; the timely change of seasons promotes health and cheerfulness; the rain grows corn, fruits, and flowers; and the alternation of day and night provides the opportunity for work and rest.

> 'Earth, water, fire and air,
> All work harmoniously.
> For thee they always food prepare,
> Thou shouldst not eat unthankfully.
> For how each day the sun shines and serves,
> All praise from thee Allah deserves.'

If you study your own body, you will find its mechanism to be the original model of the artificial mechanism of the world. Art and science fail if compared with that of His nature. The ear, eyes, and all other organs, how perfectly they are adapted in shape and mechanism to the purpose which they must serve! How liberally the needs of life, water, air, and food, are supplied; even milk is prepared in the mother's breast for the unborn infant. Should we not appreciate the liberality of the Creator, and thank him each moment with all humility and gratitude? 'Praise be to Allah, the worship of whom is the means of drawing closer to Him, and the giving of thanks to whom involves an increase of benefits. Every breath which is inhaled prolongs life, and when exhaled it quickens the frame. In every breath, therefore, two blessings are contained, and for every blessing a separate thanksgiving is due' (*Sa'di*).

He has fashioned and moulded you after His own image, and made you Ashráf al-Makhluqát, the highest of all beings and the pride of the universe, having given you command over all other beings of both worlds. As is said in the Qur'an, 'Do you not see that Allah has subjected all things on earth to you?' And at the same time He has given you, by His grace, the attributes of humanity: kindness, gratitude, faithfulness, justice, modesty, piety, sympathy, reverence, bravery, patience, love, knowledge, and wisdom. This is an open proof of your being the real object of creation and the most beloved of God.

NATURE

The argument has been raised that all manifestation is due to the interaction of natural elements, working by their own force; every cause has its effect, and the effect again becomes a cause for the reaction; thus nature works unaided. The answer is, that every cause must have some preceding cause, or first cause, to produce it; and logically one cause may produce many effects, which effects again become second causes, producing new reactions. 'While intellectual minds are seeking second causes, the wise man only perceives the first cause. Air, earth, water, being second causes, the precedent cause, which makes them act and pause, is hidden.'

THE PERSONAL BEING

Granting that we see nature, and also admitting its original cause, upon what grounds do we consider the cause to be a personal God, meriting worship? The answer is that nature itself consists of different personalities, and each of them has its peculiar attributes. The sum total of all these personalities is One, the only real personality. In relation to that One all other personalities are merely an illusion. Just as, in a limited form, a nation or a community is the sum of many personalities, just as nature manifested in numerous names and forms is still called nature, singular not plural, just as the individual combines within himself the different parts of his body, arms, limbs, eyes, ears, and is possessed of different qualities yet is one person, so the sum total of all personalities is called God. He is the possessor of all the visible and invisible attributes of the Absolute, and has different names in different languages for the understanding of man. It may be said that the personality of a man is quite comprehensible, since his actions exhibit him as a single individual, whereas God's personality has no clear identification of its own. The answer is, that variety covers unity. 'Hidden things are manifested by their opposites, but as God has no opposite He remains hidden. God's light has no opposite in the range of creation whereby it may be manifested to view' (*Jelal-ud-Din Rumi*).

The wise man by studying nature enters into the unity through its variety, and realizes the personality of God by sacrificing his own. 'He who knows himself knows Allah' (*Sayings of Mohammad*). 'The Kingdom of God is within you' (*Bible*). 'Self-knowledge is the real wisdom' (*Vedanta*).

God's relation to nature may be understood by analysing the idea expressed in the words, 'I myself'. This affirmation means the one individual; at the same time it identifies the dual aspect of the One. In this phrase 'I' is the possessor, and 'myself' is the possessed. So also God, the unmanifested, is the possessor; and nature, the manifestation, is the possessed, which has its source hidden within itself.

The possessed could not have been created from anything other than the possessor's own self, as there existed none but the possessor. Although the possessor and the possessed are considered to be two separate identities, in reality they are one. The possessor realizes the possessed through the medium of his own consciousness, which forms three aspects, the Trinity, of the one Being. The German philosopher Hegel says, 'If you say God is one, it is true; if you say He is two, that is also true; and if you say He is three, that is true too, because it is the nature of the world.'

God is regarded from three points of view: personality, morality, and reality. According to the first view, God is the most high; man is dependent upon Him and is His most obedient servant. According to the second view, God is the all-merciful and all-good Master of the Day of Judgment, while all evil is from Satan. The third is the philosophic view that God is the beginning and end of all, having Himself no beginning nor end. As a Sufi mystic has said, 'The universe is the manifestation of Allah, where from His own unity He created, by involution, variety—the state of various names and forms—, thereby distinguished as Allah, worthy of all praise and worship.'

DUAL ASPECT

According to Sufi tenets the two aspects of the supreme Being are termed *Zát* and *Sifat*, the Knower and the Known. The former is Allah and the latter Mohammad. Zát being only one in its existence, cannot be called by more than one name, which is Allah; and Sifat, being manifold in four different involutions, has numerous names, the sum of them all being termed Mohammad. The ascending and descending forms of Zát and Sifat form the circle of the Absolute. These two forces are called *Nuzul* and *Uruj*, which means involution and evolution. Nuzul begins from Zát and ends in Sifat; Uruj starts from Sifat and ends in Zát, Zát being the negative and Sifat the positive force.

Zát projects Sifat from its own self and absorbs it within itself. It is a rule of philosophy that the negative cannot lose its negativeness by projecting the positive from itself, though the positive covers the negative within itself, as the flame covers the fire. The positive has no independent existence, yet it is real because projected from the real, and it may not be regarded as an illusion. Human ignorance persists in considering Zát to be separate from Sifat, and Sifat independent of Zát.

WORSHIP

We may ask why we should worship God, and whether the theoretical knowledge of His law in nature is not sufficient for the highest realization. The answer is: no. Theoretical knowledge of a subject can never take the place of experience, which is necessary for realization. Written music cannot entertain us unless it is played, nor the description of perfume delight our senses unless we smell it, no recipes of the most delicious dishes satisfy our hunger. Nor can the theory of God give complete joy and peace; we must actually realize God or attain that state of realization which gives eternal happiness through the admiration and worship of nature's beauty and its source. 'The Beloved is all in all, the lover only veils him; the Beloved is all that lives, the lover a dead thing' (*Jelal-ud-Din Rumi*).

TRUTH

Different methods called religions and philosophies have been adopted by different nations at various periods. Though the form and teachings of the several religions appear so unlike, their source is one and the same. But from the very beginning the differences have created prejudice, envy, and antagonism between men. Such dissensions occupy a large portion of the histories of the world and have become the most important subject in life.

> 'So many castes and so many creeds,
> So many faiths, and so many beliefs,
> All have arisen from ignorance of man,
> Wise is he who only truth conceives.'

A wise man realizes that the fundamental basis of all religions and beliefs is one: *Haq*, or truth. The truth has always been covered by two garments: a turban on the head, and a robe upon the body. The turban is made of mystery known as mysticism, and the robe is made of morality, which is called religion. Truth has been covered thus by most of the prophets and saints, in order to hide it from ignorant eyes, as yet too undeveloped to bear it in its naked form. Those who see the truth uncovered, abandon reason and logic, good and bad, high and low, new and old; differences and distinctions of names and forms fade away, and the whole universe is realized as nothing other than Haq. Truth in its realization is one; in its representation it is many, since its revelations are made under varying conditions of time and space.

As water in a fountain flows in one stream but falls in many drops, divided by time and space, so are the revelations of the one stream of truth. Not everyone can comprehend the idea of different truths being derived from the one truth. Common sense has been so narrowly trained in this world of variety, that it naturally fails to realize the breadth and subtlety of a spiritual fact so far beyond the reach of its limited reasoning.

THE SUFIS

The word Sufi is derived from *Safá* meaning pure, purified of ignorance, superstition, dogmatism, egotism, and fanaticism, as well as free from limitations of caste, creed, race, and nation. The Sufis believe in God as the Absolute, the only Being; and that all creation is the manifestation of His nature.

There have been Sufis at all periods of human history. Though they have lived in different parts of the world, speaking different languages and born into different faiths and beliefs, they have recognized and sympathized with each other, through the oneness of their understanding. Yet with their deep knowledge of the world and of spiritual mysteries, they have concealed their beliefs from the multitude, and have pursued in secret their way of attainment to the highest bliss.

SELF-KNOWLEDGE

Nature has been involved through spirit into matter, and evolves through different stages. Man is the result of the involution of spirit and the evolution of matter; the final effect of this cause is 'self-realization', which means that the Knower arrives at that stage of perfection where He can know Himself.

'Thou art a mortal being,
And thou art the Eternal One;
Know thyself, through light of wisdom,
Except Thee there exists none.'

The human being is inherently capable of self-knowledge; but to know oneself means not only to know that one is John, Jacob, or Henry, or short, tall, or of normal height, or to know that one is good, bad, and so forth, but also to know the mystery of one's existence, theoretically as well as practically: to know what one is within oneself, from whence and for what purpose one was born on earth; whether one will live here for ever, or if one's stay is short; of what one is composed, and which attributes one possesses; whether one belongs to angels, contemplating the beauties of God's nature, or if one belongs to the animals, who know nothing other than to eat, drink, and be merry; or whether one belongs to the devils. It requires perfection in humanity to attain self-knowledge. To know that I am God, or we are gods, or to know that everything is a part of God, is not sufficient. Perfect realization can only be gained by passing through all the stages between man, the manifestation, and God, the only Being; knowing and realizing ourselves from the lowest to the highest point of existence, and so accomplishing the heavenly journey.

LOVE

The greatest principle of Sufism is, 'Ishq Allah, Ma'bud Allah' (God is love, lover, and beloved).

When Ahad, the only Being, became conscious of his Wahdat, only existence, through His own consciousness, then His predisposition of love made Him project Himself to establish His dual aspect, that He might be able to love someone. This made God the lover, and manifestation the beloved; the next inversion makes manifestation the lover, and God the beloved. This force of love has been working through several evolutions and involutions, which end in man who is the ultimate aim of God. The dual aspect of God is significant in Zát and Sifat, in spirit and matter, and in the mineral, vegetable, animal, and human kingdoms, wherein the two sexes, male and female, are clearly represented. The dual aspect of God is symbolized by each form of this wonderful world. This whole universe, internally and externally, is governed by the force of love, which is sometimes the cause and sometimes the effect. The producer and the product are one, and that One is nothing but love.

> 'A church, a temple or a Ka'ba stone,
> Qur'an or Bible or a martyr's bone,
> All these and more my heart can tolerate,
> Since my religion now is Love alone' (*Abul Ala*).

Sufis take the course of love and devotion to accomplish their highest aim, because it is love which has brought man from the world of unity to the world of variety, and the same force can take him back again to the world of unity from that of variety.

'Love is the reduction of the universe to the single being, and the expansion of a single being, even to God' (*Balzac*).

Love is that state of mind in which the consciousness of the lover is merged in that of the object of his love; it produces in the lover all the attributes of humanity, such as resignation, renunciation, humility, kindness, contentment, patience, virtue, calmness, gentleness, charity, faithfulness, bravery, by which the devotee becomes harmonized with the Absolute. As one of God's beloved, a path is opened for his heavenly journey: at the end he arrives at oneness with God, and his whole individuality is dissolved in the ocean of eternal bliss where even the conception of God and man disappears.

> 'Although love is a sweet madness,
> Yet all infirmities it heals.
> Saints and sages have passed through it,
> Love both to God and man appeals.'

PERFECTION

The ideal perfection, called *Baqà* by Sufis, is termed 'Najat' in Islam, 'Nirvana' in Buddhism, 'Salvation' in Christianity, and 'Mukhti' in Hinduism. This is the highest condition attainable, and all ancient prophets and sages experienced it, and taught it to the world.

Baqà is the original state of God. At this state every being must arrive some day, consciously or unconsciously, before or after death. The beginning and end of all beings is the same, difference only existing during the journey.

There are three ways in man's journey towards God. The first is the way of ignorance, through which each must travel. It is like a person walking for miles in the sun while carrying a heavy load on his shoulder, who, when fatigued, throws away the load and falls asleep under the shade of a tree. Such is the condition of the average person, who spends his life blindly under the influence of his senses and gathers the load of his evil actions; the agonies of his earthly longings creating a hell through which he must pass to reach the destination of his journey. With regard to him the Qur'an says, 'He who is blind in life, shall also be blind in the hereafter.'

The next way is that of devotion, which is for true lovers. Rumi says, 'Man may be the lover of man or the lover of God; after his perfection in either he is taken before the King of love.' Devotion is the heavenly wine, which intoxicates the devotee until his heart becomes purified from all infirmities and there remains the happy vision of the Beloved, which lasts to the end of the journey. 'Death is a bridge, which unites friend to friend' (*Sayings of Mohammad*).

The third is the way of wisdom, accomplished only by the few. The disciple disregards life's momentary comforts, unties himself from all earthly bondages and turns his eyes toward God, inspired with divine wisdom. He gains command over his body, his thoughts and feelings, and is thereby enabled to create his own heaven within himself, that he may rejoice until merged into the eternal goal. 'We have stripped the veil from thine eyes, and thy sight today is keen', says the Qur'an. All must journey along one of these three paths, but in the end they arrive at one and the same goal. As it is said in the Qur'an, 'It is He who multiplied you on the earth, and to Him you shall be gathered.'

PROPHETS

It is hard for intellect alone to believe in the possibility of prophetic inspiration.

Intellect is the consciousness reflected in the knowledge of names and forms; wisdom is consciousness in its pure essence, which is not necessarily dependent upon the knowledge of names and forms.

The gift of wisdom gives vision into the real nature of things as the X-ray penetrates material bodies. Wisdom has been specially bestowed upon certain persons, and in these rare cases the receivers of it are more than merely wise, and may be regarded as the very manifestation of wisdom. They are the prophets, who have foresight, inspiration, intuition, clairvoyance, and clairaudience as their inborn attributes.

A Sufi considers all prophets and sages, not as many individuals, but as the one embodiment of God's pure consciousness, or the manifestation of divine wisdom, appearing on earth for the awakening of man from his sleep of ignorance, in different names and forms. Just as one's own sub-consciousness would awaken one at a certain time, if previously warned, in the same way the consciousness of God is the agency for awakening His manifestation, projecting itself through different names and forms to accomplish His desire of being known. All these causes of wisdom are the manifestation of the one cause, Haq.

The prophetic mission was intended to train the world gradually in divine wisdom according to its mental evolution, and to impart it to man, according to his understanding, in forms suitable to various lands at different periods. This is why numerous different religions are still in existence, although the moral principles of all are the same.

Each prophet had a mission to prepare the world for the teaching of the next; each one prophesied the coming of the next, and the work was thus continued by all the prophets until Mohammad, the *Khatim al Mursalin*, the last messenger of divine wisdom and the seal of the prophets, came on his mission, and in his turn gave the final statement of divine wisdom: 'None exists but Allah.' This message fulfilled the aim of prophetic mission. This final definition is a clear interpretation of all religions and philosophies in the most apparent form. There was no necessity left for any more prophets after this divine message, which created the spirit of democracy in religion by recognizing God in every being. By this message man received the knowledge that he may attain the highest perfection under the guidance of a perfect murshid or spiritual teacher.

Sufis have no prejudice regarding any prophets and masters. They look upon all as divine wisdom itself, the highest attribute of God, appearing under different names and forms; and they love them with all adoration, as the lover loves his beloved in all her different garments, and throughout all the stages of her life. Sufis also respectfully recognize and offer devotion to their Beloved, the divine wisdom in all her garments, at all times, and under such different names and forms as Abraham, Moses, Jesus, and Mohammad. Mohammad's teachings are studied and followed by the orthodox as religion, and by the deep thinkers as a philosophy.

SUFISM

Sufis, who had received spiritual training from all previous prophets and leaders, likewise received training from Mohammad. The openness of Mohammad's essential teachings paved the way for them to come forward into the world without the interference they had previously experienced, and a mystic order called the Saheba-e-Safa, Knights of Purity, was inaugurated by the Prophet, and afterwards was carried on by Ali and Siddiq. The lives of these knights were extraordinary in their wisdom, piety, bravery, spirituality, and great charity of heart. This order was carried on by their successors, who were called *Pir-o-Murshid*, *Shaikh*, etc., one after another, duly connected as links in a chain.

The spiritual bond between them is a miraculous force of divine illumination, and is experienced by worthy initiates of the Sufi Order; just as the electric current runs through all connected lamps and lights them. By this means the higher development is attained without great efforts. Sufism was unostentatiously practised in Arabia during the period of Sahabis, Tába'in, and Tába'-i-tába'in. Charity, piety, spirituality, and bravery are the real proofs of Sufi advancement.

The sensational Sufi movements which took place in Persia in the later periods, have won all the credit of Sufism for the

Persians, and Sufism came to be regarded as a Persian philosophy. Imam al-Ghazali, Juneyd-e Baghdadi, Farid-ud-Din 'Attar had taken the lead in advancing Sufism in the world at large. Shams-e Tabrèz, Sa'di, Khagani, Firdausi, Omar Khayyám, Abdul Ala and other great Sufi poets, have very substantially established the reputation of Sufism by their inspired poetical works on divine wisdom. Sa'di's works (*Gulistan* and *Bostan*) illuminate the intellect; the *Divan* of Hafiz expands the heart with divine love; Jelal-ud-Din Rumi's poems, the *Masnavi e Ma'navi* inspire the soul.

These works were originally composed in Persian, but are now translated into many other languages. They have been a most important source of education for humanity, and are studied as the most popular treatises on the divine wisdom of the East.

The spiritual part of Sufism was most miraculously realized by Abdul Qadir Jilani, Moin-ud-Din Chishti, Bahá-ud-Din Naqshband, Shihab-ud-Din Sohrawardi, and others.

India, being greatly addicted to philosophy, was well suited for Sufism, where, in ancient and modern records, a great many Sufis with miraculous careers are to be found. The tombs of Moin-ud-Din Chishti, Nizam-ud-Din, Sharif-ud-Din, Bandeh Navaz, Mohammad Gauth, are visited with much reverence and devotion by people of various nations and many beliefs, in thankful remembrance of their great careers.

Sufism, as a religious philosophy of love, harmony, and beauty, aims at expanding the soul of man until the realization of the beauty of all creation enables him to become as perfect an expression of divine harmony as possible. It is therefore natural that the Sufi Order should stand foremost as a spiritual power in the East, and that it is rapidly becoming recognized in the West.

Many Sufi saints have attained what is known as God-consciousness, which is the most all-inclusive realization of the meaning of the word 'good' attainable by man. Strictly speaking, Sufism is neither a religion nor a philosophy; it is neither theism nor atheism, but stands between the two and fills the gap. Among the religious, Sufis are considered to be free-thinkers; while among intellectual philosophers they are considered religious, because they make use of subtler principles in life to elevate the soul than can readily be followed by material logic.

Sufis have in many cases realized and shown the greatest perfection in humanity. And among the lives of the Sufi saints may be found some of the most divine models of human perfection in all capacities, from a king to a labourer. The idea that Sufism sprang from Islam or from any other religion, is not necessarily true; yet it may rightly be called the spirit of Islam, as well as the pure essence of all religions and philosophies.

A true Sufi remains in the thought of truth continually, sees the truth in all things and never becomes prejudiced, but cultivates affection for all beings. A Sufi accomplishes the divine journey and reaches the highest grade of Baqà during this life, but people of all beliefs arrive, eventually, at the same level of understanding and realization which Sufism represents.

Sufism contains all branches of mysticism, such as psychology, occultism, spiritualism, clairvoyance, clairaudience, intuition, inspiration, etc., but that which a Sufi particularly wishes to acquire is not necessarily any of the above-named powers; because the object of all these powers is towards greater individuality, and individuality itself is only a hindrance on the Sufi's path towards the accomplishment of his highest perfection. Therefore the main object of initiation in the Sufi Order is to cultivate the heart through renunciation and resignation, that it may be pure enough to sow the seed of divine love and realize the highest truth and wisdom, both theoretically and practically, thereby attaining the highest attributes of humanity.

Divine perfection is perfection in all powers and mysteries. All mysteries, powers, and realizations gradually manifest themselves to the Sufi through his natural development, without his specially striving for them.

Self-realization is the highest and most difficult attainment of all; it is impossible to acquire it in the manner of sciences and arts, nor is it possible to attain it as health, wealth, honour, and power can be obtained by certain means. For the sake of self-realization, thousands have renounced family and all worldly possessions, and kings their kingdoms, and they have retired to desert, jungle, or mountain fastness, striving to find in asceticism the secret of this bliss.

SUFI TRAINING

The murshid prefers a mureed whose mind is unembarrassed by other methods of training; who is free from worldly considerations, and is possessed of whole-hearted perseverance; who is capable of committing himself with perfect faith and devotion to the guidance of his murshid.

The practice of harmony and temperance is essential, but the murshid never prescribes for his mureeds the ascetic life; rather it is a peculiarity of the Sufi training that the mureed is quickened to appreciate and enjoy the world more than others. The murshid at first creates divine love in the mureed, which, in the course of time, develops and purifies his heart so much that it permits the virtues of humanity to develop freely of themselves. He then receives more and more divine wisdom from the appointed channel, and at last arrives at complete self-realization.

There is no common course of study for mureeds; each receives the special training best adapted to his requirements. In other words, the murshid, as a spiritual physician, prescribes a suitable remedy for curing every mureed. There is no limit of time for the advancement to a certain degree. To one, realization may come the moment after initiation; to another it may not be vouchsafed during his whole life. Among the Sayings of Mohammad one finds: 'It depends upon nothing but the mercy of Allah whomever He may kindly choose for it.'

Still, there is hope of success: 'Whoever walks one step towards the grace of Allah, the Divine mercy walks forward ten steps to receive him' (*id.*).

MANIFESTATION

The only Being has manifested Himself through seven different planes of existence, to accomplish His desire of being recognized:

Tanzih:
1. Zát—the unmanifested
2. Ahadiat—plane of Eternal Consciousness
3. Wahdat—plane of consciousness
4. Wahdaniat—plane of abstract ideas

Tashbih:
5. Arwah—the spiritual plane
6. Ajsam—the astral plane
7. Insán—the physical plane

There are, again, seven aspects of manifestation:

1. Sitara—planetary
2. Mahtab—lunar
3. Aftab—solar
4. Madeniat—mineral kingdom
5. Nabitat—vegetable kingdom
6. Haywanat—animal kingdom
7. Insán—human kingdom

Insán, being the ideal manifestation, recognizes God by the knowledge of his own self. Man reaches this perfection by development through five grades of evolution:

1. Nasut—material plane
2. Malakut—mental plane
3. Jabarut—astral plane
4. Lahut—spiritual plane
5. Hahut—plane of consciousness

Each grade of development prepares a person for a higher one, and perfects him in five different grades of humanity:

1. Adam—the ordinary man
2. Insán—the wise man
3. Wali—the holy man
4. Qutb—the saint
5. Nabi—the prophet

The five natures corresponding to these five grades are:

1. Ammara—one who acts under the influence of his senses;
2. Lauwama—one who repents of his follies;
3. Mutmaina—one who considers before taking action;

4. Alima—one who thinks, speaks and acts aright;
5. Salima—one who sacrifices himself for the benefit of others.

The following is a diagram illustrating the planes of Nuzul and Uruj (evolution and involution):

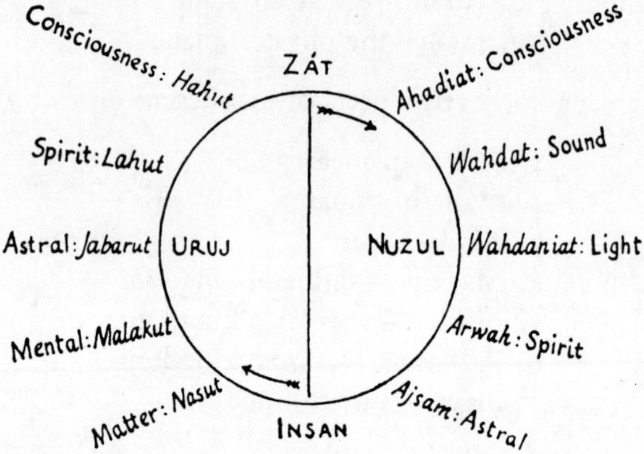

All planes of existence consist of vibrations, from the finest to the grossest kind; the vibrations of each plane have come from a higher one, and have become grosser. Whoever knows the mystery of vibrations, indeed knows all things. Vibrations are of five different aspects, appearing as the five elements:

1. Nur—ether
2. Baad—air
3. Atesh—fire
4. Aab—water
5. Khaak—earth

In relation to these elements, mankind has five senses:

Senses	*Organs*
Basárat—sense of sight . .	the eyes
Samát—sense of hearing . .	the ears
Naghat—sense of smell . .	the nose
Lazzat—sense of taste . . .	the tongue
Muss—sense of touch . . .	the skin

Through these senses and different organs of the mental and physical existence the *Ruh*, the soul, experiences life; and when the Ruh receives the highest experience of all phases of existence by the favour of the murshid, then it will have that peace and bliss, the attainment of which is the only object of manifestation.

INTEREST AND INDIFFERENCE

Interest results from ignorance and indifference results from wisdom; still it is not wise to avoid interest as long as we are in the world of illusion. It is the interest of God which has been the cause of all creation and which keeps the whole universe in harmony; nevertheless one should not be completely immersed in phenomena, but should realize oneself as being independent of interests.

The dual aspect of the only Being, in the form of love and beauty, has glorified the universe and produced harmony.

He who arrives at the state of indifference without experiencing interest in life is incomplete, and apt to be tempted by interest at any moment; but he who arrives at the state of indifference by going through interest, really attains the blessed state. Perfection is reached not through interest alone, nor through indifference alone, but through the right experience and understanding of both.

SPIRIT AND MATTER

From the scientific standpoint, spirit and matter are quite different from each other, but according to the philosophical point of view they are one.

Spirit and matter are different, just as water is different from snow; yet again they are not different, for snow is nothing other than water. When spiritual vibrations become more dense they turn into matter, and when material vibrations become finer they develop into spirit.

For a Sufi at the beginning of his training the spiritual life is desirable, but after mastering it, material and spiritual lives become the same to him, and he is master of both.

THE HEART AND SOUL

Man's heart is the throne of God. The heart is not only a physical organ but is also the function of feeling, placed in the midst of the body and soul. The heart of flesh is the instrument which first receives the feeling of the soul, and transmits its effect through the whole body. There are four aspects of the heart:

1. 'Arsh—the exaltation of the will
2. Kursi—the seat of justice and distinction
3. Lawh—the fount of inspiration
4. Kalam—the source of intuition

Breath keeps body, heart, and soul connected. It consists of astral vibrations, and has much influence upon the physical and spiritual existence. The first thing a Sufi undertakes in order to harmonize the entire existence, is the purification of the heart; since there is no possibility of the heart's development without devotion, so the faithful mureed becomes a Sahib-e Dil, as the easiest and most ideal way of development.

INTELLECT AND WISDOM

Intellect is the knowledge obtained by experience of names and forms; wisdom is the knowledge which manifests only from the inner being; to acquire intellect one must delve into studies, but to obtain wisdom, nothing but the flow of divine mercy is needed; it is as natural as the instinct of swimming to the fish, or of flying to the bird. Intellect is the sight which enables one to see through the external world, but the light of wisdom enables one to see through the external into the internal world.

Wisdom is greater and more difficult to attain than intellect, piety, or spirituality.

DREAMS AND INSPIRATIONS

Dreams and inspirations are open proofs of the higher world. The past, present, and future are frequently seen in a dream, and may also be revealed through inspiration. The righteous person sees more clearly than the unrighteous. There are five kinds of dreams:

1. Khayali—in which the actions and thoughts of the day are reproduced in sleep
2. Qalbi—in which the dream is opposite to the real happening
3. Naqshi—in which the real meaning is disguised by a symbolic representation which only the wise can understand
4. Ruhi—in which the real happening is literally shown
5. Elhami—in which divine messages are given in letters or by an angelic voice

Dreams give, sometimes clearly, sometimes in a veiled form, warnings of coming dangers and assurance of success. The ability to be conscious of dreams and their meaning varies with the degree of development attained.

Dreams have their effect sooner or later, according to the stars under which they take place. The dream seen at midnight is realized within one year, and the dream of the latter part of night within six months; the dream of the early morning is realized soon after. At the same time the manifestation of dreams is subject to qualification according to the good or bad actions of the dreamer.

Inspirations are more easily reflected upon spiritual persons than upon material ones. Inspiration is the inner light which reflects itself upon the heart of man; the purer the heart is from rust, like a clean mirror, the more clearly inspiration can be reflected in it. To receive inspirations clearly the heart should be prepared by proper training. A heart soiled with rust is never capable of receiving them. There are five kinds of inspiration:

1. Elham-e-'Ilm—inspiration of an artist and scientist
2. Elham-e-Husn—inspiration of a musician and poet
3. Elham-e-'Ishq—inspiration of a devotee
4. Elham-e-Ruh—inspiration of a mystic
5. Elham-e-Ghayb—inspiration of a prophet

Inspirations are reflected upon mankind in five ways:

1. Kushád der Khyal—in the wave of thought
2. Kushád der Hál—in emotions and feelings
3. Kushád der Jemal—in the sufferings of the heart
4. Kushád der Jelal—in the flow of wisdom
5. Kushád der Kemal—in the divine voice and vision

Some are born with an inspirational gift, and to some it appears after their development. The higher the development in spirituality, the greater the capacity for inspiration, yet the gift of inspiration is not constant; as the saying of Mohammad declares, 'Inspirations are enclosed as well as disclosed at times; they appear according to the will of Allah, the only Knower of the unknown."

LAW OF ACTION

The law of cause and effect is as definite in its results in the realm of speech and thought as in the physical world.

Evil done, when it is considered evil, is a sin; and good done, when it is considered good, is a virtue; but one who does good or bad without understanding, has no responsibility for his sins nor credit for his virtues; but he is liable to punishment or reward just the same.

Man forms his future by his actions. His every good or bad action spreads its vibrations and becomes known throughout the universe. The more spiritual a man is, the stronger and clearer are the vibrations of his actions, which spread over the world and weave his future.

The universe is like a dome: it vibrates to that which you say in it, and echoes the same back to you. So also is the law of action: we reap what we sow.

It is impossible to differentiate between good and bad, because the thing seen is coloured by the personality of the seer; to the bad view, all good is bad, and to the good view, even the bad seems good in a certain sense; so the wise keep silence in distinguishing good from bad. The most essential rule is not to do to others that which you would not have done to you. That action is desirable which results from kindness, and that action is undesirable which is unkind. Doubtless also, might is often right, but in the end, right is the only might.

There are different principles for life in different religions, but a Sufi's will is the principle for himself. He is the servant, who surrenders himself to principles; and he is the master, who prescribes principles for himself. One who has never been commanded in life, never knows how to command; in the same way, to be the master, one must first be the servant.

The murshid as a physician of the soul prescribes necessary principles to the mureed, who after accomplishing the training, arrives at that blessed state where he overcomes virtues and sins, and stands beyond good and bad. To him happiness no longer differs from sorrow, for his thought, speech, and action become the thought, speech, and action of God.

MUSIC AMONG SUFIS

Music is called *Ghiza-i-ruh*, the food of the soul, by Sufis. Music being the most divine art elevates the soul to the higher spirit; music itself being unseen soon reaches the unseen; just as only the diamond can break the diamond, so musical vibrations are used to make the physical and mental vibrations inactive, in order that the Sufi may be elevated to the spiritual spheres.

Music consists of vibrations which have involved from the top to the bottom, and if they would only be systematically used, they could be evolved from the bottom to the top. Real music is known only to the most gifted ones. Music has five aspects:

1. Tarab—music which induces motion of the body (artistic)
2. Raga—music which appeals to the intellect (scientific)

3. Qūl—music which creates feelings (emotional)
4. Nida—music heard in vision (inspirational)
5. Saut—music in the abstract (celestial)

Music has always been the favourite Sufi means of spiritual development. Rumi, the author of the Masnavi, introduced music into his Maulvi Order, and enjoyed the memory of his blessed murshid's association while listening to it. Since that time music has become the second subject of Sufi practices. They declare that it creates harmony in both worlds and brings eternal peace.

The great mystic of India, Khwaja Moin-ud-Din Chishti, introduced music into his Chishtia Order. Even today musical entertainments for the elevation of the soul, called *Suma*, are held among Sufis.

ECSTASY

Ecstasy is called *Wajad* by Sufis: it is especially cultivated among the Chishtis. This bliss is the sign of spiritual development and also the opening for all inspirations and powers. This is the state of eternal peace, which purifies from all sins. Only the most advanced Sufis can experience Wajad. Although it is the most blissful and fascinating state, those who give themselves entirely to it become unbalanced, for too much of anything is undesirable; as the day's labour is a necessary precursor of the night's rest, so it is better to enjoy this spiritual bliss only after the due performance of worldly duties.

Sufis generally enjoy Wajad while listening to music called *Qawwali*, special music producing emotions of love, fear, desire, repentance, etc.

There are five aspects of Wajad: Wajad of dervishes, which produces a rhythmic motion of the body; Wajad of idealists, expressed by a thrilling sensation of the body, tears and sighs; Wajad of devotees, which creates an exalted state in the physical and mental body; Wajad of saints, which creates perfect calm and peace; and Wajad of prophets, the realization of the highest consciousness called *Sadrat al Manteha*.

One who by the favour of the murshid arrives at the state of Wajad is undoubtedly the most blessed soul and deserves all adoration.

CONCENTRATION

The entire universe in all its activity has been created through the concentration of God. Every being in the world is occupied consciously or unconsciously in some act of concentration. Good and evil are alike the result of concentration. The stronger the concentration, the greater the result; lack of concentration is the cause of failure in all things. For this world and the other, for material as well as spiritual progress, concentration is most essential.

The power of will is much greater than the power of action, but action is the final necessity for the fulfilment of the will. Perfection is reached by the regular practice of concentration, passing through three grades of development: Fanà-fi-Shaikh, annihilation in the astral plane, Fanà-fi-Rasul, annihilation in the spiritual plane, and Fanà-fi-Allah, annihilation in the abstract.

After passing through these three grades, the highest state is attained of Báqi-bi-Allah, annihilation in the eternal consciousness, which is the destination of all who travel by this path.

Breath is the first thing to be well studied. This is the very life, and also the chain which connects material existence with the spiritual. Its right control is a ladder leading from the lowest to the highest stage of development. Its science is to be mastered by the favour of the murshid, the guiding light of God.

MALE AND FEMALE ASPECT OF GOD

The only Being is manifested throughout all planes of existence in two aspects, male and female, representing nature's positive and negative forces. In the plane of consciousness there are two aspects: *Wahdat*, consciousness, and *Ahadiat*, eternal consciousness, and thus also spirit and matter, night and day, signify the dual aspect on lower planes. In the mineral and vegetable kingdoms sex is in a state of evolution, but the highest manifestation of male and female is man and woman.

Man being the first aspect of manifestation, is the more spiritual and nearer to God; woman being the next manifestation, is finer and more capable of divine knowledge. Man's natural tendency is towards God, while woman's tendency is towards the world. These contrary tendencies result in balance. Therefore man needs woman to direct his life, and woman needs man for her guidance and protection, both being incomplete in themselves.

The problem of the emancipation of woman may be studied by a comparison of her position in the East and in the West.

The Oriental woman, whose freedom is restricted, is the better wife from the individual point of view, but the enforced inactivity of half the population is not beneficial to the nation. The Occidental woman who is given entire freedom is less anxious for and less capable of home life, but being out in the world her influence promotes the advancement of the nation.

At first sight it would appear that woman is more respected by man in the West, but in reality the East gives her the greater reverence.

Man has more freedom than woman throughout the entire world because he has more strength and power; and the fineness of woman needs protection, just as the eye, being the finest organ of the body, has been protected by nature with eyelids. Both excel in their own characteristics.

A virgin is idolized by man because she is the model of high manifestation; woman's virtue is a greater ideal than her physical and intellectual beauty. Nature has placed her under the protection of man, but what is most desirable is that man gives her freedom and that she appreciates it by making the best use of it.

There are three kinds of virgins. One, commonly considered a virgin, who has never had association with a man; another is the virgin in heart, whose love is centred in one beloved only; and the third is the virgin in soul, who considers man as God. She alone can give birth to a divine child.

A woman may become a doctor, solicitor, or minister, but it is incomparably greater if she can become a good wife and a kind mother.

Monogamy and polygamy are inborn human attributes. They also exist among birds and beasts. Each individual is born with one of these tendencies, but sometimes one rather than the other is developed by the effect of the atmosphere and surroundings. These tendencies also depend upon the climatic and physical conditions of different countries and races. Polygamy may be natural to man, and monogamy to woman, as the former helps manifestation while the latter destroys it. Illegal polygamy is worse than legal, because it creates deceit and falsehood. Monogamy is the ideal life which is a comfort in this world and the next, and perfects one in love.

Absolute renunciation is as undesirable as is the blind attachment to the world. The ideal life is detached interest in the world, which is best accomplished by man and woman together.

Woman is a mystery within herself, owing to her subtle nature. Sages who made the mistake of considering woman to be of lesser spiritual importance forgot that they themselves were the product of woman.

The majority of prophets and masters have been men because man is the higher manifestation, as is signified by the myth of Adam and Eve, in which Eve was born from the rib of Adam, meaning that woman is the later manifestation; the fruit means that woman directed man's thoughts towards procreation. The interpretation of Adam and Eve's exile from heaven is the fall of mankind from the state of innocence to the state of youth. The separation and unhappiness of Adam and Eve show the object of God to manifest in the dual aspect, that He may accomplish his real desire of love. According to the Vedanta half of the divine body, Ardhangi, is womanhood, proving that unity of both is the complete life.

Sufis consider a life of complete unity the most balanced, if it is true and harmonious. Love and wisdom create harmony between man and woman; but these being absent, harmony ceases to exist.

A child inherits more attributes from its mother than from

its father, therefore the mother is more responsible for its merits and defects; and if she has knowledge she can train the soul of her child even before its birth by the power of her concentration, moulding the child's future according to her own will.

Harmony between finer persons is more lasting than the affections of average mankind. People of angelic qualities have everlasting harmony between them, in which God Himself accomplishes His object of manifestation.

Mankind is born with a worshipful attitude, and as all attitudes demand satisfaction by expression, so the attitude of worship finds its object of adoration. The ancient Greeks and Shiva Bhaktas of India worshipped both aspects of manifestation in the names of gods and goddesses. Sufism, being the essence of all religions and philosophies, looks upon both the opposite aspects of nature as one in reality, and calls it *Sifat Allah*. Sufis reach realization of God by adoring His nature, calling on Him saying, 'Kull-i shayin Hāḷ-i kull', which means, Everything will perish except His own Face.' They look upon all names and forms as the means of realizing the One, the only Being.

AQIBAT, LIFE AFTER DEATH

CONTENTS

CHAPTER I

DEATH

WE LOVE our body and identify ourselves with it to such an extent that we are very unhappy to think that this body, which is so dear to us, will some day be in the grave. No one likes to think that it will die and be destroyed. But the soul is our true self. It existed before our birth and will exist after our death. That which holds the conception of 'I', a living entity, is not the body but the soul deluded by the body. The soul thinks that it is the body; it thinks that it walks, sits, lies down when the body does, but it does not really do any of these things. A little indisposition of the body makes it think, 'I am ill'. A slight offence makes it dejected. A little praise makes it think itself in heaven. In reality it is not in heaven nor on earth; it is where it is. The soul's dwelling in the material body deludes it so much that it thinks, 'I can live only on material food, can stand only on earth, can enjoy only material surroundings. Without these I am nowhere, I am nothing.'

There is a Persian saying: 'Do not build a house on the ground of another.' This is what the soul does. Whatever it sees, the consciousness recognizes as itself. Its purity makes it reflect whatever is before it, and then it thinks, 'This is I', just as clear water reflects our image. The soul then wants everything to be very nice and pleasant for its comfort and vanity. It wants to see its objective self well dressed; then it wants very good things about it. It sets up a good house, and all through this life it is in pursuit of these things. Then when death comes this building raised on the sand is blown away. Its collected property is taken from it. This is a very, very great disappointment. It loses all that it took interest in. Its withdrawing into its pure self, and the scattering of all earth's deluding environment from its sight impresses it with the idea of death, to its greatest horror. This horror and disappointment are the only death there is, for the body is nothing but a covering put over our soul, and when it is gone we are not dead; just as we do not think that we are dead when our coat is worn out, or if someone tears our shirt.

The moment when a person dies is the only moment when he feels that he is dead. The impression of his dying condition, the hopelessness of the doctor, the sorrow and grief of the family, all make up this impression. After death, as he recovers from this impression, he gradually finds himself alive; for the life which kept him alive in his physical garb, of course feels strange in the absence of that garb. Yet it is not dead; it is even more alive, for that great burden has been removed which for a time had made him think that the physical garb was his life.

The soul by its power has created the elements from itself, and has attracted them from outside. It has collected them and it holds them, but through use they are gradually worn out and last only for a certain period. The soul holds the body composed of all these elements as long as it has interest in the body, and as long as the magnetism of the body holds it and its activity keeps it engaged. As soon as its interest in the body is lessened, or the elements that form the body have lost their power, by feebleness or some irregularity in the system, the body loosens its hold, and the soul, whose innate inclination is to free itself, takes advantage of this opportunity given to it by bodily inability. The result of this is death.

The elements begin to disperse even before death, but after the death of the body they return straight to their affinity, earth to earth, water to water, and so on, each to its affinity. And they are very glad to return. Each thing is glad to be with its like. If there is gas near the fire, the flame will go out to the gas, because there is much of the fire element in the gas.

One might think that this is all, and that after death there will be nothing left for the ordinary person who has thought of himself as this body, so tall, so broad, so heavy, so many years old; that when the physical body is gone all is gone. But it is not so; when the body is gone the mind remains, the finer part of man's self, composed of vibrations. The elements exist in the vibrations as well as in the atoms, otherwise a person who is angry would not get red and hot. In dreams, when the body is asleep, we see ourselves walking, speaking, acting, in certain surroundings with certain people. It is only by contrast with the waking condition that we call it a dream. This self still exists after the body is gone, the exact counterpart of what we are now, not of what we were when we were five years old, or ten years old, but of what we are now.

It is sometimes said that the soul is that which remains after the death of the physical body, and that it is then in heaven or in hell; but that is not so. The soul is something much greater. How can that be burned with fire which is itself light, Nur, the light of God? But owing to its delusion, it takes upon itself all the conditions that the mind has to go through after death. Therefore the experience after death of the soul that has not attained to liberation is very depressing. If the mind is not much attached to the earthly life and has gathered up the satisfaction of its deeds, it enjoys heaven; if the contrary is the case, then it experiences hell.

The mind that is more involved in earthly cares and attachments cannot let the soul be in the light. If you throw a balloon into the air it will go up and then it will come down again. It goes up because of the air that is in it; it comes down because of the earth substance in it. The tendency of the soul is to go to the highest spheres, to which it belongs; that is its nature. The earthly substance it has gathered around it weighs it down to earth. The kite goes up, but the string in a person's hand brings it back to earth. The earthly attachments are the string that draws the soul downwards. We see that the smoke goes up and on its way it leaves in the chimney its earth substance. All the rest of its earth substance it leaves in the air, and until it has left all behind, it cannot go up to the ether. By this simile we see how the soul cannot rise from the lower regions until it has left behind all earthly longings and attachments.

People have a great fear of death, and especially the simple, tender, and affectionate people, and those who are very much attached to their father and mother and brothers and sisters and friends, to their positions and possessions. But those who are unfortunate in life also fear death. A person would rather be very ill than dead. He would rather be in hospital than in the grave with the dead people. When the thought comes to a man,

'Some day I must leave all this and go down to the grave', a great sadness comes upon him. With some people this fear lasts part of their lives; with some it lasts the whole life. The proof of how great the fear of death is, is that death has been made out to be the worst punishment, although it is not nearly so bad as the pains, sorrows, and worries of life.

Death is the great examination to which one goes prepared, another unprepared; one with confidence, another with fear. However much anyone may pretend to be spiritual or virtuous in life, at the sight of death he is tested and all pretence falls away. It is said in the Qur'an, 'Then, when the crushing calamity shall come, on that day shall man remember what he has striven after.'

There was an old man who was always crying and lamenting, saying, 'I am so unhappy, my life is so hard, every day toil and labour! It would be better if I were dead.' Every day he lamented in this way and called upon death to come and take him. One day Azrael, the angel of death, appeared and said to him, 'You have called me so often, now I am come to take you with me.' The old man said, 'Not yet! I am an old man, pray grant me only a few days more of life!' The angel of death said, 'No. You have so often asked to die, and now you must come to Allah.' The old man said, 'Wait a little while. Let me stay here a little longer.' But the angel of death said, 'Not one moment more', and he carried him off.

What thought should the mind hold at the moment of death? The thought should be, in accordance with the evolution of the person, either of God or the object of his devotion, or of pleasant surroundings and whatever he likes and has idealized. If he is an earthly person then the thought of pleasant surroundings will make a heaven for him. If he is in a state of devotion, he will unite with the object of his devotion. If he is godly, the thought of God will be right for him. 'Verily death is the bridge which unites friend to friend', one finds in the Sayings of Mohammad.

Those of whom it is said that they are in the presence of God, are those who hold the vision of their divine Beloved whom they have idealized all their life, and they rejoice for a very, very long time in the presence of their idealized One.

During our life on earth we are conscious of three conditions: that of the body, the mind, and the soul. After physical death we are conscious of two only. On the physical plane, if a thief comes, we are not so much afraid. We look about to find something to attack him with. But in a dream we are afraid, for we have nothing with which to attack him. Here the will is much stronger; there the imagination is stronger, and the will less so. In the physical life we have changes from one experience to another. If in the night we are afraid, in the morning we say, 'I had a nightmare,' or, 'in my dream I was sad,' but it means nothing. But there we have no change.

Thus it is here that we should awaken to what is the aim of our life. There we cannot improve so much as we can here. That is why there have always been some, the chosen ones of God, who have said, 'Awake, awake, while there is time!'

There are some who in a dream can do what they wish. They can cause to happen whatever they will, and the next day they see occur what they saw in the night. Such are exceptional cases. Because they have mastered their will here, they can make everything go according to their will even on the higher plane. When a person is just as glad that another should eat a good dish as that he should eat it himself, that another should wear beautiful clothes as that he should wear them himself, then he is raised above humanity. These are the saints and sages, and their hereafter is in their hands, because they are happy both in the gain and the loss.

The mind of the prophets and murshids cannot be compared with other minds. Theirs is a master mind, and they can hold it much longer. As they have lived only for others, after death they still live for others. They have thought only of what is eternal. Others have thought of things that pass away, and so in time their mind passes away.

Sufism is learned chiefly in order that a person may know what will happen to him after death, in that being which is our real being, though usually it is hidden from us.

After the physical death the life that cannot die bears man up and he remains always alive. Both on earth and on the sea we living beings exist, having both elements in our form, the earth and the water. The beings of the sea are formed of earth as well; we have water also in our constitution. Yet the sea is as strange to us as the earth is to the creatures of the sea. Neither would like their place exchanged; and if it so happens that they are out of their element, it leads them to their end. It is because the fish has not realized that it is also an earthly being and that the earth is its element too, that it cannot live on earth; and in the same way beings on land whose life depends on getting to the shore, fail when they believe that they will sink in the sea.

If we were dropped into the sea, it would be a terrible thing. We would be convinced that we would go to the bottom, that we would be drowned. It is our fear that makes us go to the bottom, and our thought; except for this there is no reason why we should sink. The sea lifts up the whole ship in which a thousand people are travelling and in which tons of weight are loaded; why should it not lift up our little body?

Our inner being is like the sea, our external being as the earth. So it is with the word called death. It is the sea part of ourselves, where we are taken from our earth part, and, not being accustomed to it, we find the journey unfamiliar and uncomfortable, and call it death. To the seaman the sea is as easy to journey upon, whenever he chooses to, as the land. Christ, in connection with this subject, said to Peter, 'O thou of little faith, wherefore didst thou doubt?' Both in Sanskrit and Prakrit, liberation is called *Taran*, which means swimming. It is the power to swim which makes water the abode of the earthly fish, and for those who swim in the ocean of eternal life, in the presence as well as in the absence of the body, it becomes their everlasting abode.

The swimmer plays with the sea. At first he swims a little way, then he swims far out. Then he masters it, and at last it is his home, his element, as the earth is. He who has mastered these two elements has gained all mastery.

The divers in the port of Ceylon, and the Arabs on the Red Sea, dive down into the sea. First they stop up their ears, eyes, lips, and their nose, then they dive and bring up pearls. The mystic also dives into the sea of consciousness by closing his senses from the external world and thus entering into the abstract plane.

The work of the Sufi is to take away the fear of death. This path is trodden in order to know in life what will be with us after death. As it is said in the Qur'an, 'Mutu kubla anta mutu' or 'Die before death.' To take off this mortal garb, to teach the soul that it is not this mortal but is that immortal being, so that we may escape the great disappointment which death brings, this is what is accomplished in life by a Sufi.

CHAPTER II

THE DAY OF JUDGMENT

IN BUDDHISM and in the Hindu religion little is said about the Day of Judgment, because they have the doctrine of Karma; but in the Qur'an it recurs often in the different suras, great emphasis being put upon it, and in the Bible the Day of Judgment is spoken of very many times.

This Day of Judgment, of which various religions have spoken, is a great secret. All that can be said about it is that not one moment of time, not the blinking of the eye passes without a judgment; that in the conscience of each individual there is the faculty of judging, which judges himself and others, and that this faculty exists in its perfection in the universal Conscience, which judges the whole universe. The former is man's justice, the latter the justice of God.

In man's justice partiality and error are found, for his conscience is overshadowed by his self; thus the seeing faculty of the conscience is dimmed. God's justice is the right justice, for no shadow of partiality falls upon His universal consciousness because the whole universe is His field of vision and therefore His sight is keen. As our justice determines our likes and dislikes and creates in us favour or disfavour for another, so it is with God. He reckons the account of deeds and bestows rewards and punishments; He also forgives in His mercy and compassion whomever He may choose to forgive, as do we human beings in our small way. To the short-sighted, man's justice is plain, but God's justice is too vague to be apprehended; and there are many apparent examples to lead him astray, such as the righteous being ill-treated while the wicked enjoy life; but the keen-sighted can see an end to the enjoyment of the wicked and to the ill-treatment of the righteous. The seer can see the blow awaiting its time to fall upon the one, and the reward being prepared for the other. It is only a matter of time.

To a material person this seems absurd. He thinks, If I rob

someone, if the police catch me, that is the judgment. If they do not catch me, it is all right; then I am safe from it. If I have a purse full of money, and I can pay barristers and lawyers, it is all right.' For he does not see anything in the hereafter; he sees only what is here.

A simple believer believes that there is a Day of Judgment, but he knows hardly anything about it. It is for the Sufi to understand that there is a record in the memory of every action, thought, and work—nature's manuscript open before our own conscience; and if a murderer escapes the police, he cannot escape from his conscience within. One might think, 'It is his own conscience, what does it matter if it is displeased for a while?' But there is the universal Conscience behind it, perfectly just and all-powerful, which, if he escaped from the land and sought refuge in the water, could hang him even by means of the waves of the sea, as a penalty for his crime.

Everything that one does, all one's works, have three parts: the beginning, the action, and the end. In the beginning there is hope, in the action there is joy, but in the end comes the realization.

In the morning when one wakes up, one is fresh and ready to plan all the work of the day. A person works all day, and in the evening he sees what result he has got from his work, how much he has gained.

When a child is born it is fresh and ready to enjoy everything. It is happy with any little thing, any little doll that it is given. It does not know where the world is nor what the cares of life are. Then a person has to go through all experiences, good and bad, in life; and when old age comes, then he sees the results of his actions. At the time of action he does not see them, because action is blinding. Then, if he has worked for riches, he has got riches; if he has worked for fame, he will have that. And if he loves, he receives the affection and sympathy of his surroundings. When he is old, that is the period of his judgment on earth. Then he sees the reward of his action. If he has murdered someone, the judgment is when he is hanged. If he has robbed, he is in gaol and he repents. But the time of action comes only once, and after that it is too late to repair one's fault.

There are many things that we do that seem all right at the moment, but afterwards our self is not satisfied. It is just like a person eating something that at the time has a pleasant taste but afterwards produces a bad odour, so that the smell of his own breath makes his head ache. Whatever was tolerated in him while he had power, magnetism, and activity, together with energy, manner, appearance, and looks, no one will tolerate any longer when the power has left him. He has become cranky; his children want to leave him, because they say that old papa has lost his head; his friends despise him, because they say that he is no use.

There are many habits and weaknesses of the mind which in youth do not seem of much consequence, such as jealousy, greed, envy, anger, and passion. When youth is gone, and the strength and magnetism of youth, then only weakness remains with its gaping mouth. Whilst we are engaged in an activity, we are blind. Our eyes are opened when the result comes.

A Badishah was once riding in the jungle. Crossing a bridge he saw a man who was quite drunk standing in the middle of the bridge. The man called out, 'Will you sell that horse, O passer-by?' for he was quite drunk and could not recognize the rider. The Badishah thought, 'He is drunk', so he paid no heed. After shooting for some hours in the jungle he returned and saw the man who had been standing in the middle of the road now sitting by the roadside. The Badishah asked the man in fun, 'Do you want to purchase this horse?' The man's drunkenness had now passed. He was astonished to think what he had said to the Badishah in his drunken state, but fortunately he thought of a very witty answer. He said, 'The purchaser of the horse has gone, the groom of the horse remains.' This amused the Badishah, who overlooked his fault.

There is a time when our ego desires all that tempts it, but when that stage of beginning and action is past, helplessness remains.

Our life has three parts, the part before our birth, the time of our life here, and the time after death. When considering our life here and hereafter we understand that our life on earth is our youth, the hereafter age, the time of reaping the fruits of our actions. And the judgment comes in age, which is the time after death.

In the arts too we see that there are these three aspects. In music there is first the introduction, then there is the music in its full grandeur, then there is the conclusion, which gives the essence of all that has gone before. In painting the artist first designs, then he colours the picture, and then he looks at it; if it is not as he likes, he wipes it off or he tears it up. A person might say, 'You yourself have made it, why do you tear it up?' It is because when he looks at it, he sometimes discovers that it is valueless; whereas when it is better the artist desires it to be sent to the exhibition, and he proudly calls his relations and friends to look at it. This world is the Creator's picture. The Creator as an artist looks at his work; and He alters it, improves it, or He wipes it off as He chooses best.

Why is the Day of Judgment called 'day'? Our day is when we are awake, our night is when we are asleep. This is not the day and night of the earth, which are limited to twelve hours each, but the day and night of the consciousness. What separates one day from another, what makes us distinguish the days, is the night.

Here our life is in the darkness of activity, where the world of illusion appears to our eyes as real, and the rapid passing of life appears to us stable; just as when in the train it seems as if the trees by the line were running while the train is standing still. When the illusionary life has proved to be not so real as for some time we had thought it to be then comes the day when things appear as clear as in daylight. To some few this happens in this world, but to all in the hereafter.

Here we have two states, the waking state and the dream. There the only reality will be the dream. That will be our day, uninterrupted by any intervening night. It will not change. And this day will last for ever, that is to say until our individuality is merged in the divine consciousness.

We dream of all the things which are in our surroundings and of all things as they appear naturally. We dream of a horse or an elephant, or of our brother, our sister, our mother, our father, or our uncle; but we do not dream of non-existent objects, such as a horse with wings or a rabbit with elephant's ears; because these are not of our world. That with which our consciousness is impressed, that only is our world. And that world comes into the judgment which is always going on. The world of the husbandman will be his cottage with his family, the world of the king will be the surroundings of his palace.

Shall we, then, not be in a great gathering where there will be millions and billions of souls in whatever form they may appear, and all the souls that have existed on earth will be tried at the same time? It will be so in appearance, but not in reality, for every individual's Judgment Day will reflect the whole world within himself and will be peculiar to himself; in other words a world will be resurrected in each soul. The affirming and denying aspects of conscience will both be in full play, sometimes in the guise of Munkir and Nakir, the recording angels.

In reality it will be like a gramophone record, which repeats all one's life's experiences, remembered and forgotten, good and bad, together with the moving picture of all who were concerned in them, whether dead before or after, or still alive on earth. This takes place before one's own soul in the presence of the perfectly just and mighty Being, the thorough Knower and Weigher of all things.

CHAPTER III

HEAVEN AND HELL

THE IDEA of heaven and hell exists in some form or another in all religions. This gives the religions a great hold upon the masses keeping them completely under their sway, inducing them to do good and to keep from evil. Without this it would be almost impossible, for man is always being tempted to evil, and great difficulties stand in his way when he attempts to do good, since the wicked seem to possess the kingdom of the earth, while the righteous look to the mercy of God. If no such promise had been given, no other reward, however great, would ever have united mankind in the religion of faith.

The reward that God gives is quite different from any earthly comforts and riches, but in early times, and even with most people now, it could only be expressed in the form of earthly rewards. That is why the Apostles received the power to speak to every man in his own language.

The early scriptures were given at a time when the evolution of the world was such that people were eager for whatever material comfort was obtainable. If it had been at this time, something else would have been promised. They were told, 'If you will keep from sin, then you will be amid thornless lota trees and banana trees laden with fruit, the shade of them spreading over you, with water flowing and couches set up. Under them shall walk youths ever-blooming, and bright ones with large eyes like hidden pearls. There shall be created for you a new creation, and maidens young and beautiful, with golden goblets and ewers and a cup of flowing wine. Brows ache not thereat nor do the senses fail. And fruits of what you like best, and flesh of birds, whatever you desire. Ye shall hear therein no vain talk nor sin, only the cry, "Peace, peace!"'

When a child is told, 'If you do this, you shall have candy', however great the sacrifice is, it will do it, for it thinks, 'I shall have candy'. The words in the scriptures about the reward of good deeds in heaven were spoken in a manner suited to the evolution of that time. The promises were made as an older person makes promises to a child and says, 'Do not take another person's apple; I will give you another apple, even sweeter than this. Don't take another child's doll; I will give you another doll, even better than this.'

This was the only way of keeping unevolved people from undesirable actions.

In the same way mankind was threatened with punishment, such as being burnt by a scorching fire, made to drink from a fountain boiling fiercely, having no food but thorns and thistles, as a mother says to her child, 'You will get a whipping if you do so.'

The Prophet once said, 'Hell is for the wicked, and heaven is striven for by the fools.'

Each religion has pictured heaven and hell according to familiar scenes upon earth, in whatever part of the world it might be.

The heaven of the Hindu is an opera house. In it are the Upsaras and Gandharvas, the singers and dancers, and in their hell are snakes and scorpions, filth and worms.

In the Christian heaven the blessed become angels robed in white, with white wings. They hold golden harps. They are in the blue sky, seated on white clouds, singing the praise of God; and their joy is in knowing God and in the communion of the blessed. The Christian hell is a blazing, fiery furnace with lakes of brimstone and burning sulphur, where the worm dieth not and the fire is not quenched. The devils goad the damned with the red-hot prongs of their pitchforks. They are parched with thirst, and there they remain either for ever or until they have paid the debt of their sins to the uttermost farthing.

In the Moslem heaven there will be Hūris and Malaks to wait upon the inhabitants of Jannat, the heavenly attendants, whose faces will be luminous and radiant with heavenly beauty and incomparably more handsome than the fair ones of the earth. Milk and honey flow in streams, and jewels and gems roll underfoot. Cooling drinks, the bracing breeze, and all fruits and delicious foods will always be ready, and fountains of Kouthar, the divine wine, will run. Every person who enters Jannat, whether he be a child or aged, will be young there. There will be the association of the holy, and the divine atmosphere will be felt throughout everything. Hell in the Moslem tradition is said to be like a raging fire, hotter beyond comparison than any fire on earth. There will be the company of those crying and shrieking, calling for water with flames in their mouths. Melancholy, miserable, helpless, and feeble will be the surroundings, and darkness, confusion, horror, and ignorance will be felt all around, while a devilish atmosphere will overwhelm all.

One might ask why the different religions have given differing accounts of heaven and hell. But the prophets never spoke what is not true, so that if we take the philosophical view, we see that the meaning is that whatever we have idealized we shall have.

The Hindus had idealized music, singing, playing, and dancing; therefore this was their heaven.

In Christianity, because from its foundation the thought of the distinction of sex was avoided, the holy place was held to be one where there are angels, sexless, singing to the God in the heavens above the clouds.

In Arabia, in the hot sand, a person wishes for a cooling drink every moment, and the climate makes the people emotional and gives them the desire to admire youth and beauty.

Heil, in almost all religions, has been described in some way or other as the place of torment, where all sources of torture are to be found.

The picture of heaven or hell had its origin in the simplest revelation as it came to the mind of the Prophet: a great horror at the idea of sin and a sense of joy and beauty at the sight of virtue. It expresses itself first in artistic imagination before it comes to the lips. The thought of horror at once brings pictures of fire, especially in the deserts and hot sand of Arabia, where water is the one salvation of all creatures, and fire is always the chief element of destruction. When the thought of joy and beauty comes, it at once pictures the beauty of the opposite sex, which has charmed the soul from the first day of creation and will do the same for ever. Then all delights which appeal to the senses and all sights which one longs to see, stood before the Prophet's artistic view, and were expressed in the language that his listeners were capable of appreciating. While the Sufi penetrates to the source of this idea, the simple believer revels in the words.

All that the traditions say is understood literally by the faithful, but the Sufi perceives them differently. To him Hūris are the heavenly expressions of beauty appearing before the eye which was open on earth, admiring the divine immanence on earth. 'God is beautiful and He loves beauty', as it is said in the Hadith. The whole creation was made that the beauty within the Creator might manifest in His creation, that it might be witnessed. The same tendency is working throughout the whole circuit. God's eye sees the heavenly beauty through the godly on their way towards the eternal goal. 'No soul knows what is reserved for them, what joy will refresh their eyes as a reward for what they have done', says the Qur'an.

Honey is the essence of all flowers. The essence of the whole being is wisdom. Wisdom is the honey which is found in heaven. Milk is the pure and essential substance prepared in the breast of the mother. The essential sustenance of our being is the spirit, which is pure like milk, and by spirituality we drink that milk on which our soul is nourished. It is said in the Bible, 'Man doth not live by bread alone, but by every word that proceedeth out of the mouth of God.' The earthly treasures such as gems and jewels, which the godly have renounced in their life upon earth, are rolling like pebbles, worthless, beneath their feet.

To the seer earthly wealth, which man pursues all his life, becomes in the end like pebbles rolling under his feet. Kouthar, wine, means the intoxicating influence of spiritual ecstasy, which is hidden in the heart as love. This purifies the mind from all impressions made upon it during the life on earth, thus preparing the soul for the at-one-ment with God.

There is a different heaven and hell for each person, in accordance with the grade of his evolution. What is heaven to one person may be hell to another. A poor man will think it heaven to have a comfortable house to live in and a carriage to drive in. If a king were made to live in the house of a rich merchant, with one or two carriages, and a few servants to wait upon him, he would think it hell. A click of the tongue is more painful to the horse than ten lashes on the back of a donkey. This shows that the hell of a horse and of a donkey cannot be the same.

There is a story told of a Badishah before whom four persons were brought, arrested for the same crime. He looked at one and said, 'Hang him.' He looked at another and said, 'Life-long imprisonment.' He looked at the third and said, 'Banish him.' Then he saw the fourth and said, 'Shame! How dare you show your face to me? Go, and never come before me again.' The one who went to be hanged killed a few more on his way to the gallows. The exiled one went away and started his trade and roguery still more prosperously in another country. The imprisoned one rejoiced shamelessly with friends in the prison. But he who was exempted from all punishment went home and committed suicide; to him the Badishah's bitter words were worse than a bowl of poison.

It is not that God from His infinite state rewards us or punishes us, or that there is one fold or enclosure called heaven, in which the virtuous are allowed to be, and another called hell, in which all the sinners are penned. In reality we experience heaven and hell in our everyday life all the time. But here we experience both states, the dream and the physical life. There is always the possibility of change. If we experience hell now, tomorrow it may be heaven. If our experience today is heaven, then there is the chance that tomorrow it may be hell. But when we return from this world of variety we do not progress in experience; our heaven and hell do not change much.

Let us take first the hell and heaven that each person makes for himself here. When a person does an action with which his conscience is not pleased, the impression remains with him, torturing him continually and keeping before his eyes the agonies that his self experiences. We see in the world people in high positions, in luxurious surroundings, possessed of wealth and power, yet whose evil deeds keep up a blazing fire within them. Sometimes their life shows outwardly what their inward state is; sometimes it does not, and people think that they are happy, but they themselves find they are in hell. And yet it is partly hidden from their eyes, because of the continual variety of their experiences. This is the vague sight of their hell, which they will in the future experience fully.

When a person does some deed which his conscience likes, it approves him. It says, 'Bravo! Well done!' His soul is glad of his deeds. In however bad an environment he may be placed, the inner joy still suffices to keep him happy. When by his righteous deeds he has satisfied his conscience, the God within is pleased. However bad his worldly situation may be, he is happy within himself. The world, perhaps, may deem him unhappy, but he is happier than kings. This is his heaven, and the same experience continues uninterruptedly on the higher plane of existence, which is heaven and hell.

Every person creates his own heaven and hell. A disciple once asked his murshid, 'Pray, Murshid, let me see heaven in a vision.' The murshid said, 'Go into the next room, child, and sit and close your eyes and you will see heaven.' The mureed went into the next room and sat in meditation. He saw in his vision a large area but nothing else. There were no rivers of honey and seas of milk, nor bricks of ruby, nor roofs of diamonds. He went to his murshid and said, 'Thank you, Murshid. Now I have seen heaven, I should like to see hell.' The murshid said, 'Very well; do the same again.' The disciple went into the next room and sat in his meditation, and again he saw a large area, but nothing in it, no snakes, no fire, no devils nor cruel animals, nothing. He went to the murshid and said, 'I saw an area, but again there was nothing in it.' The murshid said, 'Child, did you expect that the rivers of honey and the seas of milk would be there, or the snakes or the fire in hell? No. There is nothing there; you will have to take everything from here. This is the place to gather everything, either the delights of heaven or the fires of hell.'

'Heaven is the vision of fulfilled desire, and hell the shadow of a soul on fire', says Omar Khayyám.

Our self, in reality, is heaven if blessed by divine mercy, and it is our self which is hell if cursed by the divine wrath. The seven gates spoken of in the Qur'an are the seven openings of our senses, through which gates we experience our heaven or hell, and the seven pinnacles mean the seven planes of man's existence, which have each its peculiar heaven and its peculiar hell.

Things appear to us as we make them appear. If we are tolerant with our surroundings and contented with whatever we have, enduring unavoidable discomforts and inconveniences, and if we acquire knowledge of our being, if we see the divine immanence around us, and if we develop within us the love on which the whole world is sustained, our life becomes a preparation for heaven and our hereafter its full expression. Such is the state of the godly. As it is said in the Qur'an, 'The pious enter therein in peace and security. . . . There shall touch them therein no worry, nor shall they be cast out.' If they are covered with rags, if lying on the dust, that dust becomes the throne of Suleyman, and their turban of rags becomes Khussrau's crown.

Our discontent with what we have in life, our intolerance of our surroundings, and lack of endurance of those conditions that we cannot avoid, our weakness in giving way to our passions and appetites, our lack of sociability, our ignorance of our true being and our blindness to the vision of God manifest in nature, are the torment of life here and the blazing fire in the hereafter.

Heaven is for the pious whose virtues were for this end, and hell is for the wicked who themselves have kindled its fire. The Sufi says, 'I am beyond both, happy in the arms of the eternal peace. Neither can the joy of heaven tempt me, nor can the fire of hell touch me, for I have embraced the bliss and have kissed the curse, and have been raised above life's joys and sorrows.'

Of course, no soul will remain in heaven or hell for ever. It is a gradual process of dissolving in the ocean of the eternal Being the remainder of the individual being. It is this state which is called *Pulserat*, or purgatory.

CHAPTER IV

QAYAMAT, THE END OF THE WORLD

A PERSIAN poet says:

> 'Thou hast hidden Thy face under the veil of Thy creation,
> But I know that it is Thou who hast by one stroke set both the worlds in motion.'

The world is like a child's hoop; when a blow is given to it, it runs on and on; when the force of the blow is spent it stops and falls down, and this may be seen in a lesser way in all things in the world. When the activity of the world has expired the world will fall down. The course of destruction is like the course of manifestation: it is in cycles. The first action is created by the blow given, and each action afterwards causes a further action.

The course of the world's life is like that of the clock. It is wound to go for a certain time. Some clocks go for four days, some go for eight days, some you have to wind every day. When that period for which it was wound has passed the wheels stop.

The law of construction and destruction may be described as having three aspects. Uruj, the first aspect, shows the force of activity; Kemal shows the climax, the limit of its progress; and Zeval brings it back to inactivity, the end of which is the absolute Kemal. Kemal shows its destructive power in both its poles, first at the end of Uruj, the activity in force, when the progress stops; and again at the finish of Zeval, when the activity absolutely ceases. The constructive element is called Kadr, the dominated power. The destructive is the absolute power which dominates. It is called Kaza. All that is born, built, made, or that springs up, must one day or other, singly or collectively, submit to Kaza, the destructive power.

It amazes us when, owing to an explosion, a factory is accidentally blown up, and thousands of lives are lost; it horrifies us to see a big city destroyed by a flood, and millions of lives sacrificed; but to the Creator it amounts to nothing. It is as if a mathematician were to write a sum, multiply, add, subtract, and divide, up to thousands and millions of figures, and then suddenly take a fancy to destroy the whole thing.

There is a time when one finger is cut off, and a time when the whole hand is lost. There is a time when one limb perishes, and a time when the whole body is dead. There is a time when one thing in the room is broken, another when everything in the room is smashed, another when the whole house is ruined, another time when the whole city, or the whole country is destroyed. So there is a time when the whole world is destroyed, even the universe; but this comes in a much longer period of time.

Why is manifestation, although it is made of eternal life, yet subject to destruction? The answer is that the eternal life is the only life and this seeming life on earth is merely an assumption. The Prophet was once asked, What is the soul? He answered in one word, 'Amr-e Allah', an action of God. There is the same difference between God and His manifestation that there is between a man and his action. As the action perishes and man remains, so the manifestation is destroyed and God remains.

All impressions and all memory, and all stains of the world disappear from the consciousness, leaving it as pure as it was before.

If a bottle full of ink is poured into the ocean, the inky substance is absorbed, and the sea is clear and unchanged as before. When a new universe is manifested, it is without the experience of a previous manifestation. When the universe has ceased to be, it starts again, and though this is repeated numberless times, each time it is as fresh as ever.

CHAPTER V

HAUNTED PLACES

IN OUR daily life the influence of the visitors who come to our house is felt not only in their presence but remains even after they have left. In the chair on which they have sat, the room in which they have been, the hall in which they have walked a finer person can sense it, though not, if course, everybody.

Once, on a journey, I had taken a room at Kandy in Ceylon, and during the hours of my meditation in the evening, whilst I was engaged in the sacred practices, I felt very restless and disturbed, and could not fix my mind on my meditation for a single moment. I became cross with myself, and went to bed, but my uneasiness increased. Then I got up and felt I must look in the cupboards. I did not know why I was doing so. I think perhaps my inner self wanted to guide me to the reason for such an unusual experience. I found there, to my surprise, a bunch of black hair, looking as if some woman had collected her combings for a long time. I spent a bad night, and in the morning the first thing I did was to ask the landlady who had occupied this room before me. She said, 'Sir, don't remind me of her. The thought of her makes me feel ill. A woman lived here for some time. She never paid me my rent. She called me bad names, fought with the men, and quarrelled every single day, driving away all my other tenants. Now my heart is at rest since she has left this house.' I said, 'What a shame that you gave me such a room to stay in.' She said, 'Sir, I gave you that room on purpose, because you seem from your looks to be a godly man, so that I was sure that this room would be purified by your good influence.' I had no answer for her but a smile.

If the influence of the living is such, how much greater is the influence of the dead in those places where they have lived and been happy, to which they are attached, and from which death has forcibly taken them! The remembrance of their home keeps them in the home in which they lived or in the field in which they worked, and in the clubs in which they enjoyed life, and in the houses of the friends to whom they are drawn.

If the spirit, during his life, has been interested in good dishes, after his death wherever there is a good dish he will always be there. If all his life he has been fond of whisky, after his death he will be at the bar where there is whisky.

Spirits are also attracted to their graves and to the crematorium by the love of the body which they had thought was their only self, but which in fact was merely the instrument of experience. In fact there is not one inch of space, whether on land or on the water, free from the influence of spirits.

A person who has been very fond of a certain society, of the society of his friends, his parents, his brothers and sisters, will long to be in that society.

The spirits that are desperately attached to this plane, and especially those among them that have but lately left it, manifest to the view as apparitions, or else by knocking at the door, by rapping on the tables and chairs, by lifting and removing objects, and by speaking. Their voices vibrate in the spheres and become audible to some of us. Sometimes one hears singing and shouting, and sometimes dancing on the top floor, or fighting going on among them. Some spirits appear to the living without any clothes, some with their legs and feet twisted outward. The former is owing to their lust, also to the misery they went through in life; the latter is due to a life passed in the thought of duality, and because they have gone astray in life, not having kept to the thought of unity; their body itself then demonstrates their crookedness.

I had my first experience of the spirits when a boy. One night I awoke in the middle of the night feeling a wish to look out of the window into our courtyard at the beautiful moonlight shining there. I went to the window, and looking out I saw some way off a man of saintly appearance, clothed in a long white robe, with long snow-white hair and beard. I saw him as plainly as in full daylight. I was amazed at the sight of him, wondering how it had been possible for him to enter our courtyard, all the doors being locked. But for his saintly appearance I might have supposed him to be a thief, but the nearer he came the taller he grew. At each step his height increased, until I could no longer see his head, and as he came forward his figure became a mist, until at last he was like a shadow, and in a moment he vanished from my sight. My hair stood on end and I was completely overcome by bewilderment.

The next morning when I told my family what I had seen, they tried to make nothing of it in order to keep me from superstitious beliefs; but others told me that they too had often seen this phantom appearing in this quarter. This taught me that spirits are attached to those places in which they are interested, just as we are, and they are constantly drawn to the places of their interest. Their form is not solid but ethereal, and can expand. This phantom which I saw was that of a Pir who lived in the well in our courtyard.

After a few years of these first experiences I was trying to forget and disbelieve this impression, fearing that it might lead me towards superstitions. But one day, happening to arrive at our country cottage in the middle of the night, I found on our land a huge person at a distance of three yards from me, making a sign that he wished to wrestle with me in the way Indians do, who give a challenge by slapping their thighs and crossing and slapping their arms. I did not for one moment take him to be a man; I at once thought that he was a spirit. At first I was terrified, comparing my size and strength with this gigantic spirit. But I had heard that the spirits swallow the fearful, so although I did not know the art of wrestling, I determined to fight with him, and I advanced, quite prepared to give him a blow. At each step that I took forward he drew back, which naturally gave me courage to close in upon him. He retreated until he was against the wall. I was glad that now I had got him, and approaching I struck him a strong blow, which, instead of hurting the spirit, knocked my hand against the wall, and the spirit disappeared.

The reason why the spirit appears and yet has no solid form is that it exists in a vaporous state, and the image seen in this vaporous form is nothing but the impression of his former body when on earth.

Among very many different experiences I cannot forget one

which made a great impression upon my mind. I had purposely rented a haunted house in James' Street, Sekunderabad, although my friends advised me not to, and in order to experience any manifestations there I slept there alone without even a servant. After a few days I began to find that whenever I played upon the vina at night, sitting on my bed, the bed would gradually begin to move as if levitating, and to rock to and fro. It would seem to rise for an instant some way into the air, but the movement was so smooth that there was no shock. I was playing with my eyes closed, and I thought that perhaps this was the effect of imagination under the spell of music. This went on for some time. Then I happened to send my vina to be repaired, and one night to my great horror I heard a noise as if all the windows of my house were being smashed. I got up and looked everywhere. The window-panes were unbroken, and there was no reason to suppose that there might be anyone in the house who had caused the noise. For three days this went on and I could not sleep. I had no peace at night until my vina came back. The spirits seemed to be so much interested in my music that they rejoiced in it and showed their appreciation by lifting me up; when the food of their soul was not given they rebelled.

You might ask by what power the bed was lifted. The answer is that the finer forces are much more powerful than the external forces. There is nothing that they cannot lift up or carry.

There are some who master the spirits so that the spirits bring them whatever they desire from anywhere, jewels, money, fruits, food. The spirits can even carry a person from one place to another. But those who work evil by the help of a spirit, train that spirit in evil and one day the spirit throws the bomb of evil back at them.

Sometimes spirits bring news for him who has mastered them. From whatever distance it may be they can bring the news in a moment of time. Sometimes the spirits go and cause trouble to someone if they are so directed by a spiritualist master. I have myself seen a case where the spirits would set fire to a man's house. Sometimes his clothes would catch fire, sometimes his papers burned, sometimes the food disappeared from the dish in which it had been put and dirt was found in the dish instead.

In twelve years' travelling throughout India, during which I concerned myself with psychical research, I have met with great and extremely expert spiritualists, who were able to receive news in a moment from any part of the world, and could even foretell future events by the help of a seer spirit.

Mohammad Chehl, a simple, unassuming man of ordinary appearance, our greatest spiritualist in India, showed the most wonderful phenomena. He could disconnect railway carriages from a train, leaving as many as he chose with the engine. Sometimes he disconnected all the carriages when the train was starting, leaving the engine to start alone. He never cared to travel in any class but the third. He used often for fun to ask the people sitting in the same railway carriage to show him their tickets, and then he would take the tickets, tear them up, and throw them out of the window in their presence. Everybody was angry and wanted to fight with him. He said to them, 'Who has taken your tickets? You have them with you.' He said to one, 'Look in your turban,' to another, 'Look again in your pocket,' to another, 'See in your shoe,' to another, 'Find it in your sleeve.' They were all amused and thought him a wonderful conjurer. He said to them, 'You may think that I hid your tickets and then put them in your pockets by sleight-of-hand, but what do you think of this?' And he put his hand out of the window and asked for a few hundred tickets for Delhi, and a few hundred for Ajmer, and a few hundred for Agra, and he asked them what other stations they wanted. When the train reached the next station there was great excitement. The station-master had just received a telegram saying that all the tickets for those stations had been stolen in a second and nobody knew where they had gone.

Mohammad Chehl never produced such phenomena unless he wanted to amuse himself. He never cared for notoriety or money. Nothing would induce him to make a show or a trade of his power. If he had cared to show his great power in the Western world, he could have filled his house with bags of gold.

CHAPTER VI

SPIRITUALISM

THE BELIEVERS in spirit phenomena often lose their balance and go to such lengths that the pursuit of spiritualism becomes a craze with them, for it is always interesting to tell and to listen to ghost stories. The teller has a tendency to exaggerate the story, to make it more interesting and arouse the astonishment of the hearer, and a simple listener has a tendency sometimes to take the rod for a snake.

There is a well-known case which happened in India where ghosts were being discussed among friends. One of them said, 'I don't believe in such things. I am willing to go and sit half the night in the graveyard if you like.' His friends said that they would not believe him unless he did so. He went the same night to sit in the graveyard. Half the night he passed trying to avoid all the threats that his imagination produced before him during that dark night in the graveyard. When the time was over, as he started to return to his friends, his long robe caught in some thorn bushes growing there. He thought a spirit had surely caught him. He fell down and was choked with fear, and in the morning he was found dead.

Often a landlord's enemies spread rumours that the house is haunted, so that he may not be able to get a tenant. Sometimes pretended spiritualists, who have made this their life's occupation, make it as interesting a play as they can, by arranging some knocks from here and there, by lifting the chairs and tables with an arrangement of wires, by producing effects of light and shade with phosphorus; they take advantage of the simple-minded. Some pretend to carry messages from the spirit world or to it, and deceive many earnest enquirers into these matters. Many carry out their questionable purposes by holding spirit meetings. All this drives material people, unbelievers in the spirit, still further away from the knowledge of the finer existence, while the so-called spiritualists are often so much engrossed in their hobby that they never realize their own spirit.

In ordinary life we experience two planes, the physical plane in which we experience through the eyes, the ears, and all the organs of the body; and the mental plane, the plane of thought and feeling. When we are asleep and all our organs are resting, we see ourselves just as we appear when awake in various surroundings. This shows us that we have another being besides this physical being and other eyes besides these eyes. Whilst we are dreaming, the dream is real to us. When we awaken, we think, 'I was there and now I am here. If what I saw in the dream had been real, it should all still be here now that I am awake; but it is all gone.' We distinguish the dream as a dream by its contrast with the waking condition.

Whilst we are dreaming, if someone comes and tells us that it is a dream, that it is not real, we do not believe him. Or if someone tells us it is a dream, we say, 'No, it is quite real, I see the things about me.' There is an expression we use of what is past, saying, 'It is all a dream now.'

When a person after death still longs for the earthly joys, he is in a very bad state, because he has not the physical body with which to experience them. He is like a cricketer or a football player who has lost his arms: he longs to play, but he has no arms; or a singer whose throat has been operated upon: he will long to sing, but he cannot, because his voice has gone.

When the physical plane is taken from a person, then the dream remains as reality, because there is no contrast to prove it otherwise, and this state of existence is called *Mithal*. He cannot experience on the earth now because he has lost the physical means. All the impressions that he has gathered upon earth are his world. It is the nature of the mind to gather as many impressions as it can. From this store the pictures that he sees are formed. We do not dream of what we do not know, of what we have not seen. The butcher sees the meat all day, and at night he does not dream of the dairy but of meat.

Sometimes, not only in the West but also in the East, those apparitions of the departed that come to communicate, to warn, to speak with someone dear to them, are called spirits. The word is really inappropriate. The spirit is the essence, the soul that dwells beyond. But since the word is so generally used, let us accept it. These so-called spirits are not the soul alone, but the soul together with the mind; that is, all that remains of the external self after the death of the body.

It sometimes happens that ghosts wish so much to experience the life of this world, that to a certain extent they make themselves substantial. They cannot make themselves as concrete as we are; otherwise they could live here. But to a certain extent they do, by activating the elements around, either the ether or the air.

When people see a ghost, it is in part illusion and in part they may really see it. When the inner eye sees, these outer eyes think that they see. But if they try to touch the ghost, there is nothing there. Thus the actual self of the spirit might show itself in the mist; but where, one may ask, does it get the clothes in which it appears, or anything that it may hold in its hand? The answer is that it is the impression of itself that the spirit holds which mirrors in the soul of the spectator, so that by his concrete illusion he feels its presence as positively as if he saw it with his own eyes.

The dead feel the thought, the good wish of the living. Prayer and religious rites focus the mind of the living on that of the dead, so that the dead may be helped by the living, or the living may be blessed by a saintly spirit.

The custom of offering food, perfume, or incense, to the dead exists among Hindus and Muslims. If someone comes to see us and we set food before him, or whatever may please him, it is appreciated. It is so with the dead also. They enjoy by our eating, by our smelling the perfume, because, although they do not enjoy the actual thing that we put upon the table, yet the impression of our mind, the joy it gives, mirrors itself upon their soul.

The dead person becomes more interested in the things that speak to the mind than in the material satisfactions. Therefore, when the food and drink and perfume are offered, the sacred names, the suras of the Qur'an, are read before them so that their intelligence may be satisfied also.

In order to know of the existence of the spirit we must ourselves live in the spirit, and above matter. If a person loses someone whom he loved very much and in whom he was quite absorbed, and he goes about lost in the thought of that person, he will become dead to the world around him, and then wherever he goes, in the crowds, in the jungle, he feels the presence of that person, because his self is no more before his view.

Our connection with the beings upon earth is much stronger, because we are conscious of our earthly life. We think of our friends whom we see, and sympathize with them; but we think much less of those who have passed on and what their condition may be now. Those who are living on other planes also think much less of us. There may be a connection between a mother and a child, or between a lover and his beloved, but ordinarily there is no contact between the living and the dead.

In regard to spirit communion, which is a subtle subject, I will say that it is better to have more connection with the beings living upon earth than to be obsessed with the desire to meet with the people on the other side of life. It is here that we are meant to evolve, and by being absorbed in those who have passed on we are taken away from the life we are meant to have; and we live on earth as if we were dead. People in pursuit of the spirits have a dead expression on their faces.

To have a devotion for the immortal and holy beings who have passed away is allowable because they are more alive than the living and more than the dead.

There are spirits whom we attract by our love for them, by our wish for their presence. We are surrounded in life by our friends, by those whom we like, whom by our liking we attract to us. And we attract the spirits also by our love. These are usually of a higher sort, these whom we call upon for help, for guidance, the murshids and the prophets. Sometimes there are visions of the murshids, the higher beings; these come to the initiate. They come to guide and to help in all difficulties. Someone who is quite absorbed in the thought of a prophet or murshid may be so lost in him, that if he calls upon him in any difficulty, the one upon whom he calls will always come and help him. To have devotion for a murshid or a prophet who has passed on is better than to ask for his help in whatever difficulty we may be, for God Almighty is closest to us and sufficient to help us in all our difficulties. No mediation of anyone, living or spirit, is necessary. Of course, as in life we depend upon each other's help, so also on the higher plane if the help of some holy spirit is granted to us we may accept it, but only if God's being is realized in all; from whatever source the help comes it is from God.

I have had many experiences of the vision of my murshid. one of which is the following.

Once we were making a three days' journey through the jungle, in a place where there was great danger from robbers, and every night two or three travellers were killed. Ours was the smallest caravan. Generally the caravans were of twenty waggons, but it happened that ours was of three waggons only. I had with me very precious gems given to me by the Nizam of Hyderabad, and instead of arms I had musical instruments with me. All the night I saw the form of my murshid, at first faintly, afterwards distinctly, walking with the waggon. The two other waggons were attacked and robbed, and a few worthless bundles were taken; but my waggon was safe. This is not the only instance I have had in my life; I have had a thousand experiences of the sort.

Animals can see the spirits better than we, because their activity is less than ours. We, owing to the worries and anxieties of life and the comforts and temptations of the earth, live more on the surface, although our intelligence is brighter than that of the animals. Animals after their death also appear as spirits, but for a shorter period and fewer in number than human beings, for they are not so absorbed in the earthly life as man is in his person and possessions.

I once had an experience with a dog. Returning from the theatre in the middle of the night with a few friends, I saw a dog following us. He showed a special interest in us. One of us, thinking it to be a street dog, struck it with his stick. The instant that the stick hit it, the dog disappeared, and at the same moment the stick broke in pieces. This happened in the presence of many people. We then found that a dog, a pet of our family, very fond of us, had died six months before, and it was the spirit of that dog, still attached to us, that was following. This dog was an exceptional one, and a remarkable thing about it was that every Thursday, regularly, it would fast.

CHAPTER VII

OBSESSION

WE OFTEN find in our daily life that we do things that we do not wish to do, things against our will and contrary to our ideals. Sometimes we recognize that such or such a friend has induced us to do an action which otherwise we should not have done, and we ascribe to him the credit or discredit of its result. It may be because our love for him is so great that we take his word to heart, whether we agree with it or not, or we may be so under the power of another person that we cannot but act as he wishes.

Occasionally we feel inclined to do a thing which apparently we have no reason to do. This is owing to the silent influence of some other person acting upon us without any spoken word and causing us to do that which we imagine to be his wish.

Sometimes the thoughts and conditions of mind of another person make so strong an impression upon us, either in the presence of that person or in his absence, according to the extent of his power, that his condition is transferred to us. We sometimes laugh without reason on seeing the intensity of another person's laughter, and we feel sad without any reason when we are in contact with one who is sorrowful. We fulfil the wish of another, not knowing that he had any such wish, sometimes even without his own knowledge of it.

It also happens now and then that we feel a desire to eat fish, and find that the cook has prepared the very dish of which we were thinking; sometimes we think of a friend and it happens that the friend comes to see us. All such instances are proofs of silent suggestion, the inner influence directed consciously or unconsciously. Sometimes we are under the influence of another person's mind and thought, at another time someone may be under our influence; it depends upon the positive or negative state of the will.

Suggestions are of two kinds; spoken command, and suggestion by thought. One who is powerful minded often may not intentionally command or suggest, and yet every word spoken by the powerful and thought by the master mind is fulfilled. 'Word spoken and action done,' is the accomplishment which is called *Siddhi* by Yogis, and those so accomplished are called *Sahib-e Dil* by the Sufis.

Hypnotism and mesmerism are a kind of obsession for either a good or a bad purpose.

The black magicians work six different spells: murder, fascination, severance, unrest, torture, persecution. The same are also wrought by the evil soul whose occupation it still is to work evil upon earth. This it accomplishes solely by means of obsession. Those subject to its influence experience any of these ill effects.

All this is partial obsession. Thousands of such influences come and go like moving pictures upon the blank curtain of man's mind, and it rarely happens that the effect lasts longer; if it does, then people call it obsession.

The influence of the dead is the same as the influence of the living, but even stronger. Their spirit throws its reflection upon the mirror of man's mind, and man acts as the spirit wishes, knowing all the while that his wishes are other than the spirit's. The intensity of spirit obsession is much greater than that of the influence of a living person; for the living are themselves subject to influences and obsessions, and their own self is an obsession to them, reflecting the various pictures of their own life upon their soul; but the spirits, from whom the burden of external existence is removed, are much more powerful, freer, and more inclined to obsess others.

Frequently a crime is committed by a man under the influence of another. A person with an evil thought of revenge, or the desire to kill somebody, by the very concentration of his evil thought becomes so weak that he cannot do it himself. Then he may consciously or unconsciously, by the intensity of his desire, convey to some other person the suggestion of doing it. The other person is innocent of the evil desire and so has the strength to accomplish it. This is often seen with anarchists; among anarchists there are some who only plan the deed, and there are others who carry it out.

There are two sorts of obsession: one is when one soul imparts its qualities to another; the other is when one soul causes another to accomplish some deed; this may be either evil or good. In India we have often seen this with snakes. The soul focuses itself upon the snake, and then the snake will feel an inclination to go and bite a certain person.

If the influence is so strong from a living person, the obsession of a dead person, of a spirit, is much stronger still. The dead person has no other means of expression, and so he seizes upon a weak person, a weak mind, and controls that. It is not that the soul enters into the body; the soul is much too large to do that; but it reflects itself upon the other soul. A spirit focuses itself upon the soul of another; the greater power holds the lesser.

If a man has left this world full of anger, full of hatred against his enemy and longing to do him harm, he cannot find peace. If a person leaves the earth with revengeful feelings he will long to accomplish his revenge. He is restless and looking for some means to accomplish his desire. The negative soul, suited to his purpose, receives this impression; not the positive soul, but one who is weak in body or mind. The well-balanced and vigorous throw off such influences; they are not easily affected.

A spirit may obsess for a good purpose or for an evil purpose. If a mother dies before she has been able to bring her child up, and all her thoughts and affection are centred in the child, she may obsess one of the relations, who then will feel inclined to take the child and do all he can for it.

It may happen in the case of soul-mates. Especially in the East this is often seen, where a man may love a girl or a woman whom he has seen only once and there is no chance of his ever seeing her again. Then, if he dies, she may become obsessed. She can think of nothing else but his thought and she becomes half dead, and is often in a trance. It may not be that she loved him very much, but his thought obsesses her, and she feels his condition only.

The disciples of Khwaja Nizam-ud-Din Wali, a great saint of Delhi, were once sitting waiting for him to come and speak upon a very abstruse and difficult matter, when to their astonishment they saw his servant come into the room and sit down on the murshid's seat. Nizam-ud-Din then came in, made a very deep bow to the servant and took his seat before him. The servant began to speak and spoke for some time, explaining some very subtle and deep questions. Then a change came over his face, he looked around, and ran from the room in great confusion. Afterwards Nizam-ud-Din told his disciples that he had asked his murshid for the answer to some very difficult question, and that the subject was so complex that the murshid needed a human form in order to explain it exactly, and that was why he had spoken through the servant.

I have taken a great interest in this subject. As a boy, out of curiosity, I studied it very much. I have always gone where obsessed people were to be found and I have seen some very curious and remarkable cases of obsession. One was in a Parsi family. There was a young lady who sometimes once a day and sometimes two or three times, would change her mood and would speak in Arabic and Persian; and she spoke about philosophy and metaphysics which she had never been taught. She was so strongly obsessed that she did not care to speak to her father and mother or her brothers and sisters or anyone else; nor would she ever go out. She always had incense burning in her room and led a very retired life. They brought learned people to speak with her, and she discussed with them like a great philosopher and got the better of the argument. Then she would forget it all again. At Sekunderabad there was a boy who sang Telagu songs. He had never learnt them, because Telagu is not spoken there among Muslims. Sometimes he would sing many songs, and then later on he could not sing one.

Many people who are obsessed go to Ujjain in Central India to be healed at the tomb of a Sufi, Miran Datar, a saint who in his lifetime cured cases of obsession, and continued doing so even after death. I once visited this place. On the steps of the tomb a man was sitting who seemed a quiet and thoughtful person. He was praying. I spoke to him. If I had known that he was obsessed, I would not have spoken to him, but I did not know it. I asked him, 'Why are you here?' He said, 'Do not ask me such a question.' I said, 'Why not?' He said, 'Because I am afraid. Now that I am near this holy tomb I have a little strength to answer you; if I were not here I could not even do that.'

He told me that he had been a store-keeper on some British liner going back and forth between Bombay and London. One day at sea he had a strange feeling, as if some power were taking hold of him, and he was not able to do anything. After that this power would often take hold of him, and he could not do what he wanted to do. At times he wanted to eat but could not; at other times, when he did not want to eat he had to go and eat. He became quite weak. He told the ship's doctor, but the doctor could do nothing for him. Then he went to see many other doctors, but none of them could help him. At last he went to the tomb of Miran Datar to see if he could find some relief.

While I was at the tomb of Miran Datar, the Prince of Kheralu came to it, a very handsome boy of twelve or thirteen, accompanied by aides-de-camp and attendants. He was brought there to be cured. A conversation began of which we could hear only the part spoken by the prince whose words were really those of the spirit that obsessed him. He said, 'I will not leave him. I like him so much. He was in the forest, shooting, and he came near the tree on which I was sitting. Don't whip me, Miran, I am his guardian, I will not leave him. Miran, don't whip me.' The prince began to run, leaping high into the air, and showed every sign of being severely whipped. He ran round and round the tomb, leaping every time that the invisible whip struck the spirit. At last he fell down exhausted, and his attendants at once lifted him up and carried him away.

When I came to the Western world I was curious to know whether it is only we in the East who have so many obsessed people, or whether there are obsessed people in the West also. They said to me, 'Here if someone were to show such a condition, we should put him in a lunatic asylum. If you wish to see cases such as you mention you must go there.' I went, and found that there were many who were mad and also many who were obsessed. I wanted to try some experiments in casting out the influence, but the doctors would not let me, because they wanted a medical diploma, which unfortunately I lacked.

Then they took me into the laboratory where they were dissecting brains, and they showed me that this man had a certain spot in his brain that was decayed and therefore he was mad, and another man had a cavity in his skull and therefore he became mad too. I asked them whether it was the decay that caused the madness, or the madness that caused the decay. At first they were astonished, but then they thought that there might be something in my philosophy.

According to the mystic's view the cause is mostly within. It is the fever that gives heat, not the heat that gives fever. Weeping does not come first and then sadness. The sadness comes first and that causes the tears to fall.

An Arab who had lost his camel, after searching for it everywhere heard that it was in the stable of the Sherif of Mecca. He went to the Sherif and said, 'I have been told that my she-camel which I lost has been sold to you and is in your stable.' The Sherif asked him, 'How will you recognize your camel? Has she any particular marks?' The Arab said, 'She has two black marks upon her heart.' The Sherif was amazed to hear this, wondering how the Arab could know about his camel's heart; and in order to ascertain the truth the camel was cut open, and two black marks were found upon her heart. The Sherif asked, 'How could you know that your camel had these two black marks upon her heart?' The Arab replied, 'Twice my camel was in great sorrow; twice she lost her foal; she looked up and gave a deep sigh, and I knew that each time a black mark was left upon her heart.'

I have seen that there are many suffering from such influences in the West, but, science being the conqueror of religion, the casting out of devils, so often mentioned in the Bible, is today mostly regarded as only a superstition.

The East, on the contrary, has gone to the other extreme. There are a great many cases of illness there which are taken to those who cast out devils, and these, in order to get as many patients as they can, interpret every disease as the influence of a spirit.

There are, however, two advantages in this course. The first is that the patient thinks that the disease is not within himself, but is an external influence which will cease if it is cast out. This prevents his taking his illness too much to heart, for the very thought of having a disease which is rooted in the body may often lead him to his death. Instead of that, however serious the illness may be, the patient will have the impression that it is a spirit that can be cast out; and this belief may restore him to health.

The second advantage is that a wise person can, while pretending to cast out spirits, arouse the patient so that he begins to confess the secrets of his heart—some hidden thought or feeling which may have made him ill. He had not been able to speak of it, having been constrained by the situation in which he was placed, but when this poison is released, the patient can easily be cured. Faqirs often work in this way.

Sometimes women, owing to the strict customs and manners of their country and religion, cannot tell the secret of their despair to anyone, and thus they hold the poisonous seed in their heart until their death, and this consumes them within. Many have had longings which could not be attained, jealous fits which could not be explained, heart-breaks which could not be repaired. All such cases show externally as a bodily disease, which doctors try to cure by chemical prescriptions, but the root remains. This treatment is like poison within mixed with poison without; the result, without any doubt, is usually death.

As soon as the patient's secret is known to the healer, he has really made a successful operation in the invisible heart and taken out all the poisonous substance which was causing the sickness and leading the patient to his death. He then releases him from this by words of consolation, by fragrance, by music, by the recitation of the names of God, and by reflecting upon the heart of the obsessed his own wisdom and piety. No doubt there are very few, even in the East, who could give the right treatment; and mostly there are real devils amongst those who profess to cast out devils.

CONCLUSION

I have known good and bad, sin and virtue, right and wrong; I have judged and have been judged; I have gone through birth and death, joy and pain, heaven and hell; and what I realize in the end is that I am in all and all is in me.

THE PHENOMENON OF THE SOUL

CONTENTS

CHAPTER I

THE PHILOSOPHY OF THE SOUL

THE SOUL is called *Atma* in Sanskrit; in Persian it is called *Ruh*. When the Prophet was asked, 'What is the soul?' he answered in two words, Amr-e Allah, which means 'an activity of God'.

The connection between the consciousness and the soul is like the connection between the sun and the ray. The ray is formed by the activity of the sun shooting forth its light. The activity of the consciousness shoots forth its ray, which is called the soul. Activity in a certain part of the consciousness makes that part project itself towards manifestation. The ray is the sun; but we distinguish the ray as apart, distinct in itself, longer or shorter, stronger or fading away, according to the state of activity in it.

The soul, during its life on earth and after, does not change its plane of existence; if any change takes place it is in the direction of its movement. The soul has originally no weight, but on its way it gathers around it properties produced from itself and borrowed continually from the elements which compose the universe, and as our possessions are not necessarily ourselves, so the properties are not the soul. The best comparison is with our eyes, in which vast tracts of country, huge mountains and miles of horizon on the sea are reflected at one time, and yet the eyes are scarcely an inch across. Such is the nature of the soul, which is so small as to be counted one among the numberless souls contained in the universe, and yet so vast as to contain within itself the whole universe.

The external self, the mind and the body, have confined a portion of the whole consciousness; the same portion is in reality the soul. It is as if a line were drawn upon a cloth marking off a part of it as separate from the whole. Or it is as if we were to stand before a curtain with a small lantern so that the light of the lantern falls upon the curtain and forms a patch upon it. In like manner the impressions of the mind and body are reflected on the soul and separate it from the whole consciousness. Upon the soul is reflected the happiness or misery, the joy or sorrow of the external self, but the soul in itself is neither sad nor joyful. The soul is neither subject to birth and death nor does it increase or decrease; it neither evolves nor degenerates.

If we stand before a mirror clothed in rags the mirror holds the reflection of our rags, but it is not itself in misery. If we stand before the mirror covered with pearls and diamonds the reflection of our pearls and diamonds falls upon the mirror, but the mirror does not turn into diamonds or pearls. So is it with the soul: it is neither a sinner nor is it virtuous; it is neither rich nor poor. All life's joy and sorrow, ups and downs, are reflected for the time being upon the curtain of the soul, and after a time pass away. Therefore both the joy and sorrow of yesterday are nothing to us today.

The soul and the body are of the same essence; the soul has formed the body from itself, the soul being finer, the body grosser. What in the soul may be called vibration in the body becomes atom. The soul has become mind in order to experience more, it has become body in order to experience still more concretely; yet the mind is independent of the body, and the soul is independent of both mind and body.

The soul sees through the mind and the body, the body is the spectacles of the mind, and the mind is the telescope of the soul. It is the soul that sees, but we attribute sight and hearing to the eyes and ears. In absence of the soul neither the body nor the mind can see. When a person is dead the eyes are there, but they cannot see; the ears are there, but they cannot hear.

The work of the soul is to know and to see, and the work of the mind and body is to act as a magnifying glass for it. Yet they in their turn also see and hear what is external to them, as the consciousness works through them also. The soul sees the play of thought in the mind, the mind perceives the pains and sensations of the body, the body is conscious of heat, cold, and touch. Its consciousness may be seen when something is accidentally about to fall on it; before the mind can think of a plan for safety the exposed part of the body instantly contrives its escape.

The mind sees the body alone, but the soul sees both the mind and the body; neither the body nor the mind is able to see the soul. The soul is accustomed to see what is before it, and so it cannot see itself. Our soul has always looked outward, that is why our eyes, nose, ears, all our organs of perception are outward. It is our mind and our body that attract our soul outward. And as the eyes, which see all things, yet need a mirror to see themselves, so the soul cannot see itself without a mirror.

When the eyes are closed, do you think that the soul sees nothing? It sees. When the ears are closed, do you think that the soul hears nothing? It hears. This proves that it is the soul that sees and hears. In the meditative life, by the mystical experiences of Anvar and Ansar,[1] a Sufi realizes the fact that there are objects which the soul can see without the help of the eyes, and that there are sounds which it can hear without the help of the ears. The great poet Kabir has said, 'What a play it is that the blind reads the Qur'an, the deaf hears the Gita, the handless is industrious, the footless is dancing.' He refers to the soul which has the capacity of working even without instruments, such as the organs of the body and the faculties of the mind.

Sleep, the unconscious condition, is the original state of life from which all has come. As the body sleeps and the mind sleeps so the soul sleeps. The soul does not always sleep at the same time as the mind and the body. This sleep of the soul is experienced only by mystics; they are conscious of this experience in themselves, and so can recognize it in others. The body sleeps more than the mind, the soul sleeps much less than either the mind or the body. When a person is fast asleep his soul does not lose its contact with the body. If the soul lost its contact with the body, the person would die; if the soul withdrew from the mind, the mind would be dispersed, the collection of thought would be scattered, it would be like a volcanic eruption.

The soul takes pleasure in the experience of the senses, in eating and drinking, in every experience. It indulges in this, and the more it indulges in it the more it becomes bound to it. All that we eat and drink contains a narcotic, even pure water. Therefore after eating and drinking a sort of sleep comes upon us, the soul feels a little relieved, it feels rather detached from the body.

[1] Clairaudience and clairvoyance.

The soul cannot easily be free from the body and the mind. Though its real joy is to attain peace by being free from experience, yet it has forgotten this. 'He will indeed be successful who purifies it, and he will indeed fail who corrupts it.' There are people who take strong drink, hashish, opium, drugs, and all such things. Under their influence the troubles of the body are felt less and the thoughts are blurred, the soul feels relieved; but it is a transitory happiness because it is dependent upon matter instead of upon spirit.

The ordinary person knows that after deep sleep he is calm, reposed, his feeling is better, his thoughts clearer. The condition of Hál, or Samadhi, the highest condition, is the same as that of deep sleep, the difference being only that it is experienced at will. The difference between the perfect person and the ordinary person is only this, that the perfect person experiences consciously what the imperfect person experiences unconsciously. Nature provides all with the same experience, but most people are unconscious of the experience, which is to their disadvantage.

When the mind is dispersed no impression will remain on the soul, nothing will retain it from merging into the whole consciousness.

Some philosophers have said that we are parts of God. That is not so. They have said this because they have seen the physical body. What more can the intellect see? In the physical existence each individual is distinct and separate, but behind this physical existence all are one, the consciousness is one. If it were not so we should not be able to know one another, neither the face nor the voice nor the language of each other. We can know when we advance spiritually how our friend is; even if he is in Japan or in Arabia and we are here, we can know if he is ill, whether he is sad or happy; and not the state of our friends only but everything is known to the advanced soul.

CHAPTER II

MANIFESTATION (1)

IN THE beginning, when there was no earth nor heaven, there was no other phase of existence than the eternal consciousness, which in other words may be called a silent, inactive state of life or unawakened intelligence that man has idealized as God, the only Being.

In the first stage of manifestation the unconscious state of existence turns into 'Ilm, consciousness. Every soul is a ray of the consciousness. The nature of the consciousness is that it is radiant, it sends out rays. These pass through all the planes until they reach the ideal manifestation in man.

In the Vedanta the soul is called by three names which denote its three aspects, Atma, Mahatma, Paramatma. Atma is the soul conscious of the life on the surface, Mahatma is the soul conscious as well of the life within, Paramatma is the consciousness that is the soul of souls, conscious of the Absolute within and without, the God of the knower, the Lord of the seer.

In the primal stage of manifestation the consciousness has no knowledge of anything save of being, not knowing in what or as what it lives. The next aspect of the consciousness is the opposite pole of its experience, where it knows all that it sees and perceives through the vehicles of the lower world but is limited to this. When it rises above this experience and experiences the higher world as far as the highest aspect of its being, as said above, it becomes Mahatma, the Holy Ghost that unites Paramatma, the Father, with Atma, the Son, as explained in the terms of Christianity.

This whole manifestation is constituted of two aspects of the consciousness, power and intelligence, in poetical terms love and light. All power lies in the unintelligent aspect of the consciousness, and the wisdom of the Creator that we see in the creation is the phenomenon of the intelligent aspect of the consciousness.

All this creation is not created of anything that is outside of the consciousness. It is the consciousness itself which has involved a part of itself in its creation while a part remains as Creator, as water frozen turns into ice and yet water abides within and the ice lasts only for the time that it is frozen; when light reaches the ice it turns into water, its original element. So it is with the consciousness; all things have been created out of it, and when their time of existence is finished all return and merge into it.

The consciousness has taken four distinct steps in manifestation, which in Sufi terms are called *'Ilm*, *'Ishq*, *Wujud*, *Shuhud*. 'Ilm is the stage in which the consciousness acts as intelligence. 'Ishq is the stage when the activity of the rays of the consciousness has increased and this has caused confusion among the rays and made power out of the intelligence, which is will in simple terms and in poetical terms love. The third step of the consciousness, Wujud, is the creation of vehicles, such as mind and body, through which it experiences the life on the surface. And its fourth step is its conscious experience of life from the depth to its utmost height, which is called Shuhud, and this fulfils the purpose of all manifestation.

The divisions of one into many are caused by light and shade, and if we looked keenly into life, both within and without, we should realize clearly that it is one life, one light, which appears divided and made into many by different shades. Every luminous object under the shadow of a less luminous object turns darker in part, and this in terms of art is called shade. It is this secret which is hidden under the variety of things and beings.

Time and space are the cause of all creation and the source of all its variety. It is time that changes things and beings from the raw state to the ripe condition, from youth to age, from birth to death. Time brings rise and fall, and space gives success and failure. A person may meet with failure in one place and in another place with success, in one country he may rise and in another country he may fall. If one were to look closely into life one would see that all creation is changed under the influence of time and space whereas no change ever takes place in space or in time. It is in these that the mystery of the whole world abides.

The activity of the consciousness has two aspects, motion and stillness, which causes two distinct things, the expressive power and the faculty of response. From the highest to the lowest plane of existence and in the life of all things and beings we see these two forces working unceasingly, each being for the other, and in the experience of expression and response lies the joy of both; in other words, the satisfaction of the consciousness. The sun expresses, the moon responds; the voice expresses, the ear responds. All the dual aspects in life, such as male and female, show these two aspects. There is not a single thought, speech, action, or event that takes place without the activity of these two; all happiness and success are in their harmony and every fall and failure are in the lack of it. The birth of every thing and being is caused by the meeting of their glance, and death and destruction are the result of their conflict, when either merges into the other and both lose their power.

There are two different ways in which creation takes place from the highest to the lowest plane: intention and accident. The former shows the wisdom of the Creator, who makes all things suited to their purpose; and accident is that which reveals a loss of purpose in things and beings. All the opposites, such as good and evil, sin and virtue, right and wrong, beauty and ugliness, are accounted for by the above two tendencies of the Creator that work throughout creation.

The whole creation acts under the law of attraction and repulsion. Attraction is the affinity which collects and groups atoms and vibrations and all things and beings; it is power, and repulsion is the lack of it. It is these two that uphold the universe; if one of them were to cease to exist the whole universe would crumble to pieces.

The life of the universe in all its workings is entirely dependent upon the law of tone and rhythm.

The pure consciousness has so to speak gradually limited itself more and more by entering into the external vehicles, such as the mind and the body, in order to be conscious of something, for the joy of everything is experienced when it is tried.

The first state of manifestation of the consciousness is of a collective nature, in other words a universal spirit, not individual. There is a saying of a dervish, 'God slept in the mineral kingdom, dreamed in the vegetable kingdom, awakened in the animal kingdom, and realized Himself in the human race.' Therefore the ultimate aim of the eternal Consciousness in undertaking a journey to the plane of mortality is to realize its eternal being.

Each of the said kingdoms has sprung from the preceding one, and each preceding kingdom has developed into the succeeding kingdom. In the mineral kingdom one sees by a careful study how the rock has developed into metal, and from metal into softer earthy substance, until it develops into the plant. And one sees how the development of the plant creates germs and worms, which we call lives, and how from their germ and worm state of being they develop into insects, birds, and beasts. This all shows that nature is working continually to rise to a greater consciousness of life, and finds its satisfaction at last when it has accomplished its journey by rising to its natural and normal state of being, which it accomplishes in man.

CHAPTER III

MANIFESTATION (2)

WHEN a ray starts out from the universal Spirit, projecting towards manifestation, it is called *Dipak*, meaning light, which in its lower manifestation turns into Cupid, the reverse of the word 'dipak' in spelling. In Arabic it is called *Nur*, light, from which words *Nar*, man, and *Nári*, women, are derived.

It is very difficult to differentiate rays from light and light from rays. It depends on our understanding. In the rays light is more separate, more distinct, while light itself is more collected, more together. But at the same time we should remember that the truth cannot be put into words; all we can do is to make an effort to render the mystery of life intelligible to our minds. The distinction between light and sun and rays is most useful, but it must be understood by the light of intuition; then it will become clear. Take for instance the example of the rain; why must the raindrops also rear poisonous plants and weeds, why should they not fall only upon corn, fruits, and flowers? They fall in all places; and so do the rays coming from the sun. The divine light falls everywhere without distinction just as the rain does.

When science discovered the secret of electricity, on that day science was also discovering the secret of the soul. For the secret of the soul is not far removed from the secret of electricity. The current of electricity is not necessarily the same as electricity. Electricity is the power which is hidden in the current. It is the same with the soul; the soul attracts atoms by some secret current; and that current is the soul itself. It is like one globe over another. There is something within the body, but at the same time it is all collected and gathered in that current; and that current is the ray; it is the divine current.

In the angelic sphere the soul attracts angelic atoms; in the jinn sphere it attracts jinn atoms, and on the earth physical atoms. Thus mankind is clothed in the garb of an angel, of a jinn, and of a human being; but when he only sees himself in the garb of a human being without seeing the other garbs, he believes he is nothing but a human being.

The souls coming out get impressions from souls going back because they absorb, conceive, learn, and receive all that is given to them by the souls leaving the earth. But what really happens is reflection; souls coming from heaven become impressed. It is just like an impression upon a photographic plate; and when they come on earth the photographic plate is developed and finished.

As a rule the reflection of two souls meeting takes place like this; but there is a difference in the qualities of souls. There is one upon which an impression is made instantly, and another soul upon which it takes longer. That is due to the intensity of power and radiation that the soul brings along within itself.

Souls on their way to the earth plane know, and at the same time do not know exactly, that they are on the way to experience life here. There is an impulse to go forward and to experience that which they may be able to experience. That tendency gives the soul strength to advance, and those which are able to advance far enough manifest as human beings.

The soul brings on earth an accommodation for its mind, already prepared in a very negative state, from the world of the jinns; that is the plane it gets its accommodation from. It gets a body after coming on earth, but the accommodation is filled later on, after the soul's awakening on the earth plane; it is here that the soul collects everything. For instance there may be one child which listens attentively to music, while another runs away from it; this means that the latter has not got the mould in which music is engraved. It will learn to appreciate music later if it will listen to it, but with the first child the mould was already made, and the music it hears will readily fit into that mould.

The soul gathering impressions first builds up the astral being, then attracts both sexes towards each other, manifesting to them first in ether, feeling; then in air, thought; then in fire, desire; manifesting after this into water and earth elements, gathering and grouping the substance from both, choosing a clay suitable for its formation. Generally a soul chooses also its birthplace and family. The soul inherits the father's qualities and the mother's form, in other cases the reverse; attracting the heredity on the father's and the mother's side until it steps on earth as an infant.

A mother seeing the growth of her child, says that her child has gained so many pounds. In fact it has lost as much, for the soul of the child has produced from its immortal nature mortal unconsciousness in order to experience life, and the more the earthly substance is built up, the more the heavenly being is lost, the more feeble it has become and the more the almighty power is lessened.

Sex is determined in every plane where the soul forms its vehicle; first on the plane of consciousness where it emerges as dynamic force or intelligence, then on the plane of the abstract as sound or light, which gives power to man and wisdom to woman. In man this manifests as influence and in woman as beauty. In the spiritual plane it manifests as expression and response, which gives man the fatherly and woman the motherly quality.

When and why was the difference of sex produced in manifestation? One cannot say that the soul of woman or the soul of man was made first, as the soul is neither male nor female. When the soul reaches the point where the distinction of sex arises, it is first male; then if it wishes to become finer, it becomes female. We can see in the kernel of the almond and of other nuts, that where there are two kernels in one shell the female form has been formed from the male.

One sometimes calls men and women who love each other very much two parts of one soul; but this can only be said in the sense that we are all parts of one soul. Between man and woman there can be affinities of the angel plane, of the jinn plane and of the physical plane; many different ties and affinities attract them to each other.

This whole world of illusion could only be produced by duality. In reality there are not two, but one. In order to produce this world, the one Being had to turn Himself into two, and the two had to be different. We have two eyes but one sight, two ears but one hearing, two nostrils but one breath. According to whether the breath flows through the one or the other nostril, it has distinct qualities and faculties; but it is the same breath.

If we hold a mirror in the sunshine, and turn it about, some of the flashes will be stronger, others weaker; some therefore positive, others negative. In the same way the rays of consciousness differ from one another in their energy from the very beginning. Then the ray on its course towards manifestation at once meets the male and the female soul, and the impression of the male and female is made upon it. It may have great creative forces and yet appear as woman because of this impression, or it may be of feminine quality and appear as man because of the impression it has received. When the soul reaches the physical plane, its sex depends upon the parents, upon the planets, and upon the time.

The sex that it takes at the time of formation is not changed later. In the Gulman and Peri sex exists also, though in a lesser degree. We have passed through the plane of Gulman and Peri, but we are not Gulman and Peri; just as we might pass through Germany on our way to Russia, yet we would not be Germans because we had passed through that country. Those who settle in the world of Gulman and Peri, are Gulman and Peri. They have either no inclination or no power to go further.

The reason for all manifestation is that manifestation is God's nature. By this he obtains His satisfaction through the fulfilment of the purpose of the whole creation. But God's satisfaction is not something He is only conscious of; it is something which belongs to Him but is brought to fulfilment. Joy is something which belongs to us, but it is aroused by a certain emotion, a certain action; so this whole creation, which is an action, brings to God the satisfaction for which it was created. It does not bring anything new to God; it only makes Him conscious of what He is.

It is most interesting to understand how the action of God works in manifestation. For instance, sometimes a person begins to walk about the room, or starts drumming with his fingers, or looks up and down without there being any need for it. Why does he do it? Because the absence of action has the effect of paralysing the activity of the mind; and when the absence of action has paralysed the mind the soul begins to feel lonely and begins to wonder whether it is living or not. But when it begins to walk or to stop, then it realizes that it is alive, because then it lives in the outward consciousness of life. If we think about this more it opens a vast field of knowledge.

Naturally not all motion is caused by restlessness, for there are two states: weakness and strength. When a person is weak, once put in motion he will act and go on acting without any control; the other aspect, however, is strength, and that is quite different.

Manifestation takes place in time and space. The sun, the moon, and the planets all have their influence. Morning, noon, evening, night, and every hour of the day each have their special influence too. The children of one father and one mother are very different from each other in height, in breadth, in appearance, in every way, because they are born at different times. If one brother is fifteen years old and the other five, the difference between them will be very great. Twins are very much alike because there is little difference in the time of their birth. Lambs are all much alike because they are born in the same season; and fishes of the same kind are almost exactly alike because thousands of them are produced at the same moment.

This gives rise to the variety, in which the art of the Creator is shown. Since the beginning of the world there have been no two faces alike. Every artist will draw some faces that are similar; how great then must be the art of that Creator who has made all this variety!

All manifestation is made by the two forces of accident and intention, and by the creative and responsive forces. We can see the forces of accident and intention at work in our lives. For instance, if we intended to go for a walk in the park but met a friend who said, 'You must come to my house', and he took us there, we had the intention of going to the park, but accident took us to the home of the friend.

Everything in the world is creative or responsive. When someone speaks he is performing the creative part; those who are listening are performing the responsive part. The sun and the moon, male and female, the fruit and the flower, all represent nature's creative and responsive forces.

Is the Creator then not master and able to make everything work as He wishes? The mastery is there, but its working out is in accordance with the impressions which are received from the external world.

When a person has been sitting still for some time he will want to move, to rub his hands, his feet, just to feel he is alive. If someone is very fond of the society of his friends and they are not with him, he will want to go out to see them. It is not really because he wants the friends; it is because if his friends are not talking to him, if he has to miss their activity, he does not feel that he is alive.

A blind man will say, 'I am half dead. This external world is nothing to me.' He is alive, but because he cannot see the activity of the world he feels dead. If one pondered upon what one's life would be without all the organs to experience the external world, one would see that then one could realize 'I am', but nothing else. No doubt if a person is inactive but looks at his hands and feet, he realizes that he is alive; but if he were not aware of this body his feeling would be different.

Those parts of creation that do not have much activity we may call living-dead. The mineral does not feel itself alive because it has very little activity. We consider the insects, birds, and animals to be the most alive because they have the greatest activity, and we sympathize most with them.

The destruction of form during manifestation does not affect the great Breath of God, as the ebb and flow of the sea is not at all affected by the waves, whether they go this way or that way. The manner of manifestation is the same all through, from beginning to end and from God to the smallest atom. For instance as God breathes, so we breathe and so do the animals and birds breathe; and when we see that act of breathing going on in the whole manifestation, in the same manner in which it has begun, then we realize that there is one law, one way in which the whole creation took place and will go on until its end.

We can see how minerals turn into plants, and plants into animals. There are some stones that change their shape every six months or so. They are on the way to becoming plants. And there are plants that are very near the stones, that look very much like stones; their leaves are like stones, their flowers are like stones. There are plants that catch and eat flies.

The plant by its decay produces the germ and the insect. Every fruit that is not used decays and produces many germs and worms. We think that it is wasted, because we think of it as a fruit; but it turns into a higher form of life, into more activity and more consciousness.

From the insects, as their activity increases and as they develop, come the birds. Those birds that are very greedy and eat flesh become heavy and do not stay in the air. Those that do not eat so much fly in the air; but those that eat much flesh remain on the ground and their wings become legs. Then the animals come into being. On some birds one may see that among the feathers on the neck and other places there is some brown hair; this shows that they are becoming animals. The animals evolve until man is formed.

The kangaroo and the monkey are most like man. In some primitive races, which have been human for a relatively short time, one can see the likeness to the animals. Other races have been man for a very long time and are more human.

The wheel of evolution is such that the consciousness gradually evolves through rock, tree, animal, to man. In man it evolves enough to seek its own way back to its eternal state of being. Man is the most active being; he has to do with a great many things. A rock has very little activity, and it lasts long; a tree has a little more activity, and its life is not so long as that of the rock. There are many animals that live much longer than man. Man has the greatest activity, and in him the consciousness reaches its highest point of manifestation. In the human race one also finds that man's face has improved at every period of evolution.

If man and animal are both made of the same substance, why then is man superior to the animal? Man and animal are made from the same element, spirit substance, but man is the culmination of creation; that is, man was made with all the experience of the previous creation. A sculptor, as he practises his art, grows more and more expert. His earlier work is not so perfect as the later. A poet grows more and more skilful in writing verse. His earlier poems are generally less skilful and perfect than the later.

When man was manifested the Creator had all the experience of His earlier creation, and all the former creation was so to speak the framework for man, the ideal creation. The Creator is the greatest idealist. Man can have his limited ideal; the ideal of the Unlimited is far greater, and this ideal is man.

Some of the human race come straight from God, others have come from the mineral, vegetable, and animal kingdoms. Primitive man is the result of this evolution. Man in his higher development does not pass through these stages. It is like the work of a sculptor in India who wishes to model a statue. First he goes to the jungle to get the clay; then he kneads it and soaks it and prepares it. When it is prepared, he does not go back to the jungle to fetch fresh clay for every statue. He has it ready; it is always in process of preparation.

The difference between what parts of God are expressed by plants, animals, and man is in their bodies and minds. The soul is a ray; and as a ray they are all one and the same. But the body is adorned, in accordance with the fineness of the soul which inhabits it, with more or less intelligence; thus animals and plants differ from man, but among mankind one will also find differences of the same kind. Some have a vegetable quality, some an animal quality, some a human, some an angelic quality. Among Hindus there is a custom, when a couple contemplates marriage, for their family to take their horoscopes to a Brahmin. He may not see very much in the horoscopes, but he is generally a psychologist and he ponders over the question as to what category each person belongs in—whether it is angelic, human, animal, or still denser. If he finds that there is a vast difference between the categories, he will tell them it would not be right for them to marry.

All the time sparks of consciousness are thrown off by the consciousness. They reach to various points of the stages of evolution, and when man is reached the ideal creation has been attained. It is then that the return journey begins. Man only can return to that light, to that consciousness from which the whole of creation came. Neither the horse, nor the dog, nor the cat will reach that light; it is only man who is the seed of that divine fruit. If you put the rind of an orange in the ground, it will not produce an orange tree. All the lower creation was made for the creation of man, God's ideal creation. In man all creation is contained, and he alone can return to the original source, God, from whence he came.

The perfection of God's manifestation is man. When man reaches perfection, His manifestation is perfect, and without man's perfection, God's manifestation would not be perfect. Perfection is reached when man becomes truly human.

One might ask if plants and animals, mountains and streams, also have a being or an apparent individual existence on the higher planes, as human souls have. All that exists on the earth plane has its existence on the higher planes too; but what is individual? Every being and object which is distinctly separate may be called an entity, but what one calls an individual is a conception of our imagination; and the true meaning of that conception will be realized on the day when the ultimate truth throws its light upon life. On that day no one will speak about individuality; one will say 'God' and no more.

There are many beings, but at the same time there is one, the only Being. Therefore objects such as streams and mountains are also living, but they only exist separately, to our outer vision. When our inner vision opens then the separation is shown as a veil; then there is one vision alone, and that is the immanence of God.

CHAPTER IV

THE WORLD OF THE ANGELS

A MATERIALISTIC person cannot easily believe that there are such beings as angels. He says, 'How can there exist beings whom we have never seen, heard, nor known?' And as this is a materialistic age, even the religious person doubts whether there are such beings.

In Hindustani angels are called Deva; they are Devata, immortals, while the other beings are called Rakshasa, that is mortals. In reality all are immortals, but we are what we consider ourselves to be.

Where, in nature, there is a beautiful and peaceful feeling, it is said that a Deva is living there. The soul of a Deva is creative of beauty and peace. The part of the Deva in the scheme of life is loving, forgiving, and serving God and humanity. The Deva is the divine soul. We find traces of the same word *Deva* in the English words 'divinity' and 'divine'. In Persian the angel is called *Farishta*, one who is sent.

The relation of angels to human beings is that of a little child to a grown-up person; they can help human beings as an infant can help its elders.

Some souls remain angels; they are in the highest glory; and others become jinns or human beings according to the strength with which the mechanism is wound, as is the nature of the clock. The first offshoot of the divine Light is the angel; some but not all experience life on all succeeding planes. It is as if a thousand birds had started from Paris for England, and some went as far as Rouen, where they remained, as they liked the place; and enjoying themselves they forgot about England. Some went to Le Havre and stopped there; some crossed the Channel and arrived in England. The ones who stayed in Rouen did not have far to go when they returned to Paris, but the ones who reached England had farther to go on the return journey.

In the angelic heaven there is purity, but not perfection, as there is only one perfection and that is God; there cannot be perfection where there is duality. Imperfection is not learned; it is a state of being, it is limitation. Limitation is the condition of life; however great, virtuous, pure, and strong a person may be, still there is imperfection going towards perfection. The entire interest lies in going forward; if we were born perfect there would be no joy in life.

The word angel suggests *an*, without, and *jel*, mortality. Angels are souls which, coming out of the consciousness, have reached as far as the world of the angels and remain there. Every angel has a limit to its reach. When it reaches as far as man, then, by the effort of travelling so far and by the activity of man's life, its impulse is exhausted.

Angels do not experience birth and death in the sense we generally understand them; yet there is only one being: God, who is above birth and death; all else is subject.to the law of birth and death. The difference between the earth plane and the angelic plane is very great; but there is a time of youth and a time of age in everything, a time when the fruit is unripe and a time when it is ripe; and so it is with the angels, though there is no comparison possible between the life of angels and that of human beings, human life being too limited.

Just as in our life there is a time when we grow taller, broader, stronger, and everything in us increases, and then, when the limit is reached, we do not grow any more and become weaker every day, so it is with the angels. Only, the life of the angels is much longer than man's life. Theirs is a life of illumination and of praise; they are much nearer to the universal, everlasting sound, the universal, eternal light, much nearer to God, than we are. They have luminous bodies, as solid, as concrete, as the light one sees. The speed of a journey in the heavens is also much quicker and cannot be compared with that of the lower world; it is quickest in the heaven of the angels.

The question arises: do angels have a form, a face? This question is very difficult to answer in words. The reason is that every being and object that has a name has a form or a face; but we are accustomed to give a name to something only when we can distinguish a form; and what our eyes cannot see we do not call a form. One might as well ask whether our imaginations have faces. Our imaginations have the faces we give them and by which we distinguish the one from the other; our feelings too have the faces that we give them, and these faces distinguish one feeling from another feeling. However, the face of an angel is not so concrete as this physical form of ours which we call our self, 'I'; but in order to conceive, to picture, the form or the face of an angel, one needs to become an angel oneself. We are accustomed to consider every form like our own; therefore, when we picture angels, fairies, or ghosts, we picture them like ourselves. The fairies of the Chinese have Chinese features, the fairies of the Russians wear Russian hats. The form we imagine covers the angelic form.

Every atom of manifestation can be said to have a soul, because all manifestation has come from the heavenly source, the divine spheres; so every atom comes from that source and cannot exist without that heavenly radiance. Every atom has radiance, even those of dust; we see this because it has light in it. It is its own light which shows it to us, and that light is its soul. Much that seems to us devoid of intelligence is not so in reality; only the intelligence is buried in the heart; it has projected itself and it has been buried by what it has projected; one day, however, it must emerge.

One can see this in the stars and the planets, in lightning and in volcanic eruptions, when that which is captive desires to burst out. But its greatest chance is in human life, and thus spirituality is the only object in the fulfilment of human evolution.

Not only angels, jinns, and human beings, but even animals, birds, insects, trees, and plants all have a spiritual development in their lives. No creature ever born on earth will be deprived entirely of spiritual bliss, however bad or wrong it may seem. It is a matter of time and progress. Human beings all have a moment, a day, when they touch spiritual bliss; thus all other beings have a moment of promise, and that promise is the fulfilment of their life's purpose. There is nothing in this world without a purpose, and though our places in the scheme of life may seem different from one another, yet in the sum total of things we and the lower creation, together with the angels and the jinns, all have our purpose. That purpose is the realization of truth, and this realization comes to us in the form of bliss.

Is there a likeness between the bodies of an angel, a jinn, and a human being? One cannot give a definite picture of the likeness between those bodies, but they all develop towards the image of man. The physical body is the most distinct and clear; the jinn body is less clear, more phantom-like; and the body of the angel is still less distinct, that is to say less distinct to human eyes. Therefore one cannot compare the things of the earth with those of the other spheres. If there is any similarity it is only because the whole of creation is a development towards the human image.

There is one and there are many; in manifestation many, and in truth one. There is for instance the rise and fall of a nation, the prosperity and decline of a race, and there is also the birth and death of a world; yet at the same time even the lower creation is individual. Every animal, beast, or bird, every tree or plant, has its own soul and spirit; if one says that animals have collective souls, then so have human beings. Our body is one yet every organ is separate; and when we go more deeply into this we discover the wonderful phenomena of life, and we shall come to a place where the entire nature of being will unveil itself; then we shall be able to say there is nothing but God.

Every soul has come through the world of the angels, and every soul has the angelic quality and its connection with the world of the angels. Sometimes a very bad person will show a very good trait. We say that it comes through a certain influence, a certain situation. In part it is so, but mostly it is the influence of the angel. Sometimes a very good person does something very bad. This also is the angelic influence.

Muslims say that when a person performs Wuzu, the washing before prayers, from every drop of water that falls from his hand an angel is created. The meaning of this is that by that noble action for which he is preparing himself the angels are created, and to create an angel means to attract an angel, so that he can communicate with it.

The Qur'an distinguishes five principal angels, of whom Azazil was the chief, the most powerful, the favourite of Allah. The

Qur'an tells that Allah created a form made of earth. The angels were bidden to bring the substance for that form. That form was made into man, Ashráf al-Makhluqát, the Khalif of creation. All the angels were commanded to bow before him, but while all the other angels prostrated themselves, Azazil alone rebelled, saying, 'I have been chief of the angels. I will never bow before this thing made of earth.' It was pride, it was arrogance, it was hatred that made Azazil rebel, and he was degraded and deposed by God and called Shaitan (Satan).

The names of the five most important angels are: Jebrail, Israil, Israfil, Azazil, and Azrail.

Jebrail, who in the Bible is called Gabriel, is the compeller, the spirit that compels men to the way of Allah, to do something for Allah. He came to the prophets, he comes to those who have given up everything, all the desires and the interests of the world, for the sake of God.

Israil comes as inspirer. Some call what he brings inspiration, others call it revelation. This comes also to the pure-hearted musicians and poets.

Israfil is the further revelation, the explanation of the revelation. For instance, if there comes a revelation that a friend is arriving, the further revelation reveals why he is coming. The reason of everything is explained. By communication with these two influences all the metaphysics, all the philosophy that one tries to learn by study, can be acquired through inspiration, without any learning.

Azazil is the spirit that leads towards darkness, towards wrong actions, towards evil. Hatred is a wrong kind of attachment. By his evil action a person attracts this spirit. When a person goes astray he attracts this influence, communion with this spirit.

Azrail is the spirit of death. When he comes, then comes the death of everything, the destruction.

CHAPTER V

THE SOUL'S EXPERIENCE

THE CONDITION of the ordinary soul when it first leaves the body is confusion; for before death it has realized that it is dying, yet it is really only after death that it lives. It is like a person who is alive thinking that he is dead. As long as this condition remains the soul goes no further; it is this state which is called purgatory. When the soul has realized itself, when it has realized that it is still living, then the clouds of confusion are dispersed and the soul finds itself, together with the atmosphere which belongs to it.

All souls return to God, some with open eyes, some blindly. Every moment of this life is an opportunity, whose value is so great that all the pains, all the troubles, all the sorrow of existence would be too small a price for even one moment of life. It is as if God threw darts. Some reach the point at which they are aimed, others fall short, others might go much further than man is now.

The being of God is a perfect being. The riches that the souls bring from the earth, by knowledge or by anything else, are no addition to God; for God it only means that something which was in the hand has come to the elbow. What difference does it make? It is all the same. Yet it is better that the thing of the hand should be in the hand rather than at the elbow. All that is known on earth and in heaven belongs to God; it already exists and is already in Him, the perfect Being.

No soul is attracted to what we call Satan or the devil. Our soul does not like us to do what is wrong for us. Our soul does not like us to be unkind. Every soul has in it the highest attributes, and has a tendency towards the light and a tendency towards awakening. If it has not there are reasons for it. Either the soul has gathered around it vibrations that are undesirable; or it has not come through the proper channel of manifestation and therefore it is weak; or it clings to its undesirable habits and ideas and will not let them go. The condition of the soul can turn any place into heaven. Not only the earth but even hell could be turned into heaven, if only the soul attained the perfection which is its only goal.

On its return the soul passes through the same planes and states that it comes through on its way to manifestation, with all the experiences it has acquired in its life on earth. When it arrives it is blank; when it leaves it goes away with the experience that it has gathered. Souls keep their individuality after death, for individuality is not made by the physical body; individuality is covered by the physical body. When the cover disappears, individuality still remains.

All that the soul has borrowed through manifestation, it returns to its origin. It is natural that the physical body should be the earth's due. And when it is paid back to the earth it is just like giving the child into its mother's arms. It is a most natural process. The soul does not wither and get worn out, but what it has gathered around it on earth, what it has imagined itself to be, all that it has taken from the lower plane, withers and becomes worn out; not its real self but its false self.

The one who does not come to God-realization in this life will come to it on the way towards the goal. It will be perhaps easier there, but it is better to do all one can on earth. Nothing that we really value can we put off till tomorrow. What one puts off one does not value enough.

Souls which have passed away are nearer to us in one way than those on earth, but in another way they are further. They are nearer in the way that if they want to get in contact with us, or we with them, it is more easily done than with the souls on the earth. But when we look at the difference between the plane on which they live and our plane, they are further than those on earth, because there are more means of communication here.

Souls which have passed away are engaged in doing the same thing that they were doing before. Their world is more beautiful than nature on earth, for mind is nature also; mind is an improvement upon nature and it is part of nature at the same time. For instance the idea of paradise is an improvement upon nature, and while on earth paradise is an imagination, in the hereafter the same paradise will become a reality. To create happiness for oneself and others, therein lies the whole of religion and the whole of philosophy. After passing away some remain under the impression of death for a long time, but one cannot compare the time of this world with the time of the other worlds. The time of the next world is much longer than the time of this world. The deeper the impressions are, the longer one has to remain in purgatory. The sages, the prophets, have shown their spiritual advancement at the moment of their death. That is the time when the truth comes out; then there can be no falsehood, and a man has no chance of acting. When his soul is passing from the earth, where his heart was is shown—on the earth or in heaven. Besides, the person who has earned peace throughout his life then shows his wealth; he passes away peacefully and with willingness to meet what awaits him in the life beyond.

The soul upon its journey back to consciousness passes through the world of jinns until finally it reaches the infinite goal where the soul is no more individual. It still has a slight feeling of 'I'. It does not distinguish between 'mine' and 'thine', but when a man has thought of himself all his life as 'I' he will still keep a slight sense of 'I'.

The soul is hindered in its progress by being called back to earth by mediums and sorrowful friends. Suppose a person is going somewhere, and all the time people call out, 'Please stop, we want you', he will never be able to get to his destination; the purpose for which he is going is hindered. To call a soul back would be acting against nature itself. It is better to help the soul to go forward, and that one does by sending one's loving thought.

The meeting of a soul going towards manifestation and a soul returning from there may be unconscious. Also, a soul going towards the earth cannot ask for advice or help from a returning soul, because his mind has not yet become like that of a human being and he is passive. What he receives he gets without asking, in the same way that an infant does not ask for something; it only wants to have it. Just as human beings are generally not conscious of angels or jinns, so the angels are not all conscious of jinns, nor are all jinns conscious of angels, although some are. A soul can attract a jinn to help it to accomplish something on earth, and a jinn may attract a soul for the same purpose. A jinn is not really interested in accomplishing anything on earth, but when it sees what is going on there it may become interested. A person who does not go out of town has no interest outside the town, but when he goes to the country, his interest is awakened.

One may ask if a jinn who is sent to the earth looks like a human being. The jinn who is on the jinn plane is quite distinct as a jinn; but when a soul which is very much impressed by the jinn plane has come on earth, it will show something of the jinn even in form and features.

Souls return through the jinn world and the angel world by the same way by which they have come. But the ones who have realized God on earth do not stop there; they go to God while on the earth. There is no condition of having to go to God through the outer death; the condition which the Sufis call Fanà is no crucifixion, for God is nearer to them than anything else. To the jinn world is one step; to the angel world is two steps; but to God there is no journey: He is there.

The joy of life is the joy of the journey. If one could close one's eyes and be put immediately on top of the Himalayas, one would not enjoy it as much as the one who climbs and goes from one peak to another, and sees the different scenery and meets the different people on the way. The whole joy is in the journey.

There are many souls who after having passed away try to communicate with the people on earth, but generally these do not receive their communications clearly. However, unconsciously they do receive them, and very often they do errands for those who have passed away, thinking they are doing it because they themselves wish to. In order that a person should be convinced of the reality of the spiritual world, why should the spirits strive? Why should not man develop his faith? And if man is so obstinate as to avoid developing himself here, he will avoid development even in the spirit world. For in man is the possibility of faith; the jinn world is not necessary as an intermediary.

Children and infants who die also come to spiritual maturity, often on the jinn plane and sometimes on the plane of the angels. It depends upon the qualities of the soul and upon the object it is meant to accomplish.

Souls that are not in tune will enter the angelic heavens all the same; even in heaven there is no peace. The inharmonious people follow the harmonious ones even there. One soul is more harmonious than another, but in the music of the heavens they all fit in, just as in our music we would not want everything to be alike. And the souls who are still out of rhythm will continue to have the choice of becoming harmonious; for there is a choice at every step in the heavens too. Life is progressive, and that is why there is always hope of improvement.

If a link of sympathy exists, then the light of those who are our well-wishers, either in the sphere of the jinns or in the angelic heavens, will certainly be thrown upon those on earth. Their love, tenderness, and goodness shine upon those on earth just like the love, tenderness, and goodness of parents towards their children. In short, illuminated souls in whatever sphere they are will be showing their light.

The soul is continually on the way towards improvement, therefore even in the angelic world the soul is not quite perfect. The perfection is in the goal, not in the soul.

In a way there is a difference in the degree and experience of happiness of the soul going towards manifestation, and of a soul returning; but the difference is like that of notes in music. This applies particularly to the souls returning to the goal, who have acquired something from the earth or from the sphere of the jinns which has influenced the tone and rhythm of their being; and therefore they so to speak tell the legend of their past in the music they make in the heavens of the angels.

There is a relationship between the bodies of souls on the different planes, because they borrow their body from the clay of the plane where they are, and from that comes the connection caused by the clay or matter of that plane.

The soul, while being a current, has two kinds of atoms, physical atoms and mental atoms. If one garb is thrown away the other garb is not free from individuality. It goes on living;

it lives longer than the physical body. Life is limited for the very reason that substance is limited. Mind and feeling have their own life, they do not belong to the brain but to the original condition; that is why the mind lives longer than the body. The hereafter means living in the inner garb. One still continues one's life in the hereafter because the soul is consciousness itself.

The higher body of the soul is formed from the lower body of the same soul; there is no break. It is a continuation. Something is taken, although not everything can be taken.

In the jinn world there will be silence. Silence is necessary just as sleep is necessary for repose; but at the same time there will be action, and its speed will be incomparably greater than the speed of action on the earth. Spirits on the jinn plane meet with all kinds of experiences, just as on the earth; they can even have accidents or get killed. But in the jinn sphere it will be easier for us to see our goal, for the possibilities there are greater as there is less limitation.

It happens that jinns are sent to the earth with a mission, like angels. The jinns are capable of knowing their imagination to be imagination, their mind being clearer than that of man.

Jinns are able to communicate with spirits returning from the earth; but it is with them as with the inhabitants of a certain country who may have heard of other countries, but are generally much happier in their own, with their own way of living; and when some go out and bring back knowledge from the other countries, it may not be agreeable to the ones who remained at home.

The path of the jinn is the path of beauty, as the path of every soul is one of beauty; and every soul, good or bad, is seeking after beauty. When it steps wrongly on the path we call it evil, and when it steps rightly on the path of beauty we call it victory.

The scenery of the jinn world is peculiar to itself. It is a negative state of what one sees positively in this world, but there is more beauty there than one can find on earth. In a way it interpenetrates, but at the same time it has its own peculiarity which cannot be compared with the beauty of this earth. The reason is that manifestation on this plane has limitations owing to its rigidity. The higher the world, the fewer are the limitations to be met with.

Is there no illness or impression of illness on the jinn plane? There is; as there is illness on the plane of the earth so there are certain discomforts on the other planes. But the healing power of the soul is such that even on earth it can heal the body it finds itself in, and the illness it takes from the earth it heals in the hereafter. The struggle is easier there, but some of the discomfort will remain on that plane, for life is a continual struggle.

Very often it happens that a soul which had meant to go on towards the physical plane remains in the jinn plane out of love for a soul already there. It is love that takes one forward, and it is love that holds one back. The difference is that it is a higher love that takes one forward, and it is a lower love that holds one back. Once a soul has individualized itself on a certain plane, it becomes an inhabitant of that plane; it does not go forward.

CHAPTER VI

THE LAW OF HEREDITY

HEREDITY has been much thought of among all peoples and in all ages. If we look at the animal kingdom we see that the lion cub is never the offspring of the snake, nor are toads hatched from pigeon's eggs; the oak tree will not produce dates nor do roses spring from thistles.

We see in the East that of all breeds of horses the Arab horse is the best. One slight touch of the whip will make it leap any obstacle or cover any distance, while there are other horses that are like donkeys, on whose backs dozens of lashes are laid and they put one foot forward and stop, and again twenty lashes are given to them and they take one step forward. The Arabs value their horses so highly that they preserve the breed and never allow it to be mixed with any other strain. Among dogs there are some who will follow anyone. Whoever gives them a bone is their master, and if another person gives them meat, they leave the first and run after the other. And there are others who follow only one master, who obey only one and sometimes even sacrifice their life for him. It depends upon the breed, the heredity.

In the East they have considered this subject of heredity very much and have attached great importance to it. The son of a poet will always be a poet, the son of a musician is expected to be a musician. If a man handles weapons they ask him, 'Are you the son of a soldier?' The son of a miner will never do the work of a shepherd, and the son of a shepherd will never do the work of a miner. A great many words of abuse have more to do with the parents than with the person to whom they are addressed, and a great many words of praise have to do with the ancestors, not with the person of whom they are spoken.

In India, in Rajputana, there is a family of poets whose ancestors have been poets for ten or fifteen generations, and they are all of them great and wonderful poets. They are called *Shighrakavi*, improvisers, and are appointed to the courts of the

Maharajas. Their work is to stand up in the assembly upon any occasion, and to recite verses, in rhyme and metre, in a manner suitable to the occasion and to the people present.

In ancient times, when sons of kings and great people were often driven from their country and wandered unknown in other lands, the way of recognizing them was always by some test of their quality. It has happened in the history of the world that slaves have become kings, and yet they could not keep themselves from showing from the throne, through their grandeur, glimpses of their slavish nature.

Is it the soul that transmits its qualities, or is it the mind or the body that transmits qualities? This is a vast subject. Before explaining it I will say, as to the word soul, that there are some people who call soul those qualities which compose the individuality. This is not the soul but the mind. The soul has no qualities, it is the pure consciousness and therefore it does not transmit any qualities.

When the soul starts from its original point, it comes first to the world of the Farishta, the angels, and is impressed with the angelic qualities. The angels are absorbed in the hunger for beauty and the thirst for song. They do not distinguish good and bad, high and low. The infant, who represents the angel on earth, always turns to what appears to it radiant and beautiful. There are two sorts of angels, those who have never manifested as man, and those spirits who upon their way back to the infinite have reached the world of the angels. Love, light, and lyric are the attributes of the latter, and from them the soul receives these impressions. Devotion, service, and worship are the attributes of the former. The angels are masculine and feminine; the former are called Malak, the latter Hūr.

In the world of the angels the soul for years and years enjoys these experiences. When the desire for more experience urges it on, it goes forth and comes to the world of jinns, which is the astral plane. In the Bible we read that Adam was driven out of paradise; this means that the wish for more experience makes the soul leave the world of the angels and go to the astral plane and the physical plane.

The occupation of the jinns is to imagine, reason, and think.

The jinns are of two sorts: there are those who have never manifested physically and there are those spirits who have left the earth with all the load of their actions and experiences upon them. The jinns also are masculine and feminine, and are called Gulman and Peri. From the first sort of jinns, those who have not manifested physically, the soul receives the impressions of imagination and thought. The soul that leaves the earth can take to the world of the angels only whatever love, good feelings, and kindness it may have. Even its love and kindness and its good feelings it cannot take higher than the world of the angels; these are still too heavy for the higher plane. For there is a higher plane, and on that plane there is no individuality, nothing but the infinite consciousness. All the rest the soul must leave in the astral plane, and until it can leave behind all the evil that it has gathered it must remain there, as it is too heavy to go higher. It is like milk that is put over the fire: when all the watery part has evaporated, the cream, the good, the essential part of the milk remains. This plane is just like a street where someone is walking with a bundle. He says to a soul, 'Will you take this bundle?' The soul is inexperienced, and so it says, 'Yes, is it a nice bundle? Has it a good sound or a good perfume?' It takes the bundle, and receives all the impressions that go with it.

Every soul possesses the best qualities. However wicked a person may be, be assured that his soul possesses the best qualities as a special inheritance, though they are covered up by all that has been gathered afterwards. And there is always a possibility of spiritual progress for every soul, even for the most wicked.

The soul, on its journey from the unseen to the seen world, receives impressions from the souls which are on their return journey from the seen to the unseen. In this way the soul collects the first merits and qualities. It is this which forms a line for the soul to follow, and it is this line that leads it to the parents from whom it inherits its later attributes. The soul receives the impressions of another soul if it is attuned to that other soul. For instance a soul meeting the soul of Beethoven receives the impression of Beethoven's music, and then is born with the musical qualities of Beethoven. The upholders of the theory of reincarnation say that he is the reincarnation of Beethoven; the Sufi says that if they mean that Beethoven's mind is reincarnated in him, it may be so; but as the spirit comes from the unlimited, he says it need not necessarily be called reincarnation. Therefore a person of poetical gifts may be born in the family of a statesman where there was never a poet before.

The soul of a saint or murshid has remained long in the world of the angels, and being more impressed by it, it brings with it the angelic qualities of that world.

When the Bible speaks of 'the son of God', and the 'son of man', it means that he is a son of God who has recognized the eternal spirit as his parent, and that he is a son of man who has recognized himself as the son of his parents who are as limited as he. We recognize our father and mother as our origin. The parents claim the child as their own, and so delude themselves. Its origin is the universal spirit; and in this we are all brothers and sisters, without distinction of high or low, of race or caste, of creed or religion.

Each soul is like a ray of the sun or of any light. Its work is to project itself, to go forth as far as it can. It is creative and responsive. It creates its means, its expression, and it is impressed by whatever comes before it, in proportion to its interest in that. The soul goes always to what appears to it beautiful and radiant, and so it goes on and on and finds different qualities and different experiences and collects them round it, until at last it finds the mother's womb.

A child may or may not inherit the qualities and defects of its parents. If the impressions previously received by the soul are stronger it does not inherit them. Very wicked parents may have a very saintly child, and very good parents may have a very bad child.

The mental attributes of the parents are inherited by impression on the mental plane. The thought, the feeling of the parents are inherited by the child as a quality. If the father is engaged in thinking, 'I should build an orphanage', the child will have a philanthropic disposition. If the father is thinking, 'This person is my enemy, I should revenge myself on him', the child will have a vindictive disposition. If the mother admires something very much, for instance flowers, the child will have that love of beauty in its nature. Also the qualities and features of the relations and of other persons of whom one of the parents thinks a great deal are impressed on the child. To explain the relation between heredity and environment, one may say that heredity is the foundations of the house, and environment is the building itself; and from this one may conclude which has the more importance.

Often a child is like an uncle or an aunt of the father or mother; why is this? It has two aspects: it may be either that the father or mother has the qualities of this relation, although in them they have not fully developed, and those qualities develop in the child; or it may be that the grandmother or grandfather or other relation is so much attached to his descendants that his spirit watches and impresses with his qualities the child that is born in that family. Heredity is a matter of vibrations. There must be harmony in the number of vibrations, in the same way that colour and sound are made by the harmony of vibrations. Thus a person may be more like his grandfather than his father. If the grandfather has been a poet, the grandson may again be a poet if the number of the vibrations corresponds, even when the son is not one.

It is true that genius is transmitted by heredity and develops at every step, but it is sometimes found that the child of a very great person happens to be most ordinary, and sometimes the child of a most worthy person proves to be most unworthy. This may be explained in the following manner: every manifestation of genius has three stages, Uruj, Kemal, and Zeval, ascent, climax, and decline. When the genius is in the ascendant it develops more and more in every generation; when it reaches its climax it surpasses all previous manifestations of genius in that family; when it is in the decline it shows gradually or suddenly the lack or loss of genius. It is thus with families, nations, and races.

That which is outward is given in heritage more than that which is inward. A man may not be very like his father in looks or nature, yet he inherits his property; the State will give the property to the son. It is inherited because it is more outward. The qualities of the body are inherited more than those of the mind, because they are more outward.

Every physical atom of the parents becomes radiant and its qualities are imparted to the child. In the case of a father who has liked drink, the child, of course, is born without the tendency for strong drink, but as it grows and develops, the cells of its body, being the same as those of the father's, may have the same craving for drink. And so it is with all vices; though the parents would never wish to impart them to their children, yet they do so unconsciously by their weakness and neglect.

Often a man has so much concern for his posterity that he earns money and amasses it, not spending it on himself, in order that he may leave it to his children. He even gives his life on the battlefield that his children may enjoy the fruits of the victory. But if he only knew how much influence the life that he leads has on his posterity he would think it of more value to keep his life pure and elevated, both in health and mind, in order that his children may inherit the wealth of humanity, which is much more precious than earthly wealth and possessions.

Coming now to the question whether more qualities are inherited from the paternal side or the maternal side, I will say that the qualities inherited from the father are more deep-seated while those inherited from the mother may be more apparent, because the father's inheritance is the substance, while the mother's is the mould. The soul has many more attributes of the father because these are the fundamental, original attributes; the attributes of the mother are added to these, they are more active because they are later attributes. Those qualities which are first impressed upon the soul are stronger and those attributes which are acquired later are more active. From association with its mother, from her training, a child acquires very many of her attributes. A man may not like the qualities of his father and may hide them. A small child may have a face just like its mother's, but at some period of its life it will grow so like its father in looks that it is astonishing. A coward by association with brave people may become brave; he may go to the war, but then, when he hears the guns, the cowardice which was the original attribute of his soul will show itself. Although the father's qualities are stronger, the responsibility of the mother is far greater. It is she who moulds the child. The mother's responsibility is a hundred, a thousand times greater than the father's. Therefore mystical knowledge is very necessary for women; in these times of civilization this should not be withheld from them. Control of mind is very important for women.

It is the mother's fear that gives the child fear; her anger gives it anger; her contempt gives it contempt. Her bad surroundings and impressions give the child bad impressions; her good and desirable impressions give the child good and desirable impressions. It is she who moulds the human race. From her are born the prophets and murshids. The credit for all good and great people is hers; but at the same time children are often born weak and defective because of her want of control and foolishness. By putting too many coals on the fire, the fire may be covered up and the flame cannot come out.

Krishna is often represented with his mother Devaki, and Christ with his mother the Virgin Mary. This is woman's greatest merit and glory. In the Gayan it is said, 'The mother was the stepping-stone of Jesus to Christhood.' This means that human nature is such that man often forgets, seeing the great glory of the Master, that modest and humble help given at the time of need which enabled the Master to show forth his divine glory. The soul which was to expand as Christ was enabled to come on earth by the mother; and that is why in every case thought and consideration for the mother are important. Even Jesus Christ, the manifestation of the Almighty God, was dependent on his mother for his manifestation.

A child may be very like its mother in appearance, yet the quality is the father's. For instance, if the father is very generous, and the mother is finer, the child will perhaps be both generous and finer. In this way the evolution of the world goes on by the intermingling of nations and races. Those families who keep themselves segregated in the end become weak and very stupid. For this reason the Prophet in Islam allowed all races and castes to intermarry, because the time had come for the human race to evolve in this way. When a child is different from both its mother and its father, this is partly because of its heritage from other ancestors on either side, but also because of its astral impressions. Besides every thought, speech, and action of the child builds its self from the moment of its birth upon earth. It is for this reason that there can be such a difference between father and son, while there is no difference between fleas or mosquitoes of East and West.

If we inherit the attributes of our father, our mother, our grandfather and forefathers, and acquire the attributes of the jinns and angels, how can we help what our character is? A man may say, 'I have a quick temper because my father had a quick temper, I have a changeable disposition because that is in my family; I cannot help this, it is my character.' This is true in part, but it is developed by belief in it. The soul acquires and casts off attributes and qualities throughout life. A coward who joins the army through hearing always of bravery, by living with soldiers may in time feel inclined to go to the war and to fight. A joyous person from being in the society of serious people may become serious, and a sad person from being with cheerful people may become cheerful. The soul acquires only those qualities in which it is interested, it will never take on those in which it is not interested. And the soul keeps only those attributes in which it is interested, it loses those in which it is not interested. However wicked a person may be, however many undesirable attributes he may have inherited, he can throw them all off by the power of will if he does not like them.

But can we change our physical body, can we change our face? We can. People become like those of whom they think much or with whom they associate. I have seen herdsmen whose faces have become very like those of the cattle and sheep with which they lived. It is our thoughts and feelings that change our appearance, and if we had control over them we should develop the appearance that we wish to develop.

When one looks at pictures of Christ, of Zoroaster, of Moses and of other prophets, one will see that they resemble each other. These pictures are drawn from imagination; the painters have not seen their subjects. Are they then not lifelike? They are, for the mind is greater than the camera. There exist pictures of the murshids of the Sufi order, from Kwaja Moin-ud-Din Chishti onwards, and these pictures of ten or twelve murshids and their mureeds are very much alike. If it were imagination, why should not imagination produce different pictures, as the nature of imagination is more to differentiate than to unite?

But for those who are walking in the path of truth there is no heredity. By realizing their divine origin they free themselves from all earthly inheritance. As Christ said 'My Father in heaven', so they realize their origin from the spirit, and by their concentration and meditation they can create all the merits they wish for and clear away from their soul all influences which they do not like to possess.

CHAPTER VII

REINCARNATION

WHEN WE study religions, comparing them, we find that part of the world has believed in reincarnation, but most of the world has not held this belief. Krishna, Shiva, and Buddha are said to have taught the doctrine of reincarnation; Moses, Christ, and Mohammad have said nothing about it. This divides religions into two groups; but when we make a deeper study we see that we can combine the two, for the tendency of the Sufi is rather to unite than to differ.

There are four widely-spread religions, Brahminism, Buddhism, Christianity, and Islam, which have great influence upon humanity through their diffusion. Let us ask each what it has to say on the matter.

Islam is silent on this subject; Christianity says nothing. In their scriptures if there may rarely be a verse which supports this idea, there will be ten verses which disprove it.

Let us now consider Brahminism. There are four grades of Brahmins: Brahmachari, Grihasta, Vanaprasti, and Sanyasi. The three lower grades will perhaps answer, 'Yes, there is reincarnation, but it depends upon our Karma, our actions. If we, who are men, behave like animals, we may come again as animals; we may be a cow or a dog or a cat, or else we may be a human being of a lower order than we are now; and if we live a righteous life we shall find ourselves in a better condition in our next incarnation.' When we ask the highest authority among Hindus, the Sanyasi, he will say, 'You will perhaps reincarnate, I shall not. I am Jivan Mukhta, free; I am above the cycle of births and deaths.'

What has Buddhism to say about reincarnation? It says that as the world is in evolution, we shall by no means become animals, but evolve into higher and higher incarnations until we have overcome all weaknesses and have reached Nirvana, perfection; then we return no more.

By this we see that there are only two believers in reincarnation, and even these two have contrary beliefs.

We read in the Bible (John xiv. 3), 'I will come again and receive you unto myself,' and (Acts i. 11), 'This same Jesus, which is taken up from you into heaven, shall so come in like manner as ye have seen him go into heaven.' This does not refer to the person of Christ, but to the innermost being of the Master, which was in reality the Being of God. If it concerned his person he would have said, 'I shall come, but you also will come again, either in a better condition or in a worse state of being', but nothing of the kind is said. One might say, 'Why then did the Master say "I", why did he not clearly say "God"?' The answer is that divine personality is the losing of the thought of one's limited self, the absolute merging into the divine and only personality; then the ego becomes the divine ego. The 'I' is not identification with the limited personality but with the personality of God. When Christ said 'I' he meant God.

One reads the same in the Masnavi of Jelal-ud-Din Rumi, 'Seventy-two forms I have worn and have come to witness this same spring of continual change.' This also refers to the divine Consciousness which wears various forms and comes to witness this world of changes; it is not the seventy-two comings of Maulana Rumi himself. Seventy-two is symbolical of many; otherwise it would mean that since the human creation the divine Consciousness visited the earth only seventy-two times, which would be very few times for such a great length of time.

There are many statements in the Qur'an such as these: 'Some faces on that day shall be downcast', said of the wicked, and: 'They will be as monkeys, despised and hated.' The real meaning of the former is, 'We will cause the brightness, or the happiness, of their expression to fade away by throwing light upon their hidden crimes which so long have kept them bright and happy'. The meaning of the latter is, 'Those who have imitated that which they were not, will be taken for that which they are in reality, and not for that which they falsely pretend to be'; in other words, 'We will lay bare the mockery of the impostors'.

In the Gospel we read (John ix. 1-3), 'And as Jesus passed by, he saw a man which was blind from his birth. And his disciples asked him, saying, Master, who did sin, this man, or his parents, that he was born blind? Jesus answered, "Neither hath this man sinned, nor his parents: but that the works of God should be made manifest in him."' This needs no interpretation, for it plainly says that the man's blindness was not the punishment of his former sins.

In the Qur'an it is written, 'It is He who multiplied you on the earth, and to Him shall you be gathered.' This denies a return to earth. Mention is made, however, of another life in that sura. 'Every soul must taste of death, and ye shall only be paid your reward in full on the resurrection day.' Here the resurrection is spoken of, the making alive of the souls without the physical body, and it is plainly said that this existence will be as clear and distinct as is our life on earth.

As the world advances in intellectual development it becomes more and more interested in novelty; whatever is new is taken up and often the new idea is accepted and followed. The idea of reincarnation has made a great impression in the present age, because it appeals at once to the scientific faculty and reasoning natures and it also satisfies those who wish to keep a fast hold on their individuality.

I remember, when at an early age I first knew of death, how for hours I was sad, thinking, 'This, my body, the only means of experiencing life, will one day be in the grave. I shall be away from all things and beings that are the interest of life to me today. This whole environment which interests me and keeps me engaged all day long will one day be a mist; neither shall I see anybody nor will anybody see me; all whom I love now will one day be separated from me.' Now my own experience in the past clearly tells me how others must feel at the idea of turning into what seems nothing after being something. It is just like when a dream interests us so much that if we wake up in the midst of it and realize at once that we were dreaming, we yet like to close our eyes again and give ourselves up to the enjoyment of the experience. Such is the case of all those who are so much interested in the dream of life that the idea of death, which is a more real state of being, is horrible to them. They would rather live a life unreal but individual than a life real but unrealized.

The idea of reincarnation often comforts those who think that it is too soon to renounce the pleasures of life in order to commune with God. 'Perhaps,' they say, 'in our next life on earth we shall achieve what we have not achieved in this.' Also, it consoles those who have lost their loved ones, for they think these are not lost for ever, but will be born again, and often they look for them whenever a child is born among their acquaintances. It consoles those people too who have not obtained the fruit of their desires in this life and have always longed and hoped for something which they could not get; these build their whole hope on gaining it in their next incarnation.

This idea often becomes a great hindrance to real spiritual attainment, though it is helpful to a person who is discontented with his life, suffering from pain, poverty, or illness, and who thinks that it is his Karma to suffer this and that, but that when he has paid the uttermost farthing his circumstances will change. Then he has no more complaint to make; though he knows he has not in this life committed sins worthy of such punishment, still he thinks that there is justice, as he has perhaps sinned in his past life. The idea seems reasonable, especially to a person who looks at life from a practical point of view. Every man weighs the world on his own scales. And the thought of reincarnation is still more helpful to those who do not believe in God or know His being, also to those who neither believe in everlasting life nor can understand it. For some people it is very consoling to think that they will come to this earthly plane again and again, brought there by their Karma, rather than to think, as many materialists do, that when we are dead we are done with for ever.

The reason why the doctrine of reincarnation was taught to the Hindus and Buddhists must have been that the people of India at that time were very highly developed intellectually, in philosophy, in science, in logic, in the material phenomena, and believed in law rather than in love.

In the present age, especially in the West, people are now beginning to search for truth by the light of science and logic, as did the Hindus of the Vedic period. The peoples of India were working along the same lines at the origin of Brahminism and still more in the time of Buddhism.

Then, especially among the Mongols, a people most advanced in arts and sciences, the enlightened were very logical and scientific, with little devotional tendency, and the masses had innumerable objects of worship. There the average person could not conceive the idea of the soul, the hereafter, and God as it was propagated in another part of the East by the Hebrew prophets, so the theory of reincarnation was the best means of appealing to their reason instantly in order to break their former ideas. But as it is the nature of the human heart to worship someone, naturally their worship was directed to Buddha.

There is every probability that this idea came originally from the Devata, the divine messengers born among the Hindus. Each of these declared that he was the incarnation of Brahma, God, and each in turn claimed to be the reincarnation of the preceding Deva, whom he succeeded. In claiming to be the incarnation of Brahma or the Deva they succeeded, they did not mean that in their guise God was born or their predecessor reborn, but that they had realized God or that they possessed the same knowledge and mission as their predecessor. When the others asked them, 'Of what are we the incarnations?' they were obliged to give them some explanation of a like kind, and they told each one that which his condition of life suggested to them.

When the four Varnas or castes were made in India, Brahmin, Kshattria, Vaisha and Sudra, these were not in fact different castes but classes. The whole administration was arranged in this way: Brahmins to study, meditate and be worshipped, Kshattrias to fight and guard the country, Vaishas to carry on commerce, and Sudras to labour and serve. None save Brahmins had *Adhikar*, the right to study the Vedas, the books of mysticism and philosophy; even Kshattrias and Vaishas had to be content with the worship of the Brahmins and with the Purana, the religion taught in legends; Sudras, the labouring class, were denied even that.

It has always been the tendency of the stronger and more intelligent men to keep the weak and simple down. Owing to the inclination of the higher caste to keep itself pure from further admixture of the lower classes, a religious rule was made enforcing the belief that the Sudra, the lowest, could not become a Vaisha, the Vaisha could not become a Kshattria, nor a Kshattria be admitted among Brahmins, the highest and supreme class of the time, unless by his good actions he had made it possible that he should be born, in the next incarnation, in a family of the higher caste. The idea of reincarnation, as a belief generally held, was made the basis of the Hindu religion, upon which the whole building of Brahminism was erected. But everyone in the world has an inclination to raise his head and climb up higher, if he can, from that level upon which he may have been set in life. Verily the light of truth, the beauty of nature, the desire for freedom, the idea of unity cannot be covered up; sooner or later it flashes forth.

The law of Karma or action is the philosophy which a reasoning brain holds in support of reincarnation, saying, 'There is no such being as God as an intervener in our life's affairs, but it is we who by our actions produce results similar to them. There is the ever-ruling law of cause and effect, therefore every occurrence in life must be in accordance with it. If we do not get the results of our good or wicked deeds immediately that is because they need time to mature so as to produce similar results; if they do not do so in this life, then the law forces us to be born again in another incarnation, in order to experience in that the effect of our deeds.'

Looking at the wheel of evolution we see that we do not always rise, we also fall, we do not always become better people, sometimes man grows worse than he was. The nature of evolution is like a wheel turning round, not rising always. This gives us reason to doubt how far the Buddhistic idea of better and better reincarnations can prove to be logical.

In support of reincarnation a story is told of two friends who were going out on a holiday. One said, 'Let us go to the temple, there we shall hear the name of God, we shall be uplifted.' The other said, 'You are always such a melancholy boy; you always find such dull occupations. We will not go to the temple, we will go where we can enjoy ourselves; we will go to the Gaiety.'

The first said, 'I do not like that idea, I will not go with you.' So they parted. The one who went to the temple on the way met with an accident from a waggon on the road and his foot was crushed. He thought, 'What a good thing that my friend did not come with me; he too would have been injured.' The other on his way to the Gaiety had great luck, he found a purse full of gold coins. He thought, 'Thank God! If my friend had been with me, I should have had to share this with him.'

As soon as the first had recovered a little, he went to a Brahmin and asked him, 'What was the reason that I, who was on my way to the temple, had the bad luck to have my foot crushed, and my friend, who was on his way to the Gaiety, had the good luck to find this gold purse?' The Brahmin said, 'The reason is that you in your former life did some very bad action, and you were meant to be killed, and not only killed but hanged for everybody to see, but it happened that only your foot was crushed. Your friend in his former life did some very good action and he was meant to be a king, but it happened for his present sins that he only found a purse full of gold coins.'

If we believe in this idea we must first understand where evil ends and where good begins. It has never been possible even for a deep thinker to draw a line between good and evil. What distinction do we then find, from this point of view, between good and evil, if we look at it closely? None but the difference of degree and difference of point of view. What seems good to one person to another does not, and so it is with evil. Also every evil to the eye of the seer is a lesser good, which in comparison with the greater good appears different from that and so is called evil.

And if the wheel of births and deaths depended upon cause and effect, I should say it would have to go on for ever and ever and there would never be an end to it. According to this doctrine, not only the punishment of our sins, but even the reward of the good we have done would drag us back to earth; we should have to come back on earth in any case. Even should we not wish for a reward we cannot stop the wheel, for we have no power over nature's law. What a helpless condition! Neither does God intervene in our affairs, that He might stop it with

His all-might, nor can we, helpless human beings subject to the law of cause and effect.

Again, we see that everything existing can be destroyed by some other thing or substance. There is no stain that cannot be removed by some chemical solution. There is no record which cannot be erased from the surface of the paper; even if it is engraved upon stone it can be scraped off. Man, the master of the whole creation, has found the means to destroy all things; and it is very astonishing if he is unable to find a solution to wipe off the impressions of Karma, life's deeds, so as to escape the wheel of births and deaths, when he professes to know all things of the earth and claims to have solved all the mysteries of the heavens.

Some believers in God say in support of reincarnation, 'God is just. There are many who are lame or blind or unhappy in life, and this is the punishment for the faults they have committed before, in a former incarnation. If it were not so, that would be injustice on the part of God.' That makes God only a reckoner and not a lover, and it restricts Him to His justice like a judge bound by the law. The judge is the slave of law, the forgiver is its master. In fact we ourselves, limited as we are, have mercy in us, so that often if someone has done something against us we would forgive. If he only bows before us we say, 'He has humiliated himself, I will forget.' Even if a son has caused his mother much sorrow, when he is in trouble, he only needs to say, 'Mother, I have done this, but you are the one to whom I can come for sympathy', and she will say, 'My child, I forgive you, though at the time it made me sad.' If we, who are full of faults and errors, have in us that little spark of mercy inherited from God and can forgive, how can we think that God, the most Merciful, will reckon our faults like a judge? We are as little children before Him. Regarding God as a personal being, how can we think that He, whose being is love, whose action is love, who is all love, can weigh our actions as a judge would?

A judge, when someone is brought before him, after he has looked into the case, says, 'I have looked into your case and I find that you are guilty. You are given six months', or five years', or ten years' imprisonment. Your crime is very grave and so you must learn not to do it again.' But if we go to the blind and lame and ask them, 'Were you given this in punishment? Were you told so?' they say, 'No, we were told nothing.' Now how are we to imagine that God could be so unjust as to punish them and yet not tell them of their crime?

If we return, then every child that is born should know what he was before. If only exceptional ones feel that they know what they were before, in another life, then it may be a delusion, a pretence, or a scheme for gaining notoriety by appearing to know what everybody does not know.

If God is most merciful, how could He govern us only by law devoid of love and compassion, when even we human beings forget and forgive another's fault in spite of law, reason, and logic, when moved by love, our divine inheritance? God is love, not law. Love in its lower manifestation turns into law by forming habits, yet it is not law which rules love, it is love that controls law.

The idea of forgiveness is the result of our idealizing God. As we idealize God so He proves to be. Sometimes the sins of a whole life may be wiped off in one instant; sometimes all the virtue and piety of a whole life may be lost by one sin.

A story is told that Moses was going to Mount Sinai and on his way he met a very pious person, who said to him, 'Moses, speak to God of me. All my life I have been pious, I have been virtuous, I have prayed to God, and I have had nothing but troubles and misfortunes.' A little later Moses met a man sitting in the street with a bottle of liquor. He called out, 'Moses! Where are you going?' Moses said, 'To Mount Sinai.' The man called out, 'To Mount Sinai? Then speak to God of me', for he was drunk.

Moses went to Mount Sinai and he told God of the pious person whom he had met. God said, 'For him there is a place in the heavens.' Then he told God of the drunken man whom he had met. God said, 'He shall be sent to the worst possible place in hell.'

Moses went away and first he met the drunken man. He told him, 'God says you shall be sent to the worst possible place in hell.' The man said, 'God spoke of me?' and he was so overjoyed that he could not contain himself but began to dance, just as a poor man might be overjoyed if he heard that a king had spoken of him, even if the king had said nothing good of him. Then he said, 'How happy should I be that He, the Creator and Sovereign of the universe, knows me, the great sinner.' Then Moses told the pious person what God had said. He said, 'Why not? I have spent all my life in the worship of God and in piety, sacrificing all else in life; and therefore I am entitled to have it.'

Both the pious person and the drunkard died, and Moses was curious to know what had become of them. He went to Mount Sinai and asked God. God said, 'The pious person is in hell, and the drunken man is in heaven.' Moses thought, 'Does God break His word?' God said, 'The drunkard's joy on hearing that We had spoken of him has wiped out all his sins. The pious person's virtue was worthless. Why could he not be satisfied if We made the sun shine and sent the rain?'

If anyone were to weigh his righteous actions against the myriad favours of God, all the righteous actions of every moment of his life would not compare with one moment of God's favour. Therefore the devotee forgets his righteous actions, looking only at the favour of God. As Amir says, 'When the pious was looking for the beloved God among the righteous, His mercy cried out, "Come hither. I am busy among sinners, forgiving them their sins." '

CHAPTER VIII

MAN, THE SEED OF GOD

MAN MAY most justly be called the seed of God. God the Infinite, most conscious within Himself, embraces His nature full of variety; in this way He is one and He is all. The whole of manifestation is just like a tree sprung from the divine root. Nature is like its stem and all the aspects of nature are like the branches, the leaves, the fruit, and the flower; and from this tree again the same seed is produced, the human soul, which was the first cause of the tree. This seed is the spirit of man, and as God comprehends the whole universe within Himself, being one, so man contains within himself the whole universe as His miniature. It is said in the Qur'an, 'In our own image we have created man.' Therefore neither can God be anything else than what He is, for the very reason that He is one and at the same time He is all, nor can man; neither can man be reincarnated nor can God.

The men of science of today have admitted the fact that the whole skin of man is changed in so many years and they have also been able to discover that each atom of man's constitution changes so many times in life, renewing his body each time. If the body is subject to change, so is the mind, and it is only by these that man's person is identified. Again, in our food and drink we live upon so many small lives and so many small lives live upon us, dwelling in our blood, veins, tubes, and in the skin, all of which constitute our individuality. And in the mind our every thought and feeling is as alive as we, even such beings as the elementals, demons, and angels, which are created within us, from us, and of us, and yet may as fitly be called individuals as we. So in the end of the examination it is hard for a man to find out whether he exists as one or many.

In our dreams all the inhabitants of our mind resurrect, forming a world within ourselves. We see in the dream things and beings, a friend, a foe, an animal, a bird, and they come from nowhere, but are created out of our own selves. This shows that the mind of an individual constitutes a world in itself, which is created and destroyed by the conscious or unconscious action of the will, which has two aspects: intention and accident. We have experience of this world of mind even while awake, but the contrast between the world within and without makes the world without concrete and the world within abstract.

Someone may ask, 'If all that we see in the dream is we ourselves, then why do we even in the dream see ourselves as an entity separate from all the other things before us in the dream?' The answer is, because the soul is deluded by our external form, and this picture it recognizes as I, and all other images and forms manifesting before it in the dream stand in contrast to this I; therefore the soul recognizes them as other than I.

However, if it is one individual that reincarnates should we hold our changeable body to be an individual or our mind, both of which appear to be one and at the same time many? One might ask Jack, 'Which part of yourself is Jack, the eye, the nose, the ear, or the hand or foot, for each of them has a particular name? Or are your thoughts and feelings Jack? They are numerous, changeable, and diverse; you name them as such an imagination, such a feeling.' This shows that Jack stands aloof as the owner of all the finer and grosser properties that have grouped and formed an illusion before him, which, reflected upon his soul, makes him say, 'I, Jack'. He is the owner of all that he realizes around and about him, and yet each atom and vibration which has composed his illusionary self is liable to change, and to a separate and individual birth and death.

The soul on its journey to the infinite cannot turn back halfway; and when it reaches that goal, it experiences only the light, the wisdom, the love of God, and it loses two things: it loses all the marks of the experiences and thoughts of its manifestation, and it gradually loses its individuality and merges in the infinite, divine Consciousness.

If an earthen thing is thrown into the water it has a tendency to go to the bottom, to its own element. If water is accompanying fire on its journey as steam, its watery part still drips down. When fire travels with the air its smoke is taken a certain distance but in its higher spheres the air gets rid of the fire. When ether turns into spirit it drops its contact with the air element. Thus it is with the soul; on its return journey it gives back all these properties to their own sources, thus lightening its load on its way towards its own element. The earthly body goes to earth, its water part to the world of waters, its heat to the kingdom of heat, its air to the spheres of the air, its ether into the ethereal regions. Its impressions, thoughts, feelings, merits, qualities go as far as they can reach, and remain there wherever they are meant to be. Then it is the soul in its own essence that is left, merging into the ocean of consciousness where nothing of its previous properties remains.

Our personality is just like a bubble in the water. There is as little probability of a bubble once merged in the sea coming out again composed of the same portion of water, as there is of the soul once merged in the ocean of consciousness coming out again formed of the self-same portion of consciousness. The bubble may come back in the same place with the same portion of water, or it may be another portion of water. There may be half of the first drop of water in the second bubble, there may be a small part, or there may be some other portion of water added to it.

If one bubble comes, and we call that bubble John, and then we call another Jacob and a third Henry, yet they are all the same water, and if we call the water John then they are all the same John. All is the same spirit, the same life, involving itself into all the forms and the names. From this point of view there is no I, no you, no he, no she, no it, in the light of reality; all are but the differences of a moment.

Every bubble loses both reflections and any properties it possessed during its existence as soon as it merges into the water, and even if in one of a thousand chances it should come formed of the self-same portion of water, it would not retain its previous property. In the same way supposing, as a mere assumption, that the self-same portion of consciousness, which in any case is not so substantial and stable as water, could possibly appear again on the surface without any addition or deduction, it is utterly impossible that it should still possess its past qualities and impressions, for it has been absolutely purified by sinking into the consciousness. If even a drop of ink loses its ink property in the sea, why should not the ocean of consciousness purify its own element from all elements foreign to itself?

As Hinduism teaches the doctrine that bathing once in the Sangam at the confluence of the two rivers can purify man from all life's sins, how can it deny that this bath of the soul, sinking into the consciousness even once, purifies the soul from all the properties it has gathered during its previous life? In the first place, the nature of absorption into the Spirit is itself purification from the material state of being, and the very nature of manifestation is for the soul to arrive new and fresh.

Suppose we granted that cream was the reincarnation of milk, and butter was the third step of the reincarnation of milk, and its fourth reincarnation could be called ghee; then the question would arise, of what was milk the reincarnation? Milk is composed of several chemical substances, and its chemical arrangement changes the name, savour, smell, and effect. Butter cannot be called milk, nor is ghee cream. If there is anything which seems to exist through all the manifestations of the milk, it is the inner ruling current which groups and scatters atoms, compelling them to change, and which may be likened to the soul.

Also, if Jack has reincarnated as John, or John has reincarnated as Jack, what were both in the beginning? Were they two or one? If one became two, then one could become thousands, millions, and still he is one only.

The shooting forth of the soul from the consciousness can be symbolized as an arrow. The arrow shot up in the air goes up as far as the will and power of the bow-man has destined it to go, and when it reaches its utmost height its return begins. The death of the physical being is the return of that arrow. Of course, on its return it may perhaps be detained on its way, as the arrow is sometimes caught in the branches of a tree, but it returns some day or other to the earth, its own element. It does not go up again from there by any means. So it is with the human soul, which, after finishing its course on earth, returns to its origin, drawn by its power of attraction.

When we look at the world we see that everything makes a circle. The plant grows from the seed to its developed state and returns to dust. Man grows from childhood to youth, to maturity, then to old age. This, it is said, is an argument for our passing through many lives. But it is not the circle which journeys, but the point which, journeying, forms the circle and returns to the place from which it started. It is the consciousness that performs the journey and not the individual soul.

The drops of water in a fountain go up, some higher, some lower, some go a very little way, some rise very high. When each drop falls down it sinks into the stream, flowing away with it, and does not rise again, although the water of the same stream rises again and falls again in drops, which proves to us the fact that it is the water which rises and falls continually, not the drop; yet apparently it rises and falls as drops, though the portion of water in every drop is different.

One argument which the reincarnationists bring forward in support of their doctrine is that sometimes unusual genius or gifts are found in a child who does not seem to inherit them from its ancestors and cannot have acquired them from its surroundings. Sometimes in the slums a child is born which has great poetical genius which could not be traced to its father or mother nor to its forefathers; or it shows a great musical gift which was not found in its father or grandfather or ancestors.

The soul before coming to the face of the earth on its way to manifestation, for a very, very long time gathers the impressions of those souls whom it meets on its way, and takes on their attributes. In this way the attributes of the past souls are manifested again. A soul may receive the impressions of one soul or of a few souls or of many souls.

The soul on its way towards manifestation may meet the soul of a genius in poetry or music and take with it these impressions. When some very great or very good or philanthropic person has died you will find that soon after a child of like qualities will be born to balance the world. A child may be born with the qualities of Alexander the Great. This is because the new soul coming out towards manifestation has met the soul of Alexander and has become impressed with all his qualities or part of his qualities. Such a one may assert, 'I am the reincarnation of Alexander.' But the soul of Alexander does not return. If it did, then every soul that has left this life would know of his former lives.

Much of the difference of understanding is the difference of words. If someone says that the soul is the world of impressions which the consciousness holds before it, and the spirit is the consciousness, then he may say that the soul returns.

When the child of unpoetical parents sings, making up words of its own, this shows that it has received the impression of some poetical soul. The soul that comes to the surface is more responsive than creative; it is not creative, because it has nothing to give. The soul on its return is creative; it imparts its experiences there. For example, an unused photographic plate takes the impression of the object before it, but the used plate reflects its impression on to the paper. Suppose, for instance, the soul of Vishnu meets a soul on its way to manifestation, this powerful soul may impress the other with its attributes. Then that soul may say, 'I am Krishna, the reincarnation of Vishnu.' The soul is impressed with whatever comes before it. Sometimes children of quite ordinary parents may be so impressed by a great person in whose presence they are that they themselves become great. And as man's personality is nothing but an agglomeration of his thoughts and impressions, the inheritor of these may be called the reincarnation of the past one, although his soul is his own.

Sometimes a child appears to see and understand very much of what is going on around him from his infancy up. Sometimes a young man sees and understands more than an old person. Such people are supposed by the average person to be old souls, and the reincarnationists take it as a proof of the doctrine of reincarnation. But in reality knowing and understanding do not depend upon learning; knowledge is the soul's quality. The knowledge of the spirit has been man's in all ages. An old person does not need to read many books in order to learn that he was once a little child; he knows it, it is his past experience. So the soul knows its own experience; it needs only a little awakening to make it conscious of itself.

When the Shah of Persia wished to have the history of Persia written by some literary person, no one could be found to do it until the mystic poet Firdausi said that he would write it. And he wrote, from his inner knowledge, the *Shah-nameh*, the history of the Shahs of Persia. If he had this knowledge from the recollection of his own previous lives he must have reincarnated uninterruptedly in Persia and in Persia only; endowed each time with the same degree of intelligence, so as to have acquired and retained all this knowledge.

There is nothing which the soul cannot know, for the whole objective existence is made by the soul for its own use; and therefore it is not astonishing if man possesses great qualities that he has not inherited, and if he has knowledge of all things through revelation, not by learning. It is astonishing only when he lacks this, and that is owing to the globes upon globes of the objective world covering the light of the soul.

CONCLUSION

I FIRST believed without any hesitation in the existence of the soul, and then I wondered about the secret of its nature. I persevered and strove in search of the soul, and found at last that I myself was the cover over my soul. I realized that that in me which believed and that in me which wondered, that which persevered in me, and that which found, and that which was found at last, was no other than my soul. I thanked the darkness that brought me to the light, and I valued the veil which prepared for me the vision in which I saw myself reflected, the vision produced in the mirror of my soul. Since then I have seen all souls as my soul, and realized my soul as the soul of all; and what bewilderment it was when I realized that I alone was, if there were anyone; that I am whatever and whoever exists; and that I shall be whoever there will be in the future. And there was no end to my happiness and joy.

Verily, I am the seed and I am the root and I am the fruit of this tree of life.

LOVE, HUMAN AND DIVINE

CONTENTS

CHAPTER I

THE PHILOSOPHY OF LOVE

THE SOUL on its way to manifestation passes through four states, 'Ilm, 'Ishq, Wujud, Shuhud. 'Ilm is the original state of the consciousness, the pure intelligence; 'Ishq is love, the next step of the intelligence towards manifestation; therefore intelligence and love are the same in their essence. Objects, such as rocks and trees, have no intelligence, therefore they have no love, except a little perception of love that exists in plant life; but among beasts and birds intelligence develops, that is why in them love begins to show itself. Wujud is the objective world, whose purpose it is to be loved, for love could not manifest unless there were an object to love. Shuhud is the realization of love's experience, in whatever aspect it may be.

The word love is derived from the Sanskrit word *Lobh*, which means desire, wish; the same word is used in the Russian language, *Liubov*. Love may be called in other words the desire to be conscious of the object of love. Therefore Shuhud, the realization of love, is the only object of every soul. It is love in different aspects which is known by all such names as will, wish, desire, kindness, favour, and so forth.

In love abides all knowledge. It is mankind's love and interest in things that in time reveals their secret, and then man knows how to develop, control, and utilize them. No one can know anybody, however much he may profess to know, except the lover, because in the absence of love the inner eyes are blind; only the outer eyes are open, which are merely the spectacles of the inner eyes. If the sight is not keen, of what use are the spectacles? It is for this reason that we admire all those whom we love, and are blind to the good qualities of those whom we do not love. It is not always that these deserve our neglect, but our eyes, without love, cannot see their goodness. Those whom we love may have bad points too, but as love sees beauty, so we see that alone in them. Intelligence itself in its next step towards manifestation is love. When the light of love has been lit the heart becomes transparent, so that the intelligence of the soul can see through it, but until the heart is kindled by the flame of love the intelligence, which is constantly yearning to experience life on the surface, is groping in the dark.

The whole of creation is made for love. Man is the most capable of it. If we have a stone in our house and we like the stone very much, the stone will not be aware of our love to that degree to which a plant would be conscious of it. If we have a plant, and care for it and tend it, it will respond to our care and will flourish. The animals feel affection. If we keep an animal in the house, how much affection and love it can feel! The tame animals in time grow to be as affectionate as one of the family. It was Joseph's dog that fed him while in the well until he was found by travellers passing that way. It is said that the horse of an Arab who had fallen on the battlefield kept watch over him for three days, guarding his corpse from the vultures until his comrades came. But man, having the largest share of intelligence, has the most love in his nature.

All this shows that creation has evolved from mineral to plant life, from plant to animal life, and from the animal to the human being, showing a gradual development of love through every stage.

The Sufis say that the reason of the whole creation is that the perfect Being wished to know Himself, and did so by awakening the love of His nature and creating out of it His object of love, which is beauty. Dervishes, with this meaning, salute each other by saying, 'Ishq Allah, Ma'bud Allah'—'God is love and God is the beloved.' A Hindustani poet says, 'The desire to see the beloved brought me to earth, and the same desire to see the beloved I am taking with me to heaven.'

As love is the source of creation and the real sustenance of all beings, so, if man knows how to give it to the world around him as sympathy, as kindness, as service, he supplies to all the food for which every soul hungers. If man knew this secret of life he would win the whole world, without any doubt.

Love can always be discerned in the thought, speech, and action of the lover, for in his every expression there is a charm which shows as a beauty, tenderness, and delicacy. A heart burning in love's fire has a tendency to melt every heart with which it comes in contact.

Love produces such a charm in the lover that while he loves one all love him. The magnetism of love is thus explained by a Hindustani poet: 'Why should not every heart be melted into drops before the flame that my heart has sustained all through my life? As I have all my life shed tears with the pain of love, the lovers make pilgrimage to my mournful grave.' It was to teach this lesson of love that Christ said, 'I will make you fishers of men.' 'Everyone is drawn to me, to become my friend, but none divines what it is in my heart that draws him', said Jelal-ud-Din Rumi.

Love is inherent in every soul. All the occupations of life, however important or unimportant, in some way or other tend towards love; therefore no one in the world can be called entirely loveless. Love is the only thing that every soul brings to earth with it; yet after coming to earth man partakes of all the qualities of lovelessness. If it were not so, we would have been as bitter, as jealous, as angry, as full of hatred when we were born as we are now. The infant has no hatred. A little child that we have scolded will in a few minutes' time come and embrace us.

To love, to adore, to worship someone with whom we are connected neither by birth, race, creed, nor in any worldly connection, comes from the love of the soul. Sometimes people fall in love at first sight, sometimes the presence of someone draws a person like a magnet, sometimes one sees a person and feels, 'I might have known him all my life'; sometimes one speaks with another person and finds an intimacy of understanding as if the souls understood each other; all this is accounted for by the idea of soul-mates.

A heart lightened by love is more precious than all the gems and jewels of the world. There are as many different kinds of hearts as there are different substances in the world. There are hearts of metal which take a long time and much fire of love to heat, and when once heated will melt and may be moulded as you wish for the moment, but soon afterwards turn cold. There are hearts of wax which melt instantly at the sight of the fire, and if there is a wick of ideal, they will keep their flame until they become non-existent. There are hearts of paper which are set alight by a slight touch of the fire and turn into ashes in one moment.

Love is like the fire; its glow is devotion, its flame is wisdom, its smoke is attachment, and its ashes detachment. Flame rises from glow, so it is with wisdom, which rises from devotion. When love's fire produces its flame it illuminates the devotee's path in life like a torch, and all darkness vanishes.

When the life-force acts in the soul it is love, when it acts in the heart it is emotion, and when in the body it is passion. Therefore the most loving person is the most emotional, and the most emotional is the most passionate, according to the plane of which he is most conscious. If he is most awake in the soul he is loving, if awakened in the heart he is emotional, if he is conscious of the body he is passionate. These three may be pictured as fire, flame, and smoke. Love is fire when in the soul, it is a flame when the heart is kindled by it, and it is as smoke when it manifests through the body.

The first love is for the self. If illuminated, man sees his true benefit and he becomes a saint. In the absence of illumination man becomes so selfish that he becomes a devil. The second love is for the opposite sex. If it is for love's sake it is heavenly; if it is for passion's sake it is earthly. This, if it is quite pure, can certainly take away the idea of the self, but the benefit is slight and the danger is great. The third love is for the children, and this is the first service to God's creatures. To reserve it for one's children only is like appropriating to oneself what is given to us as a trust by the Creator, but if this love expands to embrace the whole creation of the Heavenly Father, it raises man to be among the chosen ones of God.

The love of the parents for the children is much greater than the love of the children towards them, for while the parents' thought is all centred in the children, the children's thought is for themselves first. Someone asked the Prophet, 'Whose love is greater, the children's love for their parents or the parents' for their children?' He said, 'The parents' love is greater, for while they do all things with the thought that their children may grow and be happy and will live after them, as if they expect to live in the life of their children after their death, even worthy children think that some day the parents will die, and with this thought they render them what little service they can.' The questioner asked, 'Of the parents, whose love is greater?' The Prophet said, 'The mother's; the greater respect and service is due to her, for heaven lies at her feet.' The love of the parents is most blessed, for this love is clear as crystal.

There is a well-known story of Shirvan Bhagat, who was devoted to his aged parents, who had reached the age when they were helpless and entirely dependent upon the service of their only son. Shirvan was so devoted to them that he sacrificed all freedom and pleasure in life in their service. He gently attended to their calls, and bore with patience all the difficulties that one finds in association with the aged.

The parents one day said that they greatly wished they had once in their lives made a pilgrimage to Kashi. This worthy son at once consented to their wish, and, as in those days there was no other means of travelling, he undertook to accomplish the journey on foot. He made baskets in which he placed his old parents and lifted them on to his back, and thus set out on a journey of thousands of miles, through many forests and mountains, crossing rivers on his way.

He travelled for months in this way, but before he arrived at their destination a misfortune happened. Shirvan, at his parents' request, set down his baskets on the ground and went to fetch some water. When he drew near to the river he was stuck by the arrow of Raja Dasheratha, who had aimed at a deer and by accident hit him. Hearing the deep sigh of a man the Raja went to him, and was grieved beyond expression. He said, 'Is there anything that I can do for you, O man?' Shirvan said, 'I am dying. I have only one desire, and that is to give my parents this water; they are thirsty in the heat of the sun.' 'That is all?' the Raja asked. 'I will do it with great pleasure as my first duty.' Shirvan said, 'If you wish to do anything more then look after them and see that they are carried to Kashi, although I doubt whether they will live any longer after I am gone.'

The Raja went, bearing water in his hands, and gave it to the old parents without saying a word to them, fearing they might not drink it, hearing the voice of a stranger. The parents said, 'O worthy son, all our life we have never seen you vexed; this is the first time that you have handed us the bowl of water without your loving word which always gives us new life.' Raja Dasheratha burst into tears, and told them of the death of their son. They, hearing this, could not live to drink the water. They lived only on the love of their son. Each of them heaved a deep sigh, 'O, our beloved Shirvan', and passed away.

This story has since become a tradition in India, and there are followers of this tradition who carry baskets on their shoulders and travel about, teaching the virtue of devotion and service to parents.

When love is centred in one object it is love. When it is for several objects it is named affection. When it is like a cloud it is called infatuation. When its trend is moral it is devotion. When it is for God, the omnipresent and omnipotent, in fact, the whole Being, then it is called divine love, the lover becomes holy.

There is no greater power than love. All strength comes with the awakening of love in the heart. People say, 'He is tender-hearted, he is weak,' but there are many who do not know what strength springs from the heart that becomes tender in love. A soldier fights on the battle-field for love of his people. Every work that one does in love is done with all strength and power. Fear and reason, which limit power, cannot stand against love. A hen, timid as she is, can withstand a lion for the love of her young ones. There is nothing too strong, too powerful for a loving heart.

The power of love accomplishes all things in life as does the power of dynamite that conquers the world. But when dynamite explodes it sets everything on fire, and so it is with love: when it is too intense it becomes a wheel of destruction, and everything goes amiss in the life of the lover. That is the mystery that accounts for all the pain and misery in the life of a lover. Still, the lover is the gainer in both cases. If he has mastered the situation he is a master; if he has lost everything he is a saint.

Love is above law, and law is beneath love. There is no comparison between them; one is from heaven and the other from earth. Where love dies law begins. Therefore law can never find a place for love, nor can love ever limit itself within law, one being limited, the other being as unlimited as life. The lover can give no reason why he loves a certain one, for there is a reason for everything except love.

Time and space are in the hands of love. A journey of miles will become a few yards in the presence of the beloved, and yards become miles in his absence. A day of separation in love is equal to a thousand years, and a thousand years of the beloved's presence are not even as long as a day.

If there is any protecting influence in the world, it is no other than love. In all aspects of life, wherever we find protection, its motive is always love, and no one can have trust in any protection, however great, except the protection that love offers. If a giant were to frighten a child, the child would say, 'I will tell my mother.' The strength and power of any man is too small in comparison with love's protection which the mother affords her child.

Love can heal better than anything in the world. There is nothing like a mother's touch when a child is in pain. There can be no greater cure than the presence of the beloved in the illness of the lover. Even cats and dogs are healed by a little pat of love.

For thought-reading, for sending and receiving telepathic messages, people try psychical processes in vain. If they only knew that the secret of all occult and psychical phenomena lies in love! The lover knows all: the pleasure, the displeasure, the happiness and unhappiness, the thoughts and imaginations, of the beloved. No time, no space, stands in his way, for a telepathic current is naturally established between the lover and the beloved. The lover's imagination, thought, dream, and vision, everything tells him all about the object of his love.

Concentration, which is the secret of every attainment in life, and the chief thing in all aspects of life, especially in the path of religion and mysticism, is a natural thing in love. The loveless will strive for years in this path, and will always fail to centre their minds on one object; but love compels the lover, holding before his admiring view the vision of the beloved. Therefore the lover need not concentrate his mind; his love itself is his concentration which gives him mastery over all things in the world. The lover attains the object of his love by the power of concentration; and if he does not attain the object, then he rises beyond it. In either case the lover has his reward.

CHAPTER II

SHIRIN AND FARHAD

LOVE IS never tempted by wealth and grandeur. Shirin, the daughter of a poor man, but rich in her ideal, was kidnapped and taken to the Shah of Fáras, who instantly became enamoured of her, and gave great rewards to those who had brought her. But, to his great disappointment, he found that Shirin was unresponsive to his love, and her ideal was too great to allow her to be tempted by the wealth and grandeur of the Shah. He did everything to please her and to make her willing to marry him, but every effort had the contrary effect.

When Shirin saw that there was no hope anywhere of rescue from the palace, which to her was a cage, and the importunity of the Shah and his servants wore out her patience so much that she was obliged to consent to their offer, she did so on one condition, which was that a canal should be made as a memorial of the occasion. This was, of course, a pretext for putting off the marriage, for the cutting of a canal was the work of years. The Shah was so much fascinated by her youth and beauty that he seized upon even the smallest sign of yielding, and at once gave command to the engineers and architects of the court to begin work on a canal without a moment's delay, and to accomplish it as soon as possible, sparing no expense or labour. Thousands of workmen were soon engaged in this, and the work went on night and day unceasingly, under the watchful eye of the king himself and his servants.

The nearer the work came to being accomplished, the stronger grew the hope of the king, and he, with great pleasure, requested Shirin to go and look at her canal. She, with despondent mind, went to see the canal, fearing that it would soon be finished and she would have to yield to the wishes of the Shah, which she regarded as worse than death. While she was walking, looking at the work going on where thousands of workmen were busy night and day, to her great surprise a workman came up, won entirely by her beauty and charm, and fearlessly exclaimed, 'O Shirin, I love you.' 'Love overlooks the difference of position of the lover and the beloved, and the height that the lover has to climb.'

It was that voice of love and that word of devotion that Shirin was looking for, and had not found until then. Shirin replied, 'Do you love me? Then break these mountains, and cut a pathway through them.' 'Gold has a test to go through.' Farhad said at once, 'Most willingly. Yes, Shirin, whatever you please.' 'There is nothing too hard for the lover to do for the beloved.'

Farhad set out on his journey whole-heartedly, not wondering why he should cut a path, nor reasoning how this great work might be accomplished. He did not stop to think how long it would take to finish, nor had he any misgiving that his efforts might ever be in vain; he went to those mountains in the wilderness and began to break the rocks with his pickaxe. He repeated the name of Shirin at every stroke he gave. The strokes of Farhad wrought a miracle. Instead of one stroke it was as if a hundred strokes fell at a time. 'Man's power is the strength of his body, but love's power is the might of God.' No sooner was the work begun than it neared completion. Work that would have taken years with many workers engaged on it was accomplished in days.

Shirin had refused the Shah since she had seen Farhad, saying, 'There is another lover who is undergoing a test, and until I know the outcome of his trial I think it better to keep from marriage.'

The king's spies had been watching Farhad from afar, and they immediately sent a report that Farhad had completed his work before the canal was finished. The Shah was very much alarmed, thinking that Farhad would most probably win Shirin's love, and that after his having done all this for her, Shirin would not be his. When he told this to his confidants one among them said, 'Sire, you are the king, Farhad is a workman. What comparison between heaven and earth? I will go, if it be the pleasure of your Majesty, and will finish him in a moment.' 'Oh, no,' said the Shah, 'Shirin will see the stain of his blood on me, and will turn her back on me for ever.' One among the king's servants said, 'It is not difficult for me, my Lord, to bring the life of Farhad to an end without shedding a single drop of blood.' 'That is much better', said the Shah.

The servant went to Farhad, who had very nearly finished his work, with great hope of a glance from Shirin. 'The lover's happiness is in the pleasure of the beloved.' This servant of the Shah said, 'O Farhad, alas, all in vain! O, that rival of the moon, your beloved Shirin, has passed away by a sudden death.' Farhad said in the greatest bewilderment, 'What? Is my Shirin dead?' 'Yes,' the servant said, 'O Farhad, alas, Shirin is dead.' Farhad heaved a deep sigh, and fell to the ground. 'Shirin' was the last word that his lips uttered, and made a way for his life to pass away.

Shirin heard from her well-wishers that Farhad had done marvels, that he had cut the path through the mountains, repeating the name 'Shirin' with his every stroke, and finished the work that might have taken a whole life in the shortest time. Shirin, the chords of whose heart had already been struck by Farhad, and through whose soul the love of Farhad had pierced, had not the patience to rest one moment, and she set out for the mountains at the first opportunity she could find. 'The higher powers separate two hearts that come together.' Shirin, who had the great fortune of having a lover like Farhad, had not the fortune to see him any more.

To her greatest grief and disappointment, Shirin found the body of Farhad lying by the side of the wonderful work he had done for her. The spies of the Shah came near to assure her of his death, hoping that now that Farhad was no more she might fix her mind on the crown of the Shah. They said, 'This is poor Farhad. Alas, he is dead.' Shirin heard from the blowing of the wind, from the running of the water, from rocks, from trees, the voice of Farhad, calling, 'Shirin, Shirin.' The whole atmosphere of the place held her soul with the magnetism of love that Farhad had created all around. She fell down, struck by the great loss that her loving heart could no longer sustain, crying, 'Farhad, I am coming too, to be with you.' 'The fate of the lover is a great disappointment in the sight of the world, but it is the greatest satisfaction in the eyes of the wise.'

Those people whose qualities harmonize, like each other. It may be the bodily qualities that harmonize, or the mental qualities, or the qualities of the soul. The physical fascination lasts least, the emotional fascination lasts longer, and the spiritual fascination lasts for ever.

Love little expressed kindles another heart, love more expressed haunts it, but when it is too much expressed it repels the object of love.

Contact makes people friends, though neither the contact of mortals nor friendship is everlasting. Being together, sitting together, eating together, breathing the same air, bring hearts closer. Two burning coals close together in time make one fire; the flames unite them. When the two hands are joined, an electric current goes from one hand to the other. This is the reason for the custom of shaking hands, that the flame in the two people may meet. This is why people have a tendency to clasp their hands, fold their arms and cross their legs when sitting or lying, for it comforts them. This is the reason of the affinity existing between those of the same nation or race.

Love has a tendency to produce the qualities, even the likeness, of the object of love in the lover. Often we see that friends, husband and wife, lovers, the murshid and mureed, in time grow to look alike. The portraits of the different Shaikhs of Khandan-i Chisht all look as if they had been moulded in the same mould. A person who goes away from his own country, and lives a long time in another country, becomes familiar with that country, likes it, and sometimes does not want to go back to his own land, because love is produced in him by association.

Meeting is the kindling of love, and separation is the blazing of love. As far as is the object of love from the reach of the lover, so wide a scope is there for the expansion of love. Therefore the love for the unattainable object has every possibility of developing, whereas when the object of love is within reach this is often a check upon love. If separation lasts a short time it increases love, but if it lasts very long the love dies. If the meeting is for a short time it kindles love, but it is hard to keep up the flame; and if the association lasts a long time, love is not so much stimulated, but it takes root, to grow and flourish and to last long. In the absence of the beloved hope is the oil which keeps the flame of love burning. Presence and absence in turn keep the fire of love blazing. Too much association chokes the fire of love, and in absence too long continued its flame dies from lack of oil.

We may spend a year in a town, and we may know people there and like them very much, and they may like us very much, so that the love increases and we think, 'If we could only spend all our life there!' When we go away it is hard to leave them. Then we go away, and our friends send letters and we answer, first every day, then every week, then every month, until the correspondence is reduced to a Christmas card or New Year's greetings; for we grow apart by the fact that we have much less to do with them and much more to do with those who may now surround us. If we go back to the same place after five or six years we first find that the climate is strange to us, and then that neither are the streets and houses familiar nor is there that warmth in the friends that there was. If a person is ignorant he blames the friends; if he understands he will blame himself too. It is growing together that increases love and being separated that has the tendency to decrease it, and so it is with our attachment to places also.

CHAPTER III

YUSUF AND ZULEIKHA

FROM THE story of Yusuf and Zuleikha we learn what part beauty plays in the world of love. Yusuf was the youngest son of Jacob, the seer, who was blest with the gift of prophecy as were several among his ancestors. He was thrown into a well by his elder brothers, who were jealous of his beauty and the influence that it had on their father and everyone that met him. 'Not love alone, but beauty also has to pay its forfeit.'

Some merchants travelling that way saw Yusuf in the well as they were drawing water, and took him up and sold him as a slave to a chief of Misr, who, charmed by the beautiful manner of this youth, made him his personal attendant.

Zuleikha, the wife of this chief, grew fonder every day of this handsome youth. She talked to him, she played with him, she admired him, and she raised him in her eyes from a slave to a king. 'Those crowned with beauty are always kings, even if they are in rags or sold as slaves.' 'A true king is always a king, with or without a throne.'

The friends and relations of Zuleikha began to tell tales about her having fallen in love with Yusuf, and, as it is natural for people to take interest in the faults of others, it eventually put Zuleikha in a difficult position.

She once invited all her relations and friends, and put into the hands of each of them a lemon and a knife, and told them all to cut the lemons when she should tell them, and then called Yusuf. When he came she told them to cut the lemons, but the eyes of every one among them were so attracted by the appearance of Yusuf, that many instead of cutting the lemon cut their fingers, thereby stamping on their fingers also the love of Yusuf. 'Beauty takes away from the lover the consciousness of self.'

Zuleikha, so entirely won by Yusuf, forgot in the love of him what is right, what is wrong. 'Reason falls when love rises.' They became more intimate every day until a spell of passion came and separated them. When the shadow of passion fell upon the soul of Yusuf, Zuleikha happened to think of covering the face of the idol, which was in her room. This astonished Yusuf and made him ask her, 'What doest thou?' She said, 'I cover the face of my god that seeth us with his eyes full of wrath.' This startled Yusuf. He saw the vision of his father pointing his finger towards heaven. Yusuf said, 'Stay, O Zuleikha, of what hast thou put me in mind! The eyes of thy god can be covered with a piece of cloth, but the eyes of my God cannot be covered. He seeth me wherever I am.' 'He is man who remembers God in anger and fears God in passion', says Zafar.

Zuleikha, blinded by the overwhelming darkness of passion, would not desist, and when he still refused, her passion turned into wrath. She hated him and cursed him and reminded him of his low position as a slave. On this he began to leave the room, and she caught him by the nape of the neck and thus Yusuf's garment was torn. The chief happened to enter the room during this. He was amazed at this sight, which neither Zuleikha nor Yusuf could hide. Before he asked her anything she complained to him, in order to hide her evident fault, that Yusuf had made an attempt to lay hands upon her, which naturally enraged the chief, and he at once gave orders that Yusuf should be taken to prison for life. 'The righteous have more trials in life than the unrighteous.'

Prison was a delight to the truthful Yusuf, who had kept his torch alight through the darkness of passion while walking in the path of love.

It was not long before the spell upon Zuleikha faded, and then came a settled melancholy. There was no end to her sorrow and repentance. 'Love dies in passion, and is again born of passion.' Years passed, and the pain of Zuleikha's heart consumed her flesh and blood. She wasted away. On one side was the love of Yusuf, on the other side the constant trouble that her guilty conscience caused her and the idea that her own beloved had been thrown into prison on her account, which almost took her life away.

Time, which changes all things, changed the conditions of Yusuf's life. Though he was in prison he had never blamed Zuleikha, by reason of her love, but he became every day more deeply immersed in the thought of her and yet remained firm in his principle, which is the sign of the godly. He was loved and liked by those in the prison, and he interpreted their dreams whenever they asked him. Yusuf's presence made the prison heaven for the prisoners. But Zuleikha, after the death of her husband, fell into still greater misery.

After many years it happened that Pharaoh dreamed a dream which greatly startled and alarmed him. Among all the soothsayers and magicians in the land there was none who could interpret his dream. Then he was told by his servants of Yusuf and his wonderful gift of interpreting dreams. He sent for Yusuf, who after having been told Pharaoh's dream gave the interpretation of it, and by his wise counsel he greatly relieved the King in his cares. Pharaoh made him chief over all his treasures, and bestowed on him honour and power that raised him in the eyes of the world. 'Verily the truth at last is victorious.'

Then his brothers came to Yusuf, and afterwards his father Jacob, who was released from the years of pain that he had suffered through his love of Yusuf. 'The reward of love never fails the lover.'

Once Yusuf, riding with his retinue, happened to pass by the place where Zuleikha in her utter misery was spending her days. On hearing the sound of the horses' hoofs many people ran to see the company passing, and all called out, 'It is Yusuf, Yusuf!' On hearing this, Zuleikha desired to look at him once again. When Yusuf saw her he did not recognize her, but he halted, seeing that some woman wished to speak to him. He was moved to see a person in such misery, and asked her, 'What desirest thou of me?' She said, 'Zuleikha has still the same desire, O Yusuf, and it will continue here and in the hereafter. I have desired thee, and thee alone I will desire.' Yusuf became convinced of her constant love, and was moved by her state of misery. He kissed her on the forehead, and took her in his arms and prayed to God. The prayer of the prophet and the appeal of long-continued love attracted the blessing of God, and Zuleikha regained her youth and beauty. Yusuf said to Zuleikha, 'From this day thou becomest my beloved queen.' They were then married and lived in happiness. 'Verily God hearkens attentively to the cry of every wretched heart.'

CHAPTER IV

THE MORAL OF LOVE

THERE is one moral, the love that springs forth from self-denial and blooms in deeds of beneficence.

The orthodox say, 'This is good, that is bad; this is right, that is wrong', but to a Sufi the source of all good deeds is love. Someone may say that this is the source of bad deeds also, but that is not so; it is lack of love.

Our virtues are made of love, and our sins are caused by lack of it. Love turns sins into virtues, and its lack makes virtues meaningless. Christ said when a woman was brought before Him accused of sin, 'Her sins are forgiven, for she loved much.' Heaven is made so beautiful with love, and life becomes a hell through the lack of it. Love in reality creates harmony in one's life on earth and peace in heaven.

A nautch girl was once watching two funerals from her window, and she said to her lover, 'The first of those two is a soul that has gone to heaven, the second is a soul that has gone to hell, I am sure.' He said, 'How can you, a nautch girl, pretend to know a thing only a saint could know?' She said, 'I know it by the simple fact that all the people who followed the first funeral had sad faces, and many had tears in their eyes; and all those who followed the second funeral had dry eyes and their faces were cheerful. The first proved that he loved and won the affection of so many, and therefore surely he was entitled to enter the heavens, and the next cannot have loved anybody, for no one grieved at his departure.'

Therefore, as this world is a hell to the loveless, the same hell will become distinct in the next world. If the soul and heart are incapable of love even a man's relations and nearest friends are strangers; he is indifferent to them, and dislikes their company.

It is easy to begin to love, and this everybody, more or less, does; but it is difficult to continue to love, because love opens the eyes of the lover to see through the beloved, though it closes the eyes of the lover to all else. First, the more the lover knows the beloved, the more he begins to see the defects as well as the merits, which naturally in the beginning of love casts the beloved down from the high pedestal on which the lover had put her.

Another thing is that besides the attributes that attract the lovers to one another, there are inclinations in each which draw them asunder. The ego always plays a trick in bringing two hearts together and then separating them. Therefore in the world nearly everyone says, 'I love', or 'I have loved', but there are rare cases where love has been ever on the increase since it began. To a real lover it is an absurd thing to hear anyone say, 'I have loved her, but now I love her no more'.

Love must be absolutely free from selfishness, otherwise it does not produce proper illumination. If the fire has no flame it cannot give light, and smoke comes out of it, which is troublesome. Such is selfish love. Whether it be for man or for God it is fruitless, for though it appears to be love for another or love for God, it is in fact love for the self. Ideas that come to the mind of a lover such as, 'If you will love me I will love you, but if you do not love me I will not love you either', or 'I love you as much as you love me', and all such declarations are false pretensions of love.

The part that a lover performs in life is much more difficult than that of the beloved. Tyranny on the part of the beloved is taken tolerantly and patiently by the lover as a natural thing in the path of love. There is a verse of Hafiz on resignation to the will of the beloved: 'I have broken my bowl of desire against the rock of the beloved's will. What may be done when my heart is won by the obstinate beloved, who does her own will and casts aside the desire of the lover?' This is the study of the lover and of the beloved's nature, that the beloved will do what she desires, while the lover lives in love; the breaking of it is the lover's death. Then the only way is resignation, either in the case of an earthly or of the divine Beloved.

The lover never can grudge or grumble about any injustice done to him, and every fault of the beloved he hides under his mantle, as a man in poverty would hide the patch on his garment. The lover takes care not to hurt the feelings of the beloved in anything he does; but as delicate as is the sense of precaution in him, even more delicate is the sensitiveness of the one who is beloved in vain.

Though love is light it becomes darkness when its law is not understood. Just as water, which cleans all things, becomes mud when mixed with earth, so love, when not understood rightly and when directed wrongly, becomes a curse instead of bliss.

There are five chief sins against love, which turn nectar into poison. The first is when the lover deprives the beloved of freedom and happiness against her desire, because of his love; the next is when the lover gives way to a spirit of rivalry and jealousy or bitterness in love; thirdly, if the lover doubts, distrusts, and suspects the one whom he loves; fourthly, if he shrinks from enduring all the sorrows, pains, troubles, difficulties, and sufferings that come in the path of love; and finally, when the lover pursues his own will instead of complete resignation to the beloved's wish. These are the natural failings of a loving heart, as maladies are natural to the physical body. As lack of health makes life miserable, so lack of love makes the heart wretched. Only the lover who avoids these faults benefits by love, and arrives safely at his destination.

Love lies in service. Only that which is done, not for fame or name, nor for the appreciation or thanks of those for whom it is done, is love's service.

The lover shows kindness and beneficence to the beloved. He does whatever he can for the beloved in the way of help, service, sacrifice, kindness, or rescue, and hides it from the world and even from the beloved. If the beloved does anything for him he exaggerates it, idealizes it, makes it into a mountain from a molehill. He takes poison from the hands of the beloved as sugar, and love's pain in the wound of his heart is his only joy. By magnifying and idealizing whatever the beloved does for him and by diminishing and forgetting whatever he himself does for the beloved, he first develops his own gratitude, which creates all goodness in his life.

Patience, sacrifice, resignation, strength, and steadfastness are needed in love, and ultimately nothing but hope, until one is united with the beloved. Sacrifice is needed in love to give all there is, wealth, possessions, body, heart, and soul; there remains no 'I', only 'you', until the 'you' becomes the 'I'. Where there is love there is patience, where there is no patience there is no love. The lover takes hope as the extract of love's religion, for hope is the only thing that keeps the flame of life alight. Hope to the lover is the rope of safety in the sea. 'Brahma collected honey from all things in life, and it was hope.'

Separation is needed according to nature's law, although it is most painful. Where there are two hearts that are united in love, separation awaits them. Separation must be accepted. A Persian poet says, 'If I had known what pain separation gives in love I would never have allowed the light of love to be kindled in my heart.' God is jealous, as the Japanese say, of any other besides Himself. Whoever it may be that you love, it is this spirit of God in nature that separates sooner or later.

This idea is symbolically expressed in an Indian story called *Indra Sabha*.

A fairy, Sabzpari, who was one of the dancers of the court of Indra, the King of Heaven, was attracted by Prince Gulfam, a man on earth, while she was flying over his palace. Her servant, the black Deva, carried Gulfam at her desire from earth to heaven. Gulfam was at first most unhappy in the strange place, but then the love of Sabzpari attracted him so much that he lived in her love. Sabzpari had to be at the court of Indra every night to dance and entertain him, and as, in the love of Gulfam, she was absent a few times, everyone at the court wondered why she was not there. But her going every night to the court of Indra made Gulfam suspect that perhaps there might be someone else who was entertained by Sabzpari's charms. He asked her about this many times, and every time she refused to tell him, until he became vexed and Sabzpari thought she could not hide it from him any longer. On hearing her explanation Gulfam requested her to take him to the court of Indra. She said, 'No man has ever been there, no man can ever go there, and if Indra should see thee it will at once end our sweet days of love and happiness. We shall surely be separated, and I know not what he will not do to thee.'

Gulfam said, 'No. It is a woman's tale. Thou art perhaps in

love with some Deva, and wishest to hide it by telling me a story.' She was most unhappy, finding herself in a helpless situation. Under the spell of the agony that his arrowlike words had produced in her heart she consented, without thinking, to take Gulfam to the court of Indra, saying to herself, 'What will be, will be.'

Sabzpari took him to the court, hiding him behind the folds of her garment and wings which spread about her. The red Deva sensed the presence of a man in the court, and, looking all around, he found that Sabzpari was dancing most skilfully before Indra, hiding Gulfam behind her. He humbly brought him before Indra, the Lord of the Heavens, who was sitting on a throne with a glass of wine in his hand, his eyes red with the wine and his high being full of glory and grandeur. When Indra saw that a man had been brought into the apex of the heavens he rose in great wrath and said to Sabzpari, 'O shameless one, how darest thou bring a man into the summit of the heavens, where no earthly creature has ever been allowed to come?' The red Deva said, 'It is her love for this earthly creature, my Lord, that has turned her faithless to the heavenly crown and made her fail in her duty at the supreme court of your Majesty.'

Sabzpari said to Gulfam, 'Seest thou, my darling beloved, what has befallen us through thy insistence?' Indra said, 'Separate them at once, that they may no more speak a word to one another. Throw him back into the depths of the earth, and tear her wings off and keep her captive until the love of Gulfam is wiped from her heart. Then purify the polluted one from the five elements. Then only can she come again, if she be allowed by our favour, forgiveness, and mercy.'

The symbolism of this story tells us of the jealous God. Indra has its origin in the word *Andar* or *Antar*, which means inner, the innermost spirit, which man idealizes as God the Almighty. The Peris are the souls that He created out of His own Being, whose dance in His praise, in His knowledge, in His presence, is the only thing He wants of them. The black Deva is the symbol of darkness, which in Sanskrit is called *Tamas*, under which the soul has built for itself a house of earthly elements, the physical body. God has created the world out of darkness.

Sabz means green, which is symbolical of water, the first

element that formed substance, matter in other words. *Sabzpari* means a soul drawn to the material body. When the soul involves itself in the earthly body, which Gulfam signifies, then the soul involved in the body becomes absorbed in earthly experiences, its love on earth, its joy on earth, and its comfort on earth. As the duty of the soul is forgotten by it, it being in the earthly pursuit, the red Deva, the power of destruction, who is constantly busy causing all change in nature by his power of destruction, then causes separation, death being the separation of body and soul. Still the soul, the dweller of the heavens, becomes wingless by the curse of the supreme Spirit and inclines earthward until it is purified from the five elements that constitute the lower world. 'Unless a man be born again of water and of the spirit, he shall in no wise enter into the kingdom of God', one reads in the Bible. It is only then that the soul rises above all earthly influences and dances for ever before the most high Indra, the Lord of lords.

The effect of love is pain; the love that has no pain is no love. The lover who has not gone through the agonies of love is not a lover, he claims love falsely. 'What love is it that gives no pain? Even if one were crazy in love it is nothing.' The pain of love is the lover's pleasure, his very life; the lack of pain is his death. Amir, the Hindustani poet, says, 'Thou wilt remember me after I am dead, O my pain in love, for I have given thee place all through life in my tender heart, and have fed thee with my flesh and blood.' Everybody can speak of love and claim to love, but to stand the test of love and to bear the pain in love is the achievement of some rare hero. The mere sight of love's pain makes the coward run away from it. No soul would have taken this poison if it had not the taste of nectar.

He who loves because he cannot help it is the slave of love, but he who loves because it is his only joy is the king of love. He who, for the sake of love, loves someone who falls short of his ideal is the ruler of love; and he who can seal his heart full of love in spite of all attraction on the part of the beloved is the conqueror of love.

Those who have avoided love in life from fear of its pain have lost more than the lover, who by losing himself gains all.

The loveless first lose all, until at last their self is also snatched away from their hands. The warmth of the lover's atmosphere, the piercing effect of his voice, the appeal of his words, all come from the pain of his heart. The heart is not living until it has experienced pain. Man has not lived if he has lived and worked with his body and mind without heart. The soul is all light, but all darkness is caused by the death of the heart. Pain makes it alive. The same heart that was once full of bitterness, when purified by love becomes the source of all goodness; all deeds of kindness spring from it.

Rumi describes six signs of the lover: deep sigh, mild expression, moist eyes, eating little, speaking little, sleeping little, which all show the sign of pain in love. Hafiz says, 'All bliss in my life has been the outcome of unceasing tears and continual sighs through the heart of night.'

The sorrow of the lover is continual, in the presence and in the absence of the beloved: in the presence for fear of the absence, and in absence in longing for the presence. According to the mystical view the pain of love is the dynamite that breaks up the heart, even if it be as hard as a rock. When this hardness that covers the light within is broken through, the streams of all bliss come forth as springs from the mountains.

The pain of love becomes in time the life of the lover; the soreness of the wound of his heart affords him a joy that nothing else can give. The heart aflame becomes the torch on the path of the lover, which lightens his way that leads him to his destination. The pleasures of life are blinding, it is love alone that clears the rust from the heart, the mirror of the soul.

Once a slave-girl, making the bed of a Badishah, felt a wish to experience how it would feel to rest in this royal bed. The great heat of the sun, the breeze coming through the windows in this regal bedroom, the flowers and perfumes sprinkled on the ground, the beautiful fragrance of the incense burning, made her so comfortable that she fell asleep as soon as she leaned against a cushion on this bed. She fell as fast asleep as if she were in the embrace of death. But presently the king and queen came, and they were astonished at the boldness and impudence of this slave-girl. The Badishah woke her with a stroke of a whip, and one or two more strokes followed after, in order to free the queen from all suspicions. The slave-girl got up in terror, and cried aloud, but it all ended in a smile. Her smile created more curiosity in the minds of the king and queen than her fault had done. They asked what made her smile. She said, 'I smiled at the thought that the comfort and joy of this bed gave me an inclination to experience its pleasure for a moment, the penalty of which is given me as these blows, and I wonder, as you have experienced the pleasure of this comfortable bed all your life, what penalty you will have to pay for this to God, the King of all kings.'

The nature of life is such that every little pleasure costs incomparably greater pain. The lover, therefore, has collected all pain that is the current coin, and his path will be smoother through life's journey from earth to heaven. There he will be rich when all others will be found poor.

The imagery of the Sufi poets portrays the nature of love, lover, and beloved with such a delicacy of metaphor, complexity, and convention in its expression that their poetry makes a true picture of human nature.

The lover is always imagined to be the victim of the tyranny of the cold-hearted and vain beloved, who gives no heed, revels with his rivals, pays no attention to his sufferings, gives no hearing to his appeal, and when she responds, responds so little that instead of being cured the malady is increased. The lover holds his unruly heart for mercy before the beloved, taking it on his palms. He places his heart at the feet of the beloved, who coldly treads upon it, while he is crying, 'Gently, beloved, gently! It is my heart, it is my heart.' The heart of the lover sheds tears of blood. The lover presses his heart, keeping it from running away to where the beloved is. The lover complains of his heart being so faithless as to have left him and gone to the beloved. The lover begs of the beloved to give his heart back if it be of no use. The abode of the heart is in the curls of the beloved.

The lover is restless, uneasy, and unhappy in the agonies of separation. Nights pass, days pass, all things change but the pain of the lover. The pain of love is his only companion through the nights of separation. The lover asks the weary night of separation,

'Where wilt thou be when I am dead?' The lover expects the coming of death before the coming of the beloved. He begs of the beloved to show herself to him once before he dies. He prays the beloved to visit his tomb, if not for love, at least for appearances' sake.

The lover only wishes the beloved to understand him, to know how much he loves and what sufferings he is going through. The lover wishes constantly that either the beloved would come to him or he might be called to the beloved; even the sight of the messenger of love makes the beloved cross. The good and ill of the world is nought to the lover. The lover complains of being robbed of ease, patience, and peace, and of having lost his religion, morals, and God. The lover is seen without hat and shoes, and regarded as crazy by his friends. He tears his garment in the agony of pain. He is tied in chains for his madness. He has lost honour before all.

The wound in his heart is as a rose to the lover, the soreness in it is its bloom. He weeps in order to sprinkle salt water upon it to make it smart, that he may fully enjoy the sweet agony. The lover is jealous of the attentions his rivals bestow on his beloved. When the lover tells the story of love to his companions of love they all begin to weep with him. The lover kisses the ground where the beloved walks. He envies the privilege of the beloved's shoes. The lover spreads his carpet at the gate of the beloved. The eyebrows of the beloved are the Mehrab, the archway in the mosque. The patch on the cheeks of the beloved is the magic spot that reveals to him the secrets of heaven and earth. The dust under the feet of the beloved is to him as the sacred earth of Ka'ba. The face of the beloved is the open Qur'an, and he reads Alif, the first and symbolical letter of Allah's name, in the straight features of the beloved. The lover drinks Kouthar, wine, out of the eyes of the beloved; her overflowing glance intoxicates him. The sound of the beloved's anklets makes him alive. The lover is satisfied to see the beloved even in the dream, if not in the waking state.

When the lover speaks of dying the beloved disbelieves him. The lover is so wasted that even Munkir and Nakir, the recording angels, cannot trace him in his grave. Fear of the lover's approach makes the beloved gather up the train of her garment and lift it when walking past his grave, lest the lover's hand may reach it.

With the deep sigh of the lover heaven and earth shake. His tears in the thought of the fair one turn into flowers as they touch the ground. Pain is his comrade in the heart of night, and death is his companion through the journey of life. He plans and imagines a thousand things to tell to the beloved, of his longing, his pain, praise, and love; but when he sees the beloved he is spellbound, his tongue motionless and his lips sealed, his eyes engaged in the vision of the desired one.

Joy in the real sense of the word is known to the lover alone. The loveless know it by name, not in reality. It is like the difference between a rock and man. Man, with all life's struggles and difficulties, would rather live as a man than become a rock, which no struggle or difficulty can ever touch; for even with struggles and difficulties the joy of living is immense. With all the pains and sorrows that the lover has to meet with in love, his joy in love is unimaginable, for love is life, and its lack is death. 'Angels would give up their free dwelling in the heavens if they knew the joy when love springs up in youth.'

There are two worthy objects of love: on the lower plane man, and on the higher God. Every person in the world first learns to love on the lower plane. As soon as the infant opens its eyes it loves whatever its eyes see, whatever seems to it beautiful. Later there comes the love for what is permanent, for what is unchanging, which leads to the ideal of God. But then the man is already fixed in such a difficult position in life that there is a struggle between the one and the other. The idol pulls from one side and the ideal draws from the other side, and it is only the rare one who rises above this difficulty.

This is explained in the life of Surdas, a very great musician and poet of India. He was deeply in love with a singer and took delight in seeing her. His fondness so increased that he could not live a single day without her. Once there was a heavy rainfall which continued for weeks and the country towns were all flooded. There was no means of getting about, the roads were impassable, but nothing would prevent Surdas from seeing his beloved at the promised time. He set out through the heavy rain, but on the way there was a river which was in flood and unfordable. There was no boat in sight. Surdas therefore jumped into the river and tried to swim. The rough waves of the river buffeted him, raised him up and threw him down as if from mountains to the abyss. Fortunately he was thrown against a corpse, of which, taking it to be a log of wood, he seized hold, and he clung to it and arrived in the end, after a great struggle, at the cottage of his beloved.

He found the doors locked. It was late at night and any noise would have roused the whole neighbourhood. Therefore he tried to climb up the house and enter through the upper window. He took hold of a cobra, which seemed like a rope hanging, thinking that it had perhaps been put there on purpose for him by his beloved.

When she saw him she was amazed. She could not understand how he had managed to come, and the impression that his love made on her was greater than ever. She was as if inspired by his love. He was raised in her ideal from a man to an angel, especially when she discovered that he had taken a corpse for a log of wood and the cobra, the enemy of man, for a rope of safety. She saw how death is slain by the lover. She said to him, 'O man, thy love is higher than the average man's love, and if only it could be for God, the supreme Deity, how great a bliss it would be! Rise, then, above the love of form and matter, and direct thy love to the spirit of God.' He took her advice like a simple child, and left her with heavy heart and wandered from that time onward in the forests of India.

For many years he roamed in the forests, repeating the name of the divine Beloved and seeking refuge in His arms. He visited the sacred places, the places of pilgrimage, and by chance reached the bank of a sacred river where the women of the city came every morning at sunrise to fill their pitchers with the sacred water. Surdas, sitting there in the thought of God, was struck by the beauty and charm of one among them. His heart, being a torch, did not take long to light. He followed this woman. When she entered her house she told her husband, 'Some sage saw me at the river and has followed me to the house and he is still standing outside.' The thoughtful husband went out immediately and saw this man with the face of a sage and spiritual dignity shed around him. He said, 'O Maharaj, what has made thee tarry here? Is there anything that I can do for thee?' Surdas said, 'Who was the woman who entered this house?' He said, 'She is my wife, and she and I are both at the service of sages.' Surdas said, 'Pray ask her to come, O blessed one, that I may see her once more.' And when she came out he looked at her once and said, 'O Mother, pray bring me two pins.' And when she brought them to him he bowed to her charm and beauty once more and thrust the pins into his eyes, saying, 'O my eyes, ye will nevermore see and be tempted by earthly beauty and cast me down from heaven to earth.'

Then he was blind for the rest of his life, and his songs of the divine ideal are still alive and are sung by the God-loving people in India, and if any Hindu is blind, people call him Surdas, which he takes as a term of honour and respect.

'Though I have loved only one, yet it is eternal', says Mohi. There can be love only where there is one object before us, not many; where there are many there can be no devotion. 'When in the place of one there are two, the peculiarity of the one is lost. It is for this reason that I did not allow the portrait of my beloved to be made.' That one is God, the formless and even nameless, the eternal, who is with us and will remain for ever.

Love for one person, to whatever depth it may have reached, is limited; perfection of love lies in its vastness. 'The tendency of love is to expand, even from one atom to the whole universe, from a single earthly beloved to God.'

When love is for the human being it is primitive and incomplete, and yet it is needed to begin with. He can never say, 'I love God', who has no love for his fellow-man. But when love attains its culmination in God, it reaches its perfection.

Love creates love in man and even more with God. It is the nature of love. If you love God, God sends His love evermore upon you. If you seek Him by night, He will follow you by day; wherever you are, in your affairs, in your business transactions, the help, the protection and the presence of the Divine will follow you.

The expression of love lies in silent admiration, contemplation, service, attention to please the beloved, and precaution to avoid the beloved's displeasure. These expressions of love on the part of the lover win the favour of the beloved, whose vanity otherwise cannot easily be satisfied; and the favour of the beloved is the only aim of the lover, nor is any cost too great a price for it.

The nature of beauty is that it is unconscious of the value of its being. It is the idealization of the lover which makes beauty precious, and it is the attention of the lover which produces indifference in the beautiful, a realization of being superior, and the idea, 'I am even more wonderful than I am thought to be'. When the vanity of an earthly beauty is thus satisfied by admiration, how much more should the vanity of the beauty of the heavens be satisfied by His glorification, who is the real beauty and alone deserves all praise. It is the absence of realization on man's part that makes him forget His beauty in all and recognize each beauty separately, liking one and disliking another. To the sight of the seer, from the least fraction of beauty to the absolute beauty of nature, all becomes as one single immanence of the divine Beloved.

It is told that God said to the Prophet, 'O Mohammad, if We had not created thee We would not have created the whole universe.' What, in reality, does it mean? It means that the heavenly beauty, the beauty of the whole Being, loved, recognized and glorified by the divine lover, moved to a perfect satisfaction, says from within, 'Well done, thou hast loved Me completely. If it were not for thee, O admirer of my whole Being, I would not have made this universe, where my creatures love and admire one part of my Being on the surface, and my whole beauty is veiled from their sight.' In other words, the divine Beloved says, 'I have no admirer, though I am standing adorned. Some admire my bracelets, others admire my earrings, some admire my necklace, some admire my anklets, but I would give my hand to him and consider that for him I have adorned myself, who would understand and glorify my Being to the fullest extent, wherein lies my satisfaction.'

CHAPTER V

LEILA AND MAJNUN

THE STORY of Leila and Majnun has been told in the East for thousands of years and has always exerted a great fascination, for it is not only a love-story, but a lesson in love; not love as it is generally understood by man, but the love that rises above the earth and heavens.

A lad called Majnun from childhood had shown love in his nature, revealing to the eye of the seers the tragedy of his life. When Majnun was at school he became fond of Leila. In time the spark grew into a flame, and Majnun did not feel at rest if Leila was a little late in coming to school; with his book in his hand, he fixed his eyes on the entrance, which amused the scoffers and disturbed everybody there. The flame in time rose into a blaze and then Leila's heart became kindled by Majnun's love. Each looked at the other; she did not see anyone in the class but Majnun, nor did he see anyone save Leila. In reading from the book Majnun would read the name of Leila, in writing from dictation Leila would cover her slate with the name of Majnun. 'All else disappears when the thought of the beloved occupies the mind of the lover.'

Everyone in the school whispered to each other, pointing them out. The teachers were worried and wrote to the parents of both that the children were crazy and intensely fond of one another, and that there seemed no way to divert their attention from their love-affair which had stopped every possibility of their progress in study.

Leila's parents removed her at once, and kept a careful watch over her. In this way they took her away from Majnun, but who could take Majnun away from her heart? She had no thought but of Majnun. Majnun, without her, in his heart's unrest and grief, kept the whole school in a turmoil, until his parents were compelled to take him home, as there seemed to be nothing left for him in the school. Majnun's parents called physicians, soothsayers, healers, magicians, and poured money at their feet, asking them for some remedy to take away from the heart of Majnun the thought of Leila. But how could it be done? 'Even Luqman the great physician of the ancients, had no cure for the love-sick.'

No one has ever healed a patient of love. Friends came, relations came, well-wishers came, wise counsellors came, and all tried their best to efface from his mind the thought of Leila, but all was in vain. Someone said to him, 'O Majnun, why do you sorrow at the separation from Leila? She is not beautiful. I can show you a thousand fairer and more charming maidens, and can let you choose your mate from among them.' Majnun answered, 'O, to see the beauty of Leila the eyes of Majnun are needed.'

When no remedy had been left untried, the parents of Majnun resolved to seek the refuge of the Ka'ba as their last resort. They took Majnun on the pilgrimage to Ka'bat-ullah. When they drew near to the Ka'ba a great crowd gathered to see them. The parents, each in turn, went and prayed to God, saying, 'O Lord, Thou art most merciful and compassionate, grant Thy favour to our only son, that the heart of Majnun may be released from the pain of the love of Leila.' Everybody there listened to this intently, and wonderingly awaited what Majnun had to say. Then Majnun was asked by his parents, 'Child, go and pray that the love of Leila may be taken away from your heart.' Majnun replied, 'Shall I meet my Leila if I pray?' They, with the greatest disappointment, said, 'Pray, child, whatever you like to pray.' He went there and said, 'I want my Leila,' and everyone present said, 'Amen.' 'The world echoes to the lover's call.'

When the parents had sought in every way to cure Majnun of his craze for Leila, in the end they thought the best way was to approach the parents of Leila, for this was the last hope of saving Majnun's life. They sent a message to Leila's parents, who were of another faith, saying, 'We have done all we can to take away from Majnun the thought of Leila, but so far we have not succeeded, nor is there any hope of success left to us except one, that is your consent to their marriage.' They, in answer, said,

'Although it exposes us to the scorn of our people, still Leila seems never to forget the thought of Majnun for one single moment, and since we have taken her away from school she pines away every day. Therefore we should not mind giving Leila in marriage to Majnun, if only we were convinced that he is sane.'

On hearing this the parents of Majnun were much pleased and advised Majnun to behave sensibly, so that Leila's parents might have no cause to suspect him of being out of his mind. Majnun agreed to do everything his parents desired, if he could only meet his Leila. They went, according to the custom of the East, in procession to the house of the bride, where a special seat was made for the bridegroom, who was covered with garlands of flowers. But as they say in the East that the gods are against lovers, so destiny did not grant these perfect lovers the happiness of being together. The dog that used to accompany Leila to school happened to come into the room where they were sitting. As soon as Majnun's eyes fell on this dog his emotion broke out. He could not sit in the high seat and look at the dog. He ran to the dog and kissed its paws and put all the garlands of flowers on the neck of the dog. There was no sign of reverence or worship that Majnun did not show to this dog. 'The dust of the beloved's dwelling is the earth of Ka'ba to the lover.' This conduct plainly proved him insane. As love's language is gibberish to the loveless, so the action of Majnun was held by those present to be mere folly. They were all greatly disappointed, and Majnun was taken back home and Leila's parents refused their consent to the marriage.

This utter disappointment made Majnun's parents altogether hopeless, and they no longer kept watch over him, seeing that life and death to him were both the same, and this gave Majnun freedom to wander about the town in search of Leila, enquiring of everyone he met about Leila. By chance he met a letter-carrier who was carrying mail on the back of a camel, and when Majnun asked this man Leila's whereabouts, he said, 'Her parents have left this country and have gone to live a hundred miles from here.' Majnun begged him to give his message to Leila. He said, 'With pleasure.' But when Majnun began to tell the message the telling continued for a long, long time. 'The message of love has no end.'

The letter-carrier was partly amused and partly he sympathized with his earnestness. Although Majnun, walking with his camel, was company for him on his long journey, still, out of pity, he said, 'Now you have walked ten miles giving me your message, how long will it take me to deliver it to Leila? Now go your way, I will see to it.' Then Majnun turned back, but he had not gone a hundred yards before he returned to say, 'O kind friend, I have forgotten to tell you a few things that you might tell my Leila.' When he continued his message it carried him another ten miles on the way. The carrier said, 'For mercy's sake, go back. You have walked a long way. How shall I be able to remember all the message you have given me? Still, I will do my best. Now go back, you are far from home.' Majnun again went back a few yards and again remembered something to tell the message-bearer and went after him. In this way the whole journey was accomplished, and he himself arrived at the place to which he was sending the message.

The letter-carrier was astonished at this earnest love, and said to him, 'You have already arrived in the land where your Leila lives. Now stay in this ruined mosque. This is outside the town; if you go with me into the town they will torment you before you can reach Leila. The best thing is for you to rest here now, as you have walked so very far, and I will convey your message to Leila as soon as I can reach her.' 'Love's intoxication sees no time nor space.'

Majnun listened to his advice and stayed there, and felt inclined to rest, but the idea that he was in the town where Leila dwelt made him wonder in which direction he should stretch out his legs. He thought of the north, south, east, and west, and thought to himself, 'If Leila were on this side it would be insolence on my part to stretch out my feet towards her. The best thing, then, would be to hang my feet by a rope from above, for surely she will not be there.' 'The lover's Ka'ba is the dwelling-place of the beloved.' He was thirsty, and could find no water except some rain-water that had collected in a disused tank.

When the letter-carrier entered the house of Leila's parents he saw Leila and said to her, 'I had to make a great effort to speak with you. Your lover Majnun, who is a lover without compare in all the world, gave me a message for you, and he continued to speak with me throughout the journey and has walked as far as this town with the camel.' She said, 'For heaven's sake! Poor Majnun! I wonder what will become of him.' She asked her old nurse, 'What becomes of a person who has walked a hundred miles without a break?' The nurse said rashly, 'Such a person must die.' Leila said, 'Is there any remedy?' She said, 'He must drink some rain-water collected for a year past and from that water a snake must drink, and then his feet must be tied and he must be hung up in the air with his head down for a very long time; that might save his life.' Leila said, 'Oh, but how difficult it is to obtain!' God, who Himself is love, was the guide of Majnun, therefore everything came to Majnun as was best for him. 'Verily love is the healer of its own wounds.'

The next morning Leila put her food aside, and sent it secretly, by a maid whom she took into her confidence, with a message to tell Majnun that she longed to see him as much as he to see her, the difference being only of chains; as soon as she had an opportunity, she said, she would come at once.

The maid went to the ruined mosque, and saw two people sitting there, one who seemed self-absorbed, unaware of his surroundings, and the other a fat, robust man. She thought that Leila could not possibly love a person like this dreamy one whom she herself would not have cared to love. But in order to make sure, she asked which of them was named Majnun. The mind of Majnun was deeply sunk in his thought and far away from her words, but this man, who was out of work, was rather glad to see the dinner-basket in her hand, and said, 'For whom are you looking?' She said, 'I am asked to give this to Majnun. Are you Majnun?' He readily stretched out his hands to take the basket, and said, 'I am the one for whom you have brought it,' and spoke a word or two with her in jest, and she was delighted.

On the maid's return Leila asked, 'Did you give it to him?' She said, 'Yes, I did.' Leila then sent to Majnun every day the larger part of her meals, which was received every day by this man, who was very glad to have it while out of work. Leila one day asked her maid, 'You never tell me what he says and how he eats.' She said, 'He says that he sends very many thanks to you and he appreciates it very much, and he is a pleasant-spoken man. You must not worry for one moment. He is getting fatter every day.' Leila said, 'But my Majnun has never been fat, and has never had a tendency to become fat, and he is too deep in his thought to say pleasant things to anyone. He is too sad to speak.' Leila at once suspected that the dinner might have been handed to the wrong person. She said, 'Is anybody else there?' The maid said, 'Yes, there is another person sitting there also, but he seems to be beside himself. He never notices who comes or who goes, nor does he hear a word said by anybody there. He cannot possibly be the man that you love.' Leila said, 'I think he must be the man. Alas, if you have all this time given the food to the wrong person! Well, to make sure, today take on the plate a knife instead of food and say to that one to whom you gave the food, "For Leila a few drops of your blood are needed, to cure her of an illness." '

When the maid next went to the mosque the man as usual came most eagerly to take his meal, and seeing the knife was surprised. The maid told him that a few drops of his blood were needed to cure Leila. He said, 'No, certainly I am not Majnun. There is Majnun. Ask him for it.' The maid foolishly went to him and said to him aloud, 'Leila wants a few drops of your blood to cure her.' Majnun most readily took the knife in his hand and said, 'How fortunate am I that my blood may be of some use to my Leila. This is nothing, even if my life were to become a sacrifice for her cure, I would consider myself most fortunate to give it.' 'Whatever the lover did for the beloved, it could never be too much.' He gashed his arm in several places, but the starvation of months had left no blood, nothing but skin and bone. When a great many places had been cut hardly one drop of blood came out. He said, 'That is what is left. You may take that.' 'Love means pain, but the lover alone is above all pain.'

Majnun's coming to the town soon became known, and when Leila's parents knew of it they thought, 'Surely Leila will go out of her mind if she ever sees Majnun.' Therefore they resolved to leave the town for some time, thinking that Majnun would make his way home when he found that Leila was not there. Before leaving the place Leila sent a message to Majnun to say, 'We are leaving this town for a while, and I am most unhappy that I have not been able to meet you. The only chance of our meeting is that we should meet on the way, if you will go on before and wait for me in the Sahara.'

Majnun started most happily to go to the Sahara, with great hope of once more seeing his Leila. When the caravan arrived in the desert and halted there for a while, the mind of Leila's parents became a little relieved, and they saw Leila also a little happier for the change, as they thought, not knowing the true reason.

Leila went for a walk in the Sahara with her maid, and suddenly came upon Majnun, whose eyes had been fixed for a long, long time on the way by which she was to come. She came and said, 'Majnun, I am here.' There remained no power in the tongue of Majnun to express his joy. He held her hands and pressed them to his breast, and said, 'Leila, you will not leave me any more?' She said, 'Majnun, I have been able to come for one moment. If I stay any longer my people will seek for me and your life will not be safe.' Majnun said, 'I do not care for life. You are my life. O stay, do not leave me any more.' Leila said, 'Majnun, be sensible and believe me. I will surely come back.' Majnun let go her hands and said, 'Surely I believe you.' So Leila left Majnun, with heavy heart, and Majnun, who had so long lived on his own flesh and blood, could no more stand erect, but fell backward against the trunk of a tree, which propped him up, and he remained there, living only on hope.

Years passed and this half-dead body of Majnun was exposed to all things, cold and heat and rain, frost and storm. The hands that were holding the branches became branches themselves, his body became a part of the tree. Leila was as unhappy as before on her travels, and the parents lost hope of her life. She was living only in one hope, that she might once fulfil her promise given to Majnun at the moment of parting, saying, 'I will come back.' She wondered if he were alive or dead, or had gone away or whether the animals in the Sahara had carried him off.

When they returned their caravan halted in the same place,

and Leila's heart became full of joy and sorrow, of cheerfulness and gloom, of hope and fear. As she was looking for the place where she had left Majnun she met a woodcutter, who said to her, 'Oh, don't go that way. There is some ghost there.' Leila said, 'What is it like?' He said, 'It is a tree and at the same time man, and as I struck a branch of this tree with my hatchet I heard him say in a deep sigh, "O Leila." '

Hearing this moved Leila beyond description. She said she would go, and drawing near the tree she saw Majnun turned almost into the tree. Flesh and blood had already wasted, and the skin and bone that remained, by contact with the tree, had become like its branches. Leila called him aloud, 'Majnun!' He answered, 'Leila!' She said, 'I am here as I promised, O Majnun.' He answered, 'I am Leila.' She said, 'Majnun, come to your senses. I am Leila. Look at me.' Majnun said, 'Are you Leila? Then I am not', and he was dead. Leila, seeing this perfection in love, could not live a single moment more. She at the same time cried the name of Majnun and fell down and died.

'The beloved is all in all, the lover only veils him. The beloved is all that lives, the lover a dead thing.'

CHAPTER VI

DIVINE LOVE

LOVE IS directed by the intelligence; therefore each person chooses his object of love according to his evolution. That appears to him most deserving of love which is in accordance with the grade of his evolution. There is a saying in the East. 'As the soul is, so are its angels.' The donkey would prefer thistles to roses.

The consciousness which is awakened to the material world has its object of love only in earthly beauties. The consciousness active through the mind finds its object in thought and among the thoughtful. The consciousness awakened through the heart loves love and the loving ones. And the consciousness awakened in the soul loves the spirit and the spiritual.

Silent love, which is the divine essence in man, becomes active, living, on seeing the vision of beauty. Beauty may be explained as perfection, perfection in every aspect of beauty. Not love alone is God or the essence of God, but beauty also, even in its limited aspects, shows itself as glimpses of the perfect Being. The mineral kingdom develops into gold, silver, diamonds, rubies, and emeralds, showing perfection in it; the fruit and flower, their sweetness and fragrance, show perfection in the vegetable kingdom; form, figure, and youth show perfection in the animal kingdom; and it is the beauty of personality which is significant of perfection in the human being. There are some people in this world whose life is absorbed in the pursuit of gold and silver, gems and jewels; they would sacrifice anything or anybody to acquire the object of their love. There are others whose life is engaged in the beautiful vision of fruits, flowers, flowerbeds, and gardens; perhaps they have no other interest besides. There are some who are absorbed in the admiration of the youth and beauty of the opposite sex, and nothing else seems to them worth more. There are others who are won by the beauty of someone's personality, and have entirely devoted to the one they love both their here and their hereafter. Everyone has his object of love according to his standard of beauty, and at the same time each one loves the perfection of the divine Being in a certain aspect. When the seer sees this no one, wise or foolish, sinner or virtuous, remains blameworthy in his sight. He sees in every heart the needle of the compass that turns to one and the same Being. 'God is beautiful and He loves beauty', as it is said in the Hadith.

Man is never capable of loving God in heaven when his sympathy has not even been awakened to the beauty of the earth.

A village maiden was on her way to see her beloved. She passed by a Mullah who was saying prayers. In her ignorance she walked in front of him, which is forbidden by the religious law. The Mullah was very angry, and when she, returning, again passed near him, he scolded her for her mistake. He said, 'How sinful, O girl, on your part to cross in front of me while I was offering my prayer.' She said, 'What does prayer mean?' He said, 'I was thinking of God, the Lord of the heavens and of the earth.' She said, 'I am sorry. I don't know yet of God and His prayers, but I was on my way to my beloved, and, thinking of my beloved, I did not see you praying. I wonder how you who were in the thought of God could see me?' Her words so much impressed the Mullah that he said to her, 'From this moment, O maiden, you are my teacher. It is I who should learn from you.'

Someone once came to Jami and asked to be his mureed. Jami said, 'Have you ever loved anyone in life?' He said, 'No'. Jami said, 'Then go, and love someone, and then come to me.'

It is for this reason that great teachers and masters have often had difficulty in awakening the love of God in the average man. Parents give their child a doll so that the child may know how to dress it, how to be kind to it, how to look after it, how to love and admire it, which trains the child to become a loving mother in the future. Without this training the later course would be difficult. Divine love would be as strange to the average person as the cares of motherhood to a girl who has not yet played enough with dolls.

A mureed had been a long time in the service of a spiritual guide, but he could make no progress and was not inspired. He went to the teacher and said, 'I have seen very many mureeds being inspired, but it is my misfortune that I cannot advance at all, and now I must give up hope and leave you.' The teacher advised him to spend the last days of his stay in a house near the Khankah, and every day he sent him very good food and told him to cease the spiritual practices and to lead a comfortable and restful life. On the last day he sent the mureed a basket of fruit by a fair damsel. She set the tray down and immediately went away, though he wished to detain her. Her beauty and charm were so great, and he was now so much disposed to admire and was so much won by them, that he could think of nothing else. Every hour and every minute he longed only to see her again. His longing increased every moment. He forgot to eat, he was full of tears and sighs, finding his heart now warmed and melted by the fire of love. After some time, when the teacher visited the disciple, with one glance he inspired him. 'Even steel can be moulded if it be heated in the fire', and so it is with the heart which is melted by the fire of love.

It is love's wine which is called *Sherab-i Kouthar*, the wine found in the heavens. When the intoxication of love increases in man, people call him blindly in love or madly in love, because people wide-awake to the illusion of the surface consider themselves to be the only ones wide-awake; but their wakefulness is to the delusion, not to reality. Although the lover is called crazy, his craze for one object of the world of illusion makes him gradually free from all delusion around him. If he succeeds in attaining to this he enjoys his union with the beloved in his happy vision. Then no time is needed to lift from his sight the veil of the one object which he loved; as is said in the Qur'an, 'We will lift the veil from thine eyes and thy sight will be keen.'

It is natural for a lover to become infatuated with someone whom he admires, with whom he desires union; but no one object in the world is so perfect as fully to satisfy the aspiration of the loving heart. This is the stumbling-block that causes every beginner in love to fall. The successful travellers on the path of love are those whose love is so beautiful that it provides all the beauty that their ideal lacks. The lover by doing this in time rises above the changeable and limited beauty of the beloved, but begins to see into the beloved's inner being; in other words, the exterior of the beloved was only a means of drawing the love out of the heart of the lover, but the love led him from the external to the innermost being of the ideal of his love. When in the ideal the lover has realized the unlimited and perfect Being, whether he loves man or God, he is in fact in either case a blissful lover.

In this the journey through the path of idealism is ended and a journey through the divine ideal is begun, for the God-ideal is necessary for the attainment of life's perfection. Man then seeks for a perfect object of love, idealizing God, the whole Being, the Infinite, who is above all the world's lights and shades, good and ill, who is pure from all limitations, births or deaths, unchangeable, inseparable from us, all-pervading, present always before the vision of his lover.

When love is true it takes away selfishness, for this is the only solution to wipe off the ego. The English phrase 'to fall in love' conveys the idea of the true nature of love. It is a fall indeed from the pedestal of the ego to the ground of nothingness, but at the same time it is this fall which leads to a rise, for as low as the lover falls so high he rises in the end. The lover falls in love as a seed is thrown in the ground. Both appear to be destroyed, but both in time spring up and flourish and bear fruit for the ever-hungry world.

Man's greatest enemy in the world is his ego, the thought of self. This is the germ from which springs all evil in man. Even the virtues of the egoist turn into sin, and his small sins into great crimes. All religions and philosophies teach man to crush it, and there is nothing that can crush it better than love. The growth of love is the decay of the ego. Love in its perfection entirely frees the lover from all selfishness, for love may be called in other words annihilation. 'Whoever enters the school of lovers, the first lesson he learns is not to be.'

Unity is impossible without love, for it is love only which can unite. Each expression of love signifies the attainment of union as its object, and two things cannot unite unless one of them becomes nothing. No one knows this secret of life except the lover. Iraqi says in his verse, 'When I, without having loved, went to Ka'ba and knocked at the gate, a voice came: "What didst thou accomplish in thy home that thou hast come forth?" And when I went, having lost myself in love, and knocked at the gate of Ka'ba, a voice said: "Come, Come, O Iraqi, thou art ours." '

If there is anything that works against the vanity of the ego, it is love. The nature of love is to surrender; there is no one in the world who does not surrender. The world of variety, which has divided life into limited parts, naturally causes every lesser one to surrender to the greater. And, again, for every greater one there is another still greater in relation to whom he is smaller, and for every smaller one there is another still smaller, in relation to whom he is greater. And as every soul is by its nature compelled to surrender to perfection in all its grades, the only thing that matters is whether it be a willing surrender or an unwilling surrender. The former comes by love, the latter is made through helplessness, which makes life wretched. It moves the Sufi when he reads in the Qur'an that the perfect Being asked the imperfect souls, the children of Adam, 'Who is thy Lord?' They, conscious of their imperfections, said humbly, 'Thou art our Lord.' Surrender is a curse when, with coldness and helplessness, one is forced to surrender; but the same becomes the greatest joy when it is made with love and all willingness.

Love is the practice of the moral of Suluk, the way of beneficence. The lover's pleasure is in the pleasure of the beloved. The lover is satisfied when the beloved is fed. The lover is vain when the beloved is adorned. 'Who in life blesses the one who curses him? Who in life admires the one who hates him? Who in life proves faithful to the one who is faithless? No other than a lover.' And in the end the lover's self is lost from his vision and only the beloved's image, the desired vision, is before him for ever.

Love is the essence of all religion, mysticism, and philosophy, and for the one who has learnt this love fulfils the purpose of religion, ethics, and philosophy, and the lover is raised above all diversities of faiths and beliefs.

Moses once begged the Lord God of Israel on Sinai, 'O Lord, Thou hast so greatly honoured me in making me Thy messenger, if there could be any greater honour I should think it this, that Thou shouldest come to my humble abode and break bread at my table.' The answer came, 'Moses, with great pleasure We shall come to thy abode.' Moses prepared a great feast and was waiting eagerly for God to come. There happened to pass by his door a beggar, and he said to Moses, 'Moses, I am ill and weary, and I have had no food for three days and am at the point of death. Pray give me a slice of bread and save my life.'

Moses, in his eagerness, expecting every moment a visit from God, said to the beggar, 'Wait, O man, thou shalt have more than a slice, plentiful and delicious dishes. I am waiting for a guest who is expected this evening, when he is gone, then all that remains I will give to thee that thou mayest take it home.' The man went away, time passed on, God did not come, and Moses was disappointed. Moses went the next day to Sinai and grieved bitterly, saying, 'My Lord, I know Thou doest not break Thy promise, but what sin have I, Thy slave, committed that Thou didst not come as Thou hadst promised?' God said to Moses, 'We came, O Moses, but alas, thou didst not recognize Us. Who was the beggar at thy door? Was he other than We? It is We who in all guises live and move in the world and yet are remote in Our eternal heavens.'

Whatever diversity may exist among religions, the motive of all has been one: to cultivate and prepare the human heart for divine love. Sometimes the spirit of guidance drew the attention of mankind to see and admire the beauty of God in the firmament, sometimes in the trees and rocks, making them sacred trees, holy mountains, and purifying streams. Sometimes it has guided men's attention to see the immanence of the Lord among the beasts and birds, calling them holy animals, sacred birds. When man realized that there is no one in creation higher than himself he gave up his worship of the lower creation, recognizing the divine light most manifest in man. Thus by degrees the world evolved to see God in man, especially in the holy man who is God-conscious.

Man, with his limited self, cannot see God, the perfect Being, and if he ever can picture Him, he can best picture Him as man;

for how can he imagine what he has never known? 'We have created man in Our own image.' Krishna to the Hindus, Buddha to the Buddhists, was God in man. Angels are never pictured in any other image than that of man. Even the worshippers of the formless God have idealized God with the perfection of human attributes, although this is only a ladder to reach the love of the perfect God, to which by degrees one attains.

This is explained very clearly in a story of the past. Moses once passed by a farm and saw a peasant boy talking to himself, saying, 'O Lord, Thou art so good and kind that I feel if Thou wert here by me I would take good care of Thee, more than of all my sheep, more than of all my fowls. In the rain I would keep Thee under the roof of my grass-shed, when it is cold I would cover Thee with my blanket, and in the heat of the sun I would take Thee to bathe in the brook. I would put Thee to sleep with Thy head on my lap, and would fan Thee with my hat, and would always watch Thee and guard Thee from wolves. I would give Thee bread of manna and would give Thee buttermilk to drink, and to entertain Thee I would sing and dance and play my flute. O Lord my God, if Thou wouldst only listen to this and come and see how I would tend Thee."

Moses was amused to listen to all this, and, as the deliverer of the divine message, he said, 'How impertinent on thy part, O boy, to limit the unlimited One, God, the Lord of hosts, who is beyond form and colour and the perception and comprehension of man.' The boy became disheartened and full of fear at what he had done. But immediately a revelation came to Moses: 'We are not pleased with this, O Moses, for We have sent thee to unite Our separated ones with Us, not to disunite. Speak to everyone according to his evolution.'

Life on earth is full of needs, but among all the different needs, the need of a friend is the greatest. There is no greater misery than being friendless. This earth would turn into heaven if one had a desired friend in life, and heaven, with all the bliss it offers, would become hell in the absence of the friend one loves.

A thoughtful soul always seeks a friendship that lasts long. The wise prefers a friend who will go with him through the greater part of his life's journey. The miniature of our life's journey may be seen in our ordinary travelling. If, when we are going to Switzerland, we make friends with someone who is booked for Paris, his company will last only so far, and, after that, all the rest of the journey we shall have to go alone. Every friendship on earth will go so far and then will stop. Our journey being through death, if there is any friendship that will last, it is only the friendship with God, which is unchangeable and unending. But if we do not see and cannot perceive His Being, it becomes impossible to be friends with someone of whom we are quite unaware. But God being the only friend and friendship with Him the only friendship that is worth while, the wise first seek the friendship of someone on earth who can guide them to the divine Beloved, just as a lover would first find someone belonging to the household or among the acquaintances of the fair one with whom he desires friendship. Among Sufis many attain to the God-ideal through Rasul, the ideal man; and one reaches the door of Rasul through Shaikh, the spiritual guide, whose soul owing to devotion is focused on the spirit of Rasul and so is impressed with his qualities. This graduated way becomes clear to the traveller on the path of the attainment of the divine Beloved.

The friendship with Shaikh has no other motive than guidance in seeking God. As long as your individuality lasts it will last, as long as you are seeking God it will last, as long as a guidance is needed it will last. The friendship with Shaikh is called Fanà-fi-Shaikh, and it then merges into the friendship with Rasul. When the mureed realizes the existence of the spiritual qualities beyond the earthly being of the murshid, that is the time when he is ready for Fanà-fi-Rasul.

The friendship with the Shaikh is friendship with a form, and the form may disappear. A person may say, 'I had a father, but now he is no more.' In fact, the impression of the father whom he has idealized remains in his mind. The devotion to Rasul is like this; his name and qualities remain though the earthly form is no more on earth. Rasul is the personification of the light of guidance, which a mureed, according to his evolution, idealizes. Whenever the devotee remembers him, on the earth, in the air, at the bottom of the sea, he is with him. Devotion to Rasul is a stage that cannot be omitted in the attainment of divine love. This stage is called Fanà-fi-Rasul.

After this comes Fanà-fi-Allah, when the love of Rasul merges in the love of Allah. Rasul is the Master who is idealized for his lovable attributes, his kindness, goodness, holiness, mercy; his merits are intelligible; his form is not known, only the name which constitutes his qualities; but Allah is the name given to that ideal of perfection where all limitation ceases, and in Allah the ideal ends.

A person does not lose the friendship with the Pir nor with Rasul, but he beholds murshid in Rasul and Rasul in Allah. Then for guidance, for advice, he looks to Allah alone.

There is a story of Rabia, the great Sufi, that once she beheld Mohammad in a vision and he asked her, 'O Rabia, whom dost thou love?' She answered, 'Allah.' He said, 'Not His Rasul?' She said, 'O blessed Master, who in the world could know thee and not love thee? But now my heart is so occupied with Allah alone that I can see no one but Him.'

From those who see Allah, Rasul and Shaikh disappear. They see only Allah in the Pir and Rasul. They see everything as Allah and see nothing else.

A mureed by devotion to the murshid learns the manner of love, standing with childlike humility, seeing in the face of every being on earth his Pir's blessed image reflected. When Rasul is idealized he sees all that is beautiful reflected in the unseen ideal of Rasul. Then he becomes independent even of merit, which also has an opposite pole, and in reality does not exist, for it is comparison that makes one thing appear better than the other, and he loves only Allah, the perfect ideal, who is free from all comparison, beyond all merits and attributes. But when a mureed has risen beyond this ideal, then he himself becomes love, and the work of love has been accomplished. Then the lover himself becomes the source of love, the origin of love, and he lives the life of Allah, which is called Báqi bi-Allah. His personality becomes divine personality. Then his thought is the thought of God, his word the word of God, his action the action of God, and he himself becomes love, lover, and beloved.

PEARLS FROM THE OCEAN UNSEEN

SUFISM

SUFISM is not a religion, for it is beyond the limitations of faiths and beliefs which make the diversity of religions in the world. Sufism, in short, is a change of outlook on life. It is like viewing from an aeroplane a town, the streets of which one has known and walked through, and yet one has never before seen the whole town at a glance.

The Sufi's idea is to view life by raising himself above it. If a man is in pain, how can he relieve the pain of another? If a person is already burdened with a load, how can he take on another person's burden? If a person is quarrelsome himself, how can he bring peace between others who are fighting? Therefore a Sufi considers it necessary to live in the world and at the same time to be not of the world. Where the Yogi lives the life of an adept in the forest or in a mountain cave, the Sufi lives it in the world. For he considers that to awaken one's heart to human sympathy, one must experience oneself the struggles and responsibilities of life in the world, and realize that man lives not for himself alone, but that his greatest joy must be to share every benefit and bliss he has in life with others.

This process of viewing life both from below and from above makes his sight keen. He not only knows the law of nature, known to all, but he understands the inner law which is working behind everything, which gives him an insight into things and awakens his sympathy for others.

The Sufi's God is the only Being that exists. His teacher is the spirit of inner guidance; his holy book is the manuscript of nature, his community is the whole of humanity. His religion is love. There is no God of any people who is not his God, no spiritual teacher of any creed who is not his teacher. There is no sacred scripture that he does not accept, since he is the worshipper of light and the follower of love, and yet he is free from all the world's distinctions and differences.

The diversity of names in the universe to him is a veil of illusion which covers unity, the one life. Only One lives, and all manifestations are to him the phenomenon of that one life. All things which are born, made, and formed, are as bubbles in life's ocean. Instead of looking at their limitations, he sees in them the unlimited life.

The Sufi's God is his divine ideal to whom he attributes all that is good and beautiful in its perfection; and he himself stands before Him in humility realizing his imperfection, being a soul, free to roam the heavens, now captive on earth in the physical body. His aim in life is to release the captive soul from the bondage of limitations, which he accomplishes by the repetition of the sacred names of God, and by constant thought of his divine ideal, and an ever-increasing love for the divine Beloved until the beloved God with His perfection becomes manifest to his vision, and his imperfect self vanishes from his sight.

This he calls *Fanà*, the merging in the ideal. In order to attain the final goal he gradually raises his ideal, first to Fanà-fi-Shaikh, the ideal seen in a mortal walking on earth, and he drills himself as a soldier before battle in devotion to his ideal.

Then comes Fanà-fi-Rasul, when he sees his ideal in spirit, and pictures Him in all sublimity, and fashions Him with beautiful qualities which he wishes to obtain himself. And after this he raises it to Fanà-fi-Allah, the love and devotion for that ideal which is beyond qualities, and in which is the perfection of all qualities.

The Sufi knows that progress in every direction in life depends upon the ideal. As high as is the ideal of a person, so high he rises in life. Then in the end he sees that each ideal was made by himself; he is the creator of every ideal that he desired for his high attainment. But the ideal itself is a limitation of the perfect Being, because there is *you* and *me* in it. Then the breaking of the ideal comes as the final attainment when the ego realizes Humamanam, 'I am All'.

THE PURPOSE OF LIFE

There are two classes of people in the world: the spectators of life and the students of life. The former class may be compared to those people who go to the theatre and see acted either comedy or tragedy, and are moved by it to laughter or tears. The latter may be compared to those who go up in an aeroplane and view at a glance a whole city where hitherto they had only seen one street at a time. The students of life understand the reason of the comedy and tragedy, while the spectators of life get only a passing impression of them.

About this the Qur'an says, 'We have removed from you your veil, so your sight shall be keen.' When this happens the spectator of life becomes the student of life. We sometimes ask ourselves, 'What is the purpose of life? Is it to eat, drink, and to make merry?' Surely not. The animals do this, and man is a higher creation than the animals. Is life's purpose then to become an angelic being? This likewise cannot be the case, for the angels were created before man, and are near to God, and continually praise Him.

Man must be created therefore for something other than either the animals or the angels; for if man by reason of his piety became like an angel, he would not have fulfilled the purpose for which he was created. Man is created that he may awaken within himself humanity, sympathy, brotherhood, love, and kindness for his fellow-man.

He may think that he is kind and sympathetic, but in thinking so he makes the greatest possible mistake, for kindness is comparative. This may be illustrated by a story that is told in India of an Afghan soldier, who was once travelling with a Brahmin. The Brahmin, who was a mild and harmless man, careful not to injure the smallest of God's creation, was repeating to himself the word *Daya*, which means 'kindness'. The Afghan, who was a warrior, and understood only the rough side of life, asked him what the word meant. The Brahmin explained that the word was the same as *Rahm* in his language. 'Ah,' he exclaimed, 'I understand very well now what it means. I remember I was kind once in my life, for on the field of battle I saw a wounded man writhing in agony, and I was touched, and I put my dagger through him and ended his suffering.'

The claim to be kind and sympathetic is like a drop of water saying, 'I am water', but which on seeing the ocean realizes its nothingness. In the same way, when man has looked on perfection, he realizes his shortcomings. It is then that the veil is raised from before his eyes and his sight becomes keen. He then asks himself, 'What can I do that I may awaken this love and sympathy in my heart?'

The Sufi begins by realizing that he is dead and blind, and he understands that all goodness as well as all that is bad comes from within. Riches and power may vanish because they are outside of us, but only that which is within can we call our own. In order to awaken love and sympathy in our hearts, sacrifices must be made. We must forget our own troubles in order to sympathize with the troubles of others.

To relieve the hunger of others we must forget our own hunger. Everybody is working for selfish ends, not caring about others, and this alone has brought about the misery in the world today. When the world is evolving from imperfection towards perfection, it needs all love and sympathy; great tenderness and watchfulness is required of each one of us. The heart of every man, both good and bad, is the abode of God, and care should be taken never to wound anybody by word or act. We are only here in this world for a short time; many have been here before, and have passed on, and it is for us to see that we leave behind an impression of good.

'BLESSED ARE THE POOR IN SPIRIT'

The words 'poor in spirit' are an unsatisfactory translation, and do not convey the real meaning of the text. There are certain words in the original which cannot be accurately translated. In Sufi terms this poorness of spirit is called *Halim Taba'*, and means mild-spirited. The more true meaning of the words is, 'Blessed are the mild in ego', and this is the teaching of Jesus throughout. He himself is spoken of in the Bible as 'the Lamb of God', conveying the meaning of the mild in ego, like a lamb.

The ego is seen in the animal creation, but much more strongly in the carnivorous than in the herbivorous animals. It is very strong in the lion, and in the dog which will not suffer the presence of another dog when it is eating a bone. Elephants, on the contrary, the largest of all animals, are docile and harmless, and obey the commands of men. They live together in herds, and seldom fight. The same is the case with horses and sheep.

When we consider the ego in connection with the whole consciousness, we first look at the earth and rocks, the lowest form of life, and find how stiff and hard, how unmovable and unbendable they are. When we come to the water element, we find that it is pliable, and can be poured from one vessel to another. The course of a river or a stream may be diverted and made to go in another direction. It is poorer in spirit than the earth, for it is a higher element. A more exalted state of consciousness belongs to the poor in spirit, the pliable and the serviceable, than to the stiff and set. When we come to the fire element, we find that it is still more pliable. It can be taken from the rock and from the atmosphere, and it is more serviceable and more pliant. Air is still more pliable and is everywhere, and man cannot live without it. Ether is the highest element, and is nearest to us, for it surrounds us and is within us.

We frequently say, 'I dislike him', 'I wish to avoid her', but if we examine this carefully we find that it is the same element in all that we dislike: the ego. And when we turn to ourselves to see if we have it in us, we find it there too. We should forget it, therefore, in other people, and first turn our attention to crushing it within ourselves; we should determine to have our house clean even if other people neglect theirs. We should be careful to take away from ourselves any thorns that prick us in the personality of others. There is a verse in the Qur'an which says, 'Arise in the midst of the night, and commune with thy Lord . . . Bear patiently what others say.' This is not only a command to arise in the night and pray, but it also means that by rising in the night we crush the ego, for the ego demands its rest and comfort, and when denied, is crushed. The mystics fast for the same reason.

The Sufis base the whole of their teaching on the crushing of the ego which they term *Nafs-kushi*, for therein lies all magnetism and power. Jesus Christ meant this power of magnetism when He told His disciples that they would become the fishers of men. This can be acquired by developing the personality in poorness of spirit.

'BLESSED ARE THEY THAT MOURN'

The idea of mourning is distasteful to the world in general. People say, Let us enjoy ourselves and be happy; there is plenty of sorrow in the world without choosing to mourn', and they strive after happiness in whatever way they can. But these passing and momentary joys do not give lasting happiness, and the people who pursue them are either asleep or dead. The soul's true happiness lies in experiencing the inner joy, and it will never be fully satisfied with outer seeming pleasures. Its connection is with God, and nothing short of perfection will ever satisfy it. The purpose of life is to become aware of our imperfections, and to mourn for them. The whole universe in miniature is within man, and as the earth is composed of land and water, so the mind of man is like land and water, the water under the land, and the land above the water. The land represents the thoughts and imaginations, while the water represents the feelings; and just as the water rises and falls, so it is with the emotions and feelings of man. The people who only know the lighter side of life, and who are afraid to have their feelings touched, represent the land through which the water has never pierced. If one wishes to see a foreign country, the water has to be crossed, and so it is with those who wish to fare forth to the world unseen; they have to cross the water of feeling, and the land needs to be pierced in order that the waters may rise.

Shiva is sometimes pictured with the sacred river flowing out of his head, showing that man becomes Shiva-like when his thoughts come not only from the head, but from the heart also. It is the thoughts that spring from the depths of the heart which become inspirations and revelations, and these come from the hearts of the awakened souls, called by the Sufis, *Sahib-e Dil.* The bringers of joy are the children of sorrow. Every blow we get in life pierces the heart and awakens our feelings to sympathize with others, and every swing of comfort lulls us to sleep, and we become unaware of all. This proves the truth of these words, 'Blessed are they that mourn'.

Thought is the more solid form of feeling, and needs to be melted in order to become water. All water is the same, but when it is bitter or sweet to the taste it is because some element of the earth has become mixed with it; and so it is with the emotions in the water of feeling which have come in contact with things of the earth.

There are two classes of people in the world: those who like comedy and those who like tragedy. Those who like tragedy are the wise and thoughtful; not because they like what is tragic, but because they experience life through the pain of tragedy, and they want to keep this experience at the cost of pain.

Everybody has an ideal in life, and that ideal is the religion of his soul, and coming short of that ideal is what we term sin. The thoughtful and serious-minded man repents in tears for his shortcomings, and thus proves himself to be alive, while the shallow man is angry at his fall, and is ready to blame those who seem to him to have caused it. He is apparently dead. This shows that it is blessed to mourn over our imperfections, and by so doing we are striving after perfection, and thus fulfilling the command of Christ, 'Be ye perfect even as your Father which is in heaven is perfect.'

'REPENT YE, FOR THE KINGDOM OF HEAVEN IS AT HAND'

These words were spoken in the first place by John the Baptist in reference to the coming of Jesus Christ. But apart from this there is a spiritual meaning in the words 'Kingdom of Heaven'.

All things that belong to any person constitute his kingdom, be they great riches and power, or petty possessions. The Kingdom of Heaven means the perfect possession of anything, when the thing possessed is in itself sufficient. There was once a well-known dervish in Gwalior, Mohammad Ghauth, who sat in the jungle, unclothed, and only ate when food was brought to him. He was poverty-stricken in the eyes of the world, but was respected by all. Evil days came on Gwalior. The state was threatened by a powerful enemy, with an army twice the size of that belonging to the ruler who in his distress sought Mohammad Ghauth. The sage at first asked to be left in peace, but his help being further entreated by the Maharaja himself, he at last said, 'Show me the army that is threatening you.' They took him outside the city and showed him the vast host that was advancing.

Mohammad Ghauth waved his hand, repeating the word *Maktul*.[1] As he did so the army of the Maharaja of Gwalior appeared immense to the oncoming army, which turned in fear and fled. This Sufi saint was the possessor of the Kingdom of Heaven. His tomb is now in a palace, and the kings of the earth come and bow before it.

The Kingdom of Heaven is in the hearts of those who realize God. This is recognized in the East, and great respect and regard is always shown for the holy ones.

Sufi Sarmad, a great saint who was absorbed in the vision of the One, lived in the time of Aurangzeb, the great Moghul emperor. Aurangzeb demanded that Sufi Sarmad should come to the mosque. On his refusing to do so, he was beheaded at the command of the emperor. From that time dates the downfall of the Moghuls. This story shows that the possessor of the Kingdom of Heaven has the power even when dead to overthrow the kingdoms of the earth.

We see this same truth again in the story of Krishna and Arjuna. Arjuna and his five brothers had to fight alone against a mighty host. The prince sought the god, and wanted to renounce the kingdom. But Krishna said, 'Nay, thou must first win back what thou hast lost, and then come to me.' And the story goes on to tell how Krishna himself drove the chariot, and the enemies of Arjuna were defeated, for the possessor of the Kingdom of Heaven was with Arjuna.

Speaking from a metaphysical point of view, the Kingdom of Heaven may be attained by the way of repentance. If we have

[1] 'Maktul' = Be destroyed.

offended a friend, and he turns away from us, and we in fullness of heart ask forgiveness, his heart will melt towards us. If, on the other hand, we close our heart, it becomes frozen. Repenting and asking for pardon not only melt the heart of those we have offended, but also of those in the world unseen. These words can also be explained scientifically. Warmth melts, while cold freezes. Drops of water falling on a warm place and on a cold place are affected differently. The drop in the warm place spreads and becomes larger, covers a larger space, whereas a drop in the cold place freezes and becomes limited. Repentance has the effect of a drop spread in the warm sphere: it causes the heart to expand and become universal, while the hardening of the heart brings limitation.

The bubble does not last long; it soon breaks, but with its break it joins the mighty ocean. So with us. When by warmth of heart we can break our limited self, we merge in the One, the unlimited. When our limited kingdom is lost from our sight, we inherit the Kingdom of God.

CAUSE

There is an innate desire in every human being for knowledge. The child wants to know the cause of everything, and asks countless questions. The desire for knowledge, if our eyes were but open to perceive it, is even in the plants. It is this desire which develops the mineral into the vegetable, and the vegetable into the animal, and the animal into the human being. It is well developed in man, and fully attained in the master mind. The Sufis say that the whole of creation took place to satisfy the desire for knowledge.

With man this desire is never satisfied. He always wants to know more. There is ever a restless craving within him for knowledge. This is because he does not look for the cause in the right way; he only sees the external causes, and not the cause underlying the cause, and below that, the primal cause. For example, a man who has become estranged from his friend only sees perhaps the superficial cause, and calls his friend unkind; or he may even admit that he himself is at fault, or he may go still deeper and say that owing to a certain planetary influence they cannot be friendly; yet he has not probed the cause of this cause.

If we study nature aright, we shall find that its whole being is wisdom; life itself is wisdom. Look at the delicate structure of the eye, and the protection afforded it by the eyelid. Does not this prove that nature's wisdom is much more developed than the science and art of man? Has man ever been able to create what is not in nature? We know that the rain falls and waters the ground, and makes the plants grow, and we say that rain is the cause of all this, but if we delved deeper we should discover the cause of the rain. Even then the inner cause remains hidden.

For this reason the religions taught the God-ideal, that the primal cause might be sought through the pursuit of God.

It is when man has lost the idea of duality and feels himself at one with all creation, that his eyes are opened and he sees the cause of everything. A scientific man comes forward and claims to have made some new and wonderful discovery, but as Solomon says, 'There is nothing new under the sun.' Christ said he had come not to give a new law, and Mohammad said he had come to reveal the same law given by the teachers in the past, which had been corrupted, misunderstood, and forgotten by its followers. The mystics have possessed all knowledge from the beginning, and yet have never claimed it as their own, recognizing that all knowledge is possessed by one Being alone, and will always be so.

What is called supernatural becomes natural to one who understands, but to the ignorant it remains supernatural. He calls it a miracle or a phenomenon if he believes in it; if not he mocks at it.

There is a light within every soul. It only needs the clouds which hide it to dissolve, for it to beam forth. This is the light of revelation. It is like a lantern to us, it lights up every dark corner we wish to examine, and gives an answer to every question we would ask. This light can only shine where the heart is pure, and in order to purify the heart, the Sufi has a contemplative process suited to the evolution of each individual.

There is a beautiful Indian tale that illustrates the meaning of this light. It is said that there is a certain kind of cobra which has a diamond in its head, and when it goes into the jungle, it takes out the diamond and places it on a tree; and by means of its light it searches out all it wants, and when it has finished it puts the diamond back in its head. The cobra represents the soul, and the diamond the light of inspiration guiding it.

The same truth is portrayed in the story of Aladdin and his lamp. The lady he loved represented the ideal of his soul, and the lamp he had to find was the light of inner guidance, which, when found, would lead him to the attainment of his ideal. Starting on the spiritual path is like descending into the dark, as man knows not what he will find.

Mystics in the East have spent many years in the jungle on this spiritual quest, and later have come forth to show the way to mankind. This is a path, however, which cannot be taught; it must be realized, for language is inadequate to express even the experience of the heart, so how can the soul's experience of its highest attainment be explained in words?

HIGHER ATTAINMENT

Higher attainment in the material sense of the word is easily explained; if we possess a hundred pounds, we may hope for the higher attainment of two hundred, or we may look upon higher attainment as a rise in the social world. In spiritual matters there is nothing we can recognize as higher attainment. The striving for higher attainment on the spiritual path is like shooting an arrow into the mist. We know that we have shot it, but we do not know whither it has gone, or where it has struck. It is so with our spiritual progress. We cannot see where we are, or how far we have advanced on the spiritual path, for there is nothing to show. Some people say that higher attainment in the spiritual life means communion with God. But this would not satisfy the agnostic, for God to him is a stranger, and he would not wish for communion with a stranger. Some would travel along this path if they could attain their worldly desires, wealth or fame. To such the answer may be given: seek for things of the earth on the earth, and for heavenly things in heaven.

There are some who follow this path in order to gain occult and psychic powers, but the attainment of these powers is not necessarily higher attainment. There are only a few who travel along the path for higher spiritual attainment.

What then is higher attainment? If we look at our five fingers, we realize that all the power in them comes from the one arm. If we want to arrive at higher attainment in the spiritual life, we must enter the plane of the abstract, for we find everything there. We must come to the realization of the one life running through all. To a certain degree we attain to the realization of unity by contemplation, religion, and prayer; but what is most necessary is sincerity in our way of life. What we are is all that really matters; contemplation and meditation help in this, but our manner of life is what is all-important, sincerity in our actions, and living life practically and not in theory.

There is a story told in India of the boyhood of Bullah Shah, a great saint. He went to school when a young boy, and was set to learn the alphabet. He was given the first letter Alif, the figure one (a straight line), and he never progressed any further than this one letter. His master was in despair, also his parents. In the end they became weary of him, and he went to live in the jungle. After many years he returned and sought out his old master. He told him that he had now learned Alif, and had he anything else to teach? He then made the sign of Alif on the wall, saying, 'Look, is it right?' Immediately the wall split in two, making the sign of Alif. On seeing this phenomenon, the master exclaimed, 'Thou art my teacher; I am thy pupil.'

From this story we learn what it actually means to realize what unity is, because we always see the one. Two is one and one, and it is the same with three, four, or five, hundreds or thousands; in the end all numbers, even millions and billions, are nothing but multiples of one. Thus we may say that the higher spiritual attainment is the realization of unity.

WORSHIP

There are three aspects of worship: the worship of God in heaven by those who understand Him as a separate being; the worship of God on earth, as a god or goddess, in the form of an idol, or of some being who is considered as an incarnation of God and who is worshipped by the multitudes; and the worship of the God within, the innermost self of our being. It is this aspect of God that is understood by the Sufis, the Vedantists, and the great teachers such as Christ and Mohammad.

In the beginning, the great masters taught the worship of some concrete object to those who could not understand any higher ideal of worship, in order to lead them up to the God-ideal, that they might finally come to know the God within.

There are some people who have realized that the innermost self is God, and who say, 'Why should we approach God in forms of worship?' believing themselves to be self-sufficient. This self-knowledge can lead man either astray or towards perfection. It seldom leads him to perfection, but it frequently leads him astray, for although man is unlimited in the unseen world, in the outer world he is a very limited being. He is dependent on the whole of creation around him, and is in every way dependent on his surroundings. At one end of the pole he is unlimited and self-sufficient; at the other end of the pole he is limited and dependent. It is therefore a great mistake for a man to claim self-sufficiency. In Muslim terms these states are called *Allah* and *Bandeh*. The Allah state is the unlimited and self-sufficient, and the Bandeh state is the limited and dependent. As a man's ideal is, so is his state of evolution. The man who is only interested in himself is very narrow and limited, whereas the man who has expanded his interests to his family and surroundings is greater; while he who expands them still further to his nation is yet greater, and he who extends them to the world at large is the greatest. But in all these cases man is limited. It is the same with material ideals: one person may be content with a hundred pounds, while another may aspire to a million; in accordance with his ideal, so man becomes.

The highest ideal of man is to realize the unlimited, the immortal self within. There is no need for any higher ideal, for when man holds this ideal in his vision, he expands and becomes all he wants to be, and in time he attains to that peace which is the longing of every soul.

The worship of God expands the soul towards perfection. This is illustrated in the words of Sa'di, who says, 'Praise be to Allah, whose worship is the means of drawing closer to Him, and in giving thanks to whom is involved an increase of benefits. Every breath which is inhaled prolongs life, and, when exhaled, quickens the body. Thus in every breath two blessings are contained, and for every blessing a separate thanksgiving is due.'

THE PRAYERFUL ATTITUDE

There are five attitudes that are assumed by different classes of people with regard to prayer. In the first place there is the praiseful attitude of those who are grateful for their daily bread. The second class of people are those who are not only grateful for material benefits, but who hope also for power and position, or for forgiveness of their sins. The third class of people are those whose eyes are opened, who recognize the beauty of God in nature and in all around them, and glorify Him for that beauty.

The fourth class of people are those who recognize the greatness of God in His power, who is able to provide for all His creation, from man to the smallest worm or germ. And in the fifth class are the mystics and thinkers. Their attitude to prayer is far higher than that of the four preceding classes; they understand the truth of the being of man: that God and man are not separate. Notable among these are the Sufis. Many people who are free-thinkers, and have this understanding, do not bother about prayer, and some even say, 'To whom should we pray?' The Sufi realizes the truth of his being, and his whole life becomes an attitude of prayer, in spite of his free thought and his rising above good and bad, right and wrong. When a person loves, he may be in the crowd, and yet be unaware of those around him, being absorbed in the thought of the beloved; and so it is with the love of God. He who loves God may be in the crowd, yet, being in the thought of God he is in seclusion. To such a person the crowd makes no difference. Sa'di says, 'Prayer is the expansion of the limited being to the unlimited, the drawing closer of the soul to God.'

Hazrat Ali, the most distinguished among Sufis of the past, says, 'To know the self is to know God', yet he spent much of his day and most of his nights in prayer. The Sufi's prayer is his journey to the eternal goal, his realization of God.

The question now arises how to attain to this prayerful attitude in life. In the first place, for those whose prayer is one of praise, if their whole life is to assume a prayerful attitude they must carry this praise and gratitude into the smallest details of life, and feel grateful for the slightest act of kindness done to them by anybody. Man falls very short of this ideal in life; he is so stiff, he misses so many chances of giving thanks. It is sometimes because of his riches, while at other times he is blinded by his power; all that is done for him he thinks is his due because of his money or his influence. When a man has been able to attain this attitude of praise and thanksgiving for all things in life, then his life may indeed be called a prayerful life.

Those who express a hope when they pray can turn their everyday striving into prayer, provided they maintain this hope in every pursuit of life, putting their trust in God, and provided they consider all the objects of their desire as coming from one and the same source when they have gained them.

Those people who glorify God for His beauty, should see the beauty of God in all His creatures. It is of no use to praise God for His beauty, and then to criticize and find faults in His creation; for one's life to be prayerful one must always seek the good in man. Even the worst man has a good spot, and this should be sought and not the bad points. We can learn virtue even from the greatest sinner, if we consider him as a teacher. There is a tradition that Moses asked Satan to tell him the secret of life.

Those who glorify God for the greatness of His power must be able to see greatness in His creation. There are some who so pride themselves on their power, position, and money, that they cannot see the greatness in another. For these it is of no avail to worship God for His greatness; it is only lip service.

As for the fifth class of people, those who realize the truth of their being, they recognize their God-ideal in all of His creation. They see their divine Beloved in all manifestation, in every name and form.

PRAYER

The necessity for prayer has been taught at all times by all religions, and forms of prayer have been given to their followers.

People hold different opinions with regard to prayer. Some maintain that as God knows all their wants, why should they pray? Others wonder if it is right to pray, when God knows best what is good for them. Others say that praise is the only prayer, while some even claim that they themselves are God, so that for them there is no necessity for prayer. Regarding the latter class of people it may be said that all the masters and holy ones have not only taught the necessity of prayer, but their own lives have been lives of continual prayer. The following little story gives us an illustration of this.

Abdul Qadir Jelani, a great Sufi saint, was one day engaged in prayer, when in a vision he saw the semblance of an angel, who addressed him, saying, 'O thou who hast prayed continuously all thy life, to thee God sends the good tidings that no more prayers are required of thee.' The saint, recognizing the tempter, replied, 'Begone, thou wicked one, I recognize thee in spite of thy angelic guise: thou art a devil come to tempt me. All the holy ones have passed their lives in prayer, and how can I deem myself worthy to be exempt from it?' On hearing these words the evil one vanished.

To those who ask, 'Is it right to pray for our wants?' it may be said that man has always sought to express himself. If for instance he has conceived some scheme or plan that he wants to carry out, as a rule he seeks out a capable and trusted friend whose advice he values, to whom he can confide his ideas; or if he is in trouble or distress, he goes to a loving and kind friend for sympathy. In both cases he shows his limitation. If man with his sense of justice judges himself worthy of that for which he prays, then he is amply justified, regardless of the opinion of the world as to its rightness, and he attracts the answer to his prayer. If a man has agreed to work for a certain sum of money, and knows he has worked well and earned it, he feels himself justified in claiming his money; and so it is with prayer, when a man knows he deserves that for which he prays.

Before praying for the mercy of God, man must first learn to recognize God in all around him, in the care and protection he receives from all; God's mercy shows its hands and eyes everywhere in nature, so man must try to imitate it in his own life. He will then attract to himself the mercy of God.

If our actions are harsh, we naturally attract the wrath of God. To the class of people who claim that they are God, the answer may be given in the words of the Urdu poet, who says, 'Man is not God, but man is not apart from God.' One drop cannot call itself the ocean, yet the drop is a part of the ocean. Those who lay claim to this should bear witness to it in their lives, and if they can do this, then they will keep silent and not speak one word about it in the presence of others.

There is a necessity for praise in prayer, praise of the beauty of God, for man must learn to recognize and praise the beauty of God as manifested in all His creation. In this way he impresses beauty on his soul, and he is able to manifest it in himself, and he becomes the friend of all and is without prejudice. For this reason the Sufi cultivates his heart. The emblem of the Sufi is a heart between two wings, meaning that when the heart is cultivated man can soar up into the heights of heaven.

When man is on the lower planes, he sees things as tall, short, beautiful, or ugly; but if he ascends in an aeroplane and looks down from above, things appear uniform and the same. So it is when man has raised himself to the higher planes: all things are the same to him, he only sees the One.

Man is perfectly justified and right in praying for all his desires, and there is nothing that God is not able and willing to grant; but man should distinguish between what is transitory and what is lasting, what is worth while for his own benefit, and what is worthless. Beauty of personality, devotion, love, are all desirable, but not those things that are transitory and unsatisfying. There are some people who have reached the stage at which they are beyond all desires, both earthly and heavenly, but they still continue to pray, because prayer brings them still closer to God in their limitation, and they expand from the state of limitation to the state of unlimited being. This is the highest meaning of prayer.

A man who does not believe in prayer, in times of illness seeks a doctor, for no one is self-sufficient. In life everyone needs kindness, sympathy, and the help of others, however rich or mighty he may be, and this explains the need for prayer. What man cannot do, God can do, and what is done through man, is also done by the command of God. 'Not even the weight of one atom is concealed from the Lord', says the Qur'an.

There is a story that illustrates this need of prayer. A king was once hunting in the forest, when he was overtaken by a storm and had to take refuge in the hut of a peasant. The peasant set before the king a simple meal, which he partook of with gratitude. On his departure he asked the peasant if there was any service he could render him. The man, not knowing that it was the king who was speaking to him, replied that his needs were simple, and that he had all he required. The king then drew off a ring from his finger, and gave it to the peasant, saying, 'Take this ring, and if ever you are in need of anything, bring it to the city and show it to some official, and ask for me.'

Some months later bad times came and famine was rife in the land, and the peasant was near starvation, when he bethought himself of his ring. He set out for the city, and on arrival there showed it to an official, who immediately conducted him to the king's presence. When he arrived he found the king on his knees in prayer. When the king had finished he rose from his knees, and asked the peasant what he could do for him.

The man, who was surprised to find that his friend was the king, and still more surprised to find him on his knees, asked him why he was in that posture. The king replied that he was praying to Allah. The peasant asked, 'Who is Allah?' The king replied, 'One even higher than myself, the King of kings, and

I am asking Him for my own needs and those of my people.

The peasant on hearing these words said, 'If you, the king, have to pray to somebody above you, then why should not I ask Him direct, and not trouble you?'

This story teaches us that every seeming source is a limited one when compared with the real Source, the God whose dominion is over all.

ISLAM

It is well for all those who are interested in religion to understand the essential meaning of Islam. The word *Islam* comes from *Sala'm*, which means peace, and the mistake which followers of all religions have made is to call the means by the name of the goal. Peace is the longing of every soul, and the soul seeks it either wisely or unwisely. Those who seek it wisely are called pious, and those who seek it in ignorance are called worldly. Islam, or peace, is the goal of every soul, and the different teachers of humanity have all come to show the way that leads to this goal.

The first ship to sail to America had to discover the way, and it took very long; but afterwards a course was mapped out, the way became known, and ships made the journey in a shorter time. America is the goal, and the ship is the means of getting there. In the same way religion is a means of getting to the goal, but it is not the goal itself. It is possible to reach the goal without a ship, but it is quicker and easier to reach it with a ship.

The God-ideal was taught to man gradually. There was a time when a certain rock was recognized as God. People at one period considered certain plants as sacred; at another, certain animals and birds. For instance, the cow and the eagle were considered as sacred creatures. Many worshipped the primal elements in nature, such as earth, water, fire, and air. People worshipped the spirits of mountains, hills, trees, plants, birds, and animals, until the God-ideal was raised to the Absolute.

The planets and their gods were worshipped, and prayer was offered to the moon and sun. This lasted until God was realized in man. The light of the soul of man was recognized as higher than the light of the sun. Then came hero-worship.

Warriors, speakers, physicians, musicians, poets, prophets, and teachers were idealized and worshipped by Hindus as incarnations of God, until from the Semitic race came Abraham, the father of religions, who taught the ideal of the formless God, which was explained gradually by different prophets who came after him. It was openly proclaimed by Moses and spiritually taught by Christ; and this same truth was disclosed in plain words by Mohammad, who bore the final message: 'None exists save God.' This final message expands the ideal of worship to the invisible as well as to the visible Being, in other words to the Absolute.

The perfection of the God-ideal leads up to the goal which is the true Islam or peace.

THE EFFECT OF DEEDS

All religions have taught that there will be either punishment or reward for our deeds. But if we examine more closely we shall see that the punishment or reward is the outcome of our deeds; it is our tendency towards indealization that causes us to name as punishment and reward what is simply the outcome of our actions. Good cannot be the outcome of evil, neither can evil be the outcome of good. If a thoughtless child is sent to buy eggs, and on the way home becomes so interested in its surroundings that it does not notice where it is going, and falls and breaks all the eggs, we are apt to say, 'You have broken all the eggs, and this is a punishment for your carelessness'; but in reality there was no one who dealt out this punishment; it followed as the natural result of carelessness.

If we look down deeper within ourselves, we shall find that our deeds have a great effect on our inner being, and react and manifest on the surface as good or bad results. This explains right and wrong, good and evil. In other words, our body, mind, and heart, the factor of feelings, react on each other. If the body controls the mind, or the mind the feelings, the result is bad, for it is the lower plane having a control over the higher plane of existence. On the other hand, when the heart controls the mind, and the mind the body, the result can only be good, as the higher self then has control over the lower self. The body having control over the mind is as if the horse were to ride on the man, and not the man on the horse. If the horse were to ride on the man, he would lead him astray, but if the man rides on the horse he will guide it rightly.

For instance, if the soldier were to control the sergeant, and the sergeant the captain, matters would naturally go wrong. The captain must have the control over the sergeant, and the sergeant over the soldier. To take another example: a kind-hearted person, when controlled by his thoughts, may lose his kindness, and may keep another from some good thing by thinking that he should have it for himself; but when his kind feelings have risen above his thoughts, he may repent and say to himself, how could I have thought such a thing?

There are three grades of activity in our lives called in the Hindu religion: Satva, the activity that always brings good; Rajas, the balanced activity that brings sometimes good, sometimes bad results; and Tamas, the intense activity that always results in destruction.

The extreme intensity of Tamas is bad in all its aspects, for the vibrations increase so in speed that they clash together and cause destruction. When there is an intense love on the part of one for another, something usually happens to destroy it. This is also the case with intensity of desire or action, which ends in destruction.

Rajas, the balanced activitiy, is always desirable. The result of our action may be good or bad, but it can never be very bad, as there is a balance.

Satva, the activity that always results in good, is the controlled activity, when we have a rein over it. This is the most difficult to attain, and needs the work and effort of a whole lifetime. All the saints and sages have had to journey through these grades and learn from experience, and they understand how difficult it is to attain control over our activity in life.

There are two ways in which we may attain control over our activity. The first is confidence in the power of our own will; to know that if we have failed today, tomorrow we will not do so. The second is to have our eyes wide open, and to watch keenly our activity in all aspects of life. It is in the dark that we fall, but in the light we can see where we are going.

So it is in life: we should have our eyes wide open to see where we walk. We should study life, and seek to know why we say a thing, and why we act as we do. We have failed perhaps hitherto because we have not been wide awake. We have fallen, and felt sorry, and have forgotten all about it, and perhaps may have fallen again; this is because we have not studied life. A study of life is the greatest of all religions, and there is no greater and more interesting study. Those who have mastered all grades of activity, they above all experience life in all its aspects; they are like swimmers in the sea who float on the water of life and do not sink. It is they on whom the deed has no effect; they are both the doers of the deed, and the creators of its effect.

BALANCE

In balance lies the whole secret of life, and the lack of it explains death. All that is constructive comes from balance, and all destruction comes from lack of balance. It is when balance goes that sickness and death come. There are many people who are sickly and ill for years, yet their life is prolonged because they have some balance. They are physically on the decline, but to counterbalance this they have an ambition in life that keeps them alive. It may be the desire to see the success of a loved son, or the happiness of a daughter.

All religions and philosophies have laid down certain principles such as kindness, truthfulness, and forgiveness, but the mystic lays no stress on principles, he allows everyone to have his own principles, each according to his point of view and evolution. For example, there are two men, one is so merciful that he will not even harm an insect, and he could not draw a sword to kill another human being, while the other man for the sake of his people is content to fight and to die.

These are two opposite points of view, and both are right in their way. The Sufi therefore believes one should let each hold on to the principle suited to his evolution, but for himself he looks beyond the principle to that which is at the back of it, the balance; and he realizes that what makes one lose balance is wrong, and what makes one keep it is right. The main point is not to act against one's principles. If the whole world says a thing is wrong, and you yourself feel that it is right, it is so, perhaps, for you.

The question of balance explains the problem of sin and virtue, and he who understands it is the master of life. There should be a balance in all our actions; to be either extreme or lukewarm is equally bad. There is a saying, 'Jack of all trades, and master of none'. This is very true, as there has been too little effort given, so that no one thing has been done thoroughly.

A balance in repose and activity is necessary, as too much weight on the side of repose leads to idleness, and even sickness, whereas an unbalanced activity results in nervousness, and frequently in a mental or physical breakdown.

THE SEEN AND THE UNSEEN

All religions and philosophies speak of the seen and the unseen, perhaps understanding something about them, but always differing in the explanation they give. The Christian explanation of the soul differs from the Muslim explanation, while the Vedantic explanation differs from that of the Buddhist, and these differences are very confusing to the student. The confusion, however, arises from the variety of names and forms; in other words it is due to differences of words, not of meanings. To the illuminated soul these differences mean nothing. He sees the one truth underlying all, for he listens to his soul for the truth; and he compares what he learns with all scriptures and finds his conception of truth in harmony with all.

Many different beliefs are held by the followers of various religions and philosophies about life after death, manifestation, liberation, and reincarnation. Some people believe in one God and some in many gods, and others do not believe in the existence of God at all; but in all these beliefs the mystic sees the same truth, for he can look at it from different points of view: just as a photographer realizes, when taking photographs of a large palace from the four points of the compass, that each photograph shows a different view of the palace, yet that they are all views of one and the same palace.

The real teaching comes from within, and when the holy ones received illumination from the original Source, their souls understood it, but the words in which they gave the message differed, for one spoke in Zend, one in Hebrew, another in Sanskrit, and another in Arabic. This explains why the same truth is told in different words. The sense and meaning are the same, the only difference being in the explanation, for it was meant to be given at different times to different peoples, of different evolutions. The study of the unseen is the most important study in life, but it cannot be pursued in the same way as the study of the seen.

The study of the seen is always disappointing, as it is ever changing. Therefore one should look from the seen to the source of all things. In the study of the unseen one must not look for signs. The spiritual pursuit, as Al-Ghazali says, is like shooting an arrow into the dark: you cannot see whither it has gone, or what it hits. The two important things in life are the praise of God and the pursuit of God.

The praise of God is important, and it gives bliss in life, but it is not the real attainment. The all-important work in life is the attainment of God. God cannot be explained; an attempt to do this always ends in failure. The knowledge of Him can only be attained in the silence and in solitude, and how to do this cannot be explained better than in the words of the Urdu poet Zahir, 'He who attaineth best the peace of God, his very self must lose.'

THE OTHER SIDE OF DEATH

The intelligent thinker always asks sooner or later, 'What is on the other side of death?' To the materialist, who believes in the brain as the only factor of perception, there is no hereafter. To those who believe in tradition, there is another life, but mostly they are very vague as to its real meaning. For those who are seeking the truth there is a right way and a wrong way of finding out about it. The right way consists in the study of the self, and the wrong way is in seeking to communicate with spirits.

When we are awake, the consciousness is for the most part on the physical plane, and a very small part is on the mental plane. This is proved by the fact that we are sometimes unconscious of what is going on around us, because our consciousness is at that time on another plane, and we are apt then to call any thought or feeling an imagination. The dream plane is higher than the physical plane, for everything that happens there is a reality to the consciousness. It is only in our waking state that we say that what we experienced then was a dream. It is the physical body that makes the contrast between the dream and the wakeful state of being; in the dream we are free of this body, and the consciousness experiences things as reality and not as a dream or imagination, for it is the tendency of the consciousness to take as real what it is experiencing at the moment.

All experiences, thoughts, feelings, and emotions are stored in the mental plane, and when rid of the physical body, the consciousness experiences all these to their full extent. If a man has been cheerful and happy all through life, the consciousness, when it has left the physical body, experiences the state of happiness to its full extent on the mental plane, and if he has been unhappy and miserable all through life, the consciousness experiences that state to its full extent on the mental plane. This explains the meaning of heaven and hell. We experience heaven or hell in this way each day of our lives, and our heaven or hell depends on what impressions we allow ourselves to store in our mental plane.

Our minds need to be dusted and swept just as much as our houses, and this we do by meditation and concentration, which wipe away all wrong impressions. We must be masters of our minds as well as of our houses, and not allow them to be like a furniture warehouse with all the furniture mixed up together. We must direct where everything is to be placed, so that complete order may reign therein. We must not allow any impression we do not wish, to impress itself on our mental plane. On this side of life we have more will-power to control our impressions than we have on the other side. There we experience the impressions we have formed in our life.

What chiefly concerns us is to study what makes things right or wrong, good or bad; and we shall find that good, bad, right, or wrong is according to the point of view in which we look at each one of them, and when we understand this thoroughly, then we shall know the secret of making things right or wrong, good or bad at will.

This stage of understanding gives mastery, and raises men above heaven and hell.

THE ALCHEMY OF HAPPINESS

The word 'alchemy' comes from an Arabic word, *al-Kimia*, which means the art of making gold.

There are two kinds of gold: the gold that we obtain from outside, and the gold that the Eastern alchemist knew how to make for himself. The same may be applied to happiness. Every soul seeks for happiness, and either depends on external objects for it, or like the alchemist of old, creates happiness for himself.

Those who seek for happiness from external sources are never really satisfied. A man imagines that if he could have a certain sum of money he would be happy, but if he gets it he is not really content; he wants more. No earthly happiness is lasting: it never remains. The only cause of this lack of happiness is the discomfort of the spirit. If we were offered all the homage and riches of the world if only we would remain floating in the air, we would forego them all, for our body belongs to the earth; and if a like offer were made to us if we would always stand in the water, we should refuse for the same reason. For our earthly body has its comfort only on earth.

So it is with our spirit. The Bible says, 'The spirit quickeneth, the flesh profiteth nothing.' Our spirit is the real part of us; the body is but its garment. There is absolute peace in the abode from whence the spirit came, and the true happiness of the soul lies in that peace. As man would not find peace at the tailor's just because his coat came from there, so the spirit cannot get true happiness from the earth just because the body belongs to the earth. The soul experiences life through the mind and body and enjoys it, but its true happiness lies in peace.

In order to gain this peace we have to begin with ourselves. There are fights going on within us between spirit and matter. Struggles for our daily bread, and want of peace in our surroundings; we must first get this peace within ourselves before we can talk of peace in the world. Then we must be at peace with our surroundings, and never do or say anything that disturbs that peace. All thoughts, words, and actions that disturb the peace are sin, and all thoughts, words, and actions that create peace are virtue. In our dealings with those with whom it is difficult to keep peace, a constant effort to do so has a great effect.

There are two forces in us, love and reason. We must keep an even balance between the two. If we give too much expression to love we become unbalanced and fall into trouble, and if on the other hand we lean too much on the side of reason we become cold.

WISDOM AND IGNORANCE

Mystics, philosophers, and thinkers have all agreed that the greatest blessing in life is wisdom, and the greatest curse is ignorance. All people, according to their evolution, are seeking for what they consider to be the greatest bliss in life. For some it takes the form of wealth or power, for others renown, while for others it may be religion or spiritual bliss. All of these, when there is lack of wisdom, turn into a curse, for wealth brings no happiness when there is absence of wisdom. The law courts are fed and kept going by the wealth of the foolish. Then again, what a curse power, in the hands of an unwise person, becomes to himself and to others, whereas wielded by the hand of wisdom power brings a blessing with it! Fame, unless used wisely, only breeds enemies. The wise man on the contrary may lack wealth, but he is quite happy, and he can, if he desires, create it for himself. The same may be said of power and renown. A man may start life in a humble position, but by reason of his wisdom may become powerful and famous. The wise man knows how to make his life, while the foolish man for the most part mars his.

It is the same with the spiritual life. So often a really religious person, earnestly striving after good, mars its effect by some foolish thought, word, or action, and thus destroys the work of years. The wise man never allows himself to be caught in such a net. He carefully watches his every thought, word, and action, and thus ever progresses on the spiritual path. He may at times have a set-back, but he knows how to profit even by his falls, and uses them as stepping-stones to higher things. There is no real happiness in life where there is a lack of understanding. This is the case with wife or husband, child or friend. The closest and finest relationship in life is that with one who understands, and this again is only experienced by the wise.

KAZA AND KADR

There are two forces in the universe, Kaza, the divine force that is working through all things and being; and Kadr, the free will of the individual.

If the divine will is working through all things and beings, and man is but the instrument through which the divine will works, he is helpless, and how can he be responsible for his deeds? Man is nevertheless held responsible, for the free will of the individual is the perfect will, working through the intelligence of the individual. This may be illustrated in the following way. A merchant who owns a factory employs many hands to work in it. It is his will and wish that all shall work harmoniously together, but the success of the factory is equally the responsibility of each individual worker, for the owner of the factory runs it by means of the workers. If anyone works contrary to his will, things go wrong, and the one working thus is responsible for it. In like manner the will of the whole Being works through all, yet it is the responsibility of the individual to carry out that will; if we consider this carefully we shall find that this will is also our will, and when we act contrary to it we get no satisfaction, for we have not carried out our own will. We are, as it were, a pole, at one end of which is the limited individual and at the other end the perfect Self.

In seeking to carry out the will of God our attitude should be that of a child who is kept from doing wrong by the thought that he might vex his parents. In the same way we should watch our every thought and action lest they should be displeasing to God, the perfect Self. The question may be asked, 'Is it just that human beings with intelligence should have to give in to the perfect or divine will, which seems so contrary to the ideal of freedom?' This question may be answered in the following way. Let us suppose that one wishes to move forward, and the feet move in the opposite direction, or one wants to look straight up while the eyes, against one's will, look down; would life be happy although the feet and the eyes in acting so are only using their free will? The answer is no, for in so doing they are working against the will of the whole individual being. In like manner the inharmonious free will, which may be called sin, disturbs the whole Being, the harmony of which is maintained by each individual, from greatest to least, and from highest to lowest.

THE PHILOSOPHY OF THE RESURRECTION

We find the word 'resurrection' not only in the Bible, but also in the Qur'an and other scriptures. What is truth becomes false when wrongly understood, and even the false is made true when rightly understood.

The following story will help to explain the meaning of the word resurrection. There was once a king who desired that his son should experience all aspects of life, and for this reason kept him in ignorance of the fact that he was a prince. He ordered a palace to be built with seven stories. The ground floor was very simple and plain. Each story was a little more elaborate than the last, until the seventh, which was most magnificently furnished, and was in every way a worthy habitation for a king. The little prince was put to live on the ground floor with his nurses and attendants, and in his simple surroundings lived happy and contented for many years.

When he grew older he became curious, and asked if there was anything to see on the other floors of the house. The servants replied that there were six other floors, and that he was at liberty to see them. He was also told that he might ascend by means of the lift. The boy entered the lift, but he was careful not to let go his hold on the rope, for he wanted to make sure of his return to the ground floor with which he was so familiar. In this way he explored all the seven stories. The father had determined that he should not be called the Crown Prince until he could ascend alone and investigate the palace, which was after all his own.

The seven stories mentioned in this tale can be interpreted as the seven planes of existence, and these are ours by right of inheritance. We are placed on the ground floor, the earth, as we have work to accomplish there. The most important work we have to do in life is to take charge of all seven floors. The Master, Jesus Christ, passed through all the seven planes, and gave the command, 'Be ye perfect even as your Father which is in heaven is perfect.' This state of perfection is the passing from the limited to the unlimited state of existence. The lift is breath, and when our physical body passes on to the next floor and loses hold on the breath, that is its death.

In point of fact, through death the soul enters the higher planes of existence freely, and that is the meaning of resurrection. There are two aspects of resurrection, the negative and the actual. The negative resurrection takes place when we pass to the higher planes of existence in the lift by means of the breath, and hold on to the rope, the physical body, and come back to the first floor, the earth, again. This is the meaning of those words in the Qur'an, 'Die before death'. This negative resurrection is the teaching of the Sufis, and is the whole object of the contemplative life which they lead. It takes away the fear of death, and death becomes 'the bridge that unites friend with friend'. Jesus, when passing from the earth, left behind his physical body for ever, and that was his positive resurrection.

When we are asleep and dream, we leave our physical body and live in our finer body for the time being. The finer body is a replica of our physical body; both bodies have been impressed with each other, and are exactly alike. This answers the question as to how it was that Jesus appeared to his disciples in what they believed to be his physical body. He had promised them that he would come to them again, and it was their earnest desire and loving devotion that created his presence. This whole universe was created by the power of mind. This power is in each one of us, and our power of creating is in proportion to the earnestness and reality of our desires. Such was the case with the faithful disciples. It was their earnest love and longing that created the presence of their Lord.

THE MURSHID

The Murshid is one who is passive to the word of God from within, who is illuminated, and who holds communion with God.

There are two kinds of murshid. In the first place there is the murshid who receives inspiration in the jungle or in the solitude, and when he arrives at the fullness of the message he comes forth to find a suitable Talib or Mureed, one who is responsive, to whom he can give this message, for the light must find expression. For this light to manifest, no learning is necessary. The most unlettered have been the greatest teachers in the world. One notable example is Kabir, the weaver who wrote volumes of inspired verse. His poems were in the language of an illiterate man, but in spite of this they have been read and admired all over India, and Kabir is looked upon as one of the greatest and most enlightened teachers. This class of murshid therefore gathers round him mureeds who are responsive, and who will make themselves passive to receive his training. This is difficult for some people who say that they cannot give up their individuality to another. But when we consider this question, we may ask ourselves, 'Who is another?' Then we realize that in the true sense of being there is but one. When the veil of ignorance is raised there is no longer any 'I' and 'you', but only the One exists. This is the teaching of the Bible and of all scriptures. The murshid and the mureed are one.

The other murshids are Khalifs, those who belonged to a special school such as the Chishtiyas, Qadiri, Naqshibandi, Sohrwardi, and who base their training on a careful and special observation of human beings, and their character and tendencies. They teach exactly the same truth as the other class of Sufi, but they follow a method adapted to suit the faith, belief, nature, and manner of the people who come under their care. The system is only the outer garment, the coat as it were. Many people claim to know all about Sufism from simply reading about it in books, but what such people know is in reality only the system, the outer garment, not the inner truth.

Some people who see Sufism taught by a Muslim, preaching in the mosque, naturally call it a branch of Islam; but they do not know that the seed which is found in the fruit was in its origin the root of that same plant. Those who see it in the garb of Hinduism, say it is derived from Hinduism. Those who see its resemblance to Buddhism, say that its origin is Buddhism.

Now the message of Sufism is being proclaimed in the West where the people are mostly Christian, and as it is given to suit the faith, belief, customs, and manners of the inhabitants, a person who does not know the real idea of Sufism may say that this is a new sect of Christianity. Let people call it what they will; Sufism being the essence of all religion, it matters little what faith people profess, provided they understand rightly.

In the East there are many such schools. There is a great spiritual advantage in being initiated into one of them, as the initiate has the help, not only of his murshid, but of all the former murshids who have passed over to the other side. He is, in fact, as a link in a chain. The murshid is like a gardener who knows all the flowers, plants, and fruits in his garden, and carefully tends them. In like manner the murshid tends all those who have entrusted themselves to his guidance.

The murshid is also like a physician. He prescribes to each mureed medicine suited to his needs. The same medicine could not be given to all.

A true murshid is looked upon as a bridge to unite his mureeds with their Lord. He is, as it were, the gatekeeper of the king's palace, and he can guide only to the inner door which leads to the presence chamber. The murshid is far greater than an earthly sovereign, for by his glance or his word he can change the life of another who comes to him in faith, for his kingdom is the Kingdom of Heaven, which has its domain over all the kingdoms of the earth. Hafiz says, 'Do not mistake the ragged sleeves of the dervish, for under those sleeves that are full of patches, most powerful arms are hid.'

The murshid desires all earthly as well as heavenly blessings for his mureeds; but he can do but little where there is no response and faith. The murshid sets far greater stress on the life of his mureed than on the punctuality of his meditation. He teaches that it is of far greater importance to cultivate in one's life attributes such as kindness, gentleness, and love. It is when the mureed fails in this that the murshid is unable to inspire him, for the mureed is standing in his own light.

A story is told of a mureed who had been under the guidance of a murshid for some years, and had not yet attained his goal. He had seen many come and depart inspired. In the end he went to the murshid, and asked why this was so. The murshid said in answer, 'My son, the fault is not with me, but in thyself.' A mad dog was passing at the time, and the murshid glanced at it, and the dog was cured instantly of its madness. He then pointed out that it was not lack of power on the part of the murshid, but lack of response on the part of the mureed. About this, Hafiz says, 'The dark-fated ones cannot be guided even by the illuminated ones.'

METAPHYSICS

THE EXPERIENCE OF THE SOUL THROUGH THE DIFFERENT PLANES OF EXISTENCE

CONTENTS

CHAPTER I

OUR CONSTITUTION

i

Our Physical Constitution

OUR PHYSICAL body is constituted of the five chief elements, which compose even the whole universe. The skin, flesh, and bones show earth properties; and the blood, perspiration, and saliva represent the water element. The heat in the body and the digestive fire in the system denote the fire element. The breath and its inner work within the body, which enable us to stretch and contract, and the power of movement, which does not allow us to keep still for one moment, represent the air element. The ether element in us is that which controls our activities and gradually consumes all other elements. It is for this reason that a child is more active, while an aged person is still and inclined to inactivity.

The above is a rough explanation of the different parts of the body representing the different elements. They correspond in the following way: the bones with the earth element; the flesh with the water; the blood with the fire; the skin with the air; the hair with the ether.

Bone is as void of sensation as the earth. The shrinking and swelling of the muscles, the festering of the flesh, and the effect of water on it both inwardly and outwardly, prove that the flesh corresponds to the water element. The circulation of the blood depends absolutely upon the degree of heat; it flows as the fire element makes it. The air influences the skin. In hot weather the skin becomes darker, and in cold fairer; in rough weather it becomes rough, and in fine weather smooth. All different shades of the skin are mainly due to the climatic conditions of our place of birth and dwelling. The hair corresponds with the ether and is the least sensitive. If the hair is cut or burned there is no sensation.

The outlet of each different kind of refuse is caused by a

certain element. The motion is caused by earth; urination by the water element; perspiration by fire; saliva by air; semen by ether.

ii

The Mystical Significance of the Body

Man's body may be divided into two parts: the head and the body. The head represents Shuhud, the spiritual part, and the body represents Wujud, the material part. In the former, from the crown of the head to the chin is the expressive part; in the latter, the upper half of the body is the expressive part.

Two parts of the body, the brain and the heart, are considered to be the most important factors, for the scientist thinks that the brain thinks and the orthodox believes that the heart feels. In the view of the Sufi, both are wrong in a way and right in a way. In fact it is not that the brain thinks, but the brain is the means by which the mind distinguishes thought in its concrete form; just as the piano does not compose, but the composer tries his composition on the piano and makes it clear to himself. It is not the camera which takes the photograph, but the light and the plate. The camera is the medium for both, and so it is with the brain. By disorder in the brain, the scientist says, man becomes unsound in mind. But the Sufi holds that nothing is wrong with the mind; it is the instrument through which the mind functions that is out of order.

The same misconception exists among those who believe that the heart feels. The heart, being the centre of the body, partakes of the effect of the feeling from within—which is the real heart, not the piece of flesh—and it feels suffocated and oppressed. Depression is felt as a heavy load upon the breast; and when the heavy vibrations are cleared, then especially a person has a feeling of joy and his heart is lighter than usual. This explains the *Shaqq-i sadr*, the opening of Mohammad's breast by the angels, when fear, gloom, bitterness, and conceit were all cleared away before the manifestation of divine revelation. It is as the darkness clearing away at the rising of the sun.

As the brain is the instrument of the mind which is invisible, and the heart of flesh is the vehicle of the heart within which is above substance, so it is the illumination of the soul, our invisible being, whose light is reflected within this physical body. When active it beams through the eyes, through the radiance of the countenance, charging the whole environment with a magnetic atmosphere. This light being originated from sound, both light and sound echo in the dome of the temple of this physical body, though neither in reality belongs to it. To the Sufi, the seeker of the self within, they are vouchsafed when he has control over the gateways of this holy temple, the physical body. Then, instead of reflecting outward through the expression, the light and sound both manifest within.

iii

The Nature of the Senses and Their Organs

There are five senses: sight, hearing, smell, taste, and touch. The senses of sight and hearing are the principal ones, and of these two the principal is the sense of sight. The sense of touch is perceived through the medium of the skin, which represents the earth element, and is sensitive to cold and heat. The sense of taste is perceived through the medium of the tongue, which represents the water element; all salt, sour and sweet, pungent and bitter tastes are distinguished by it. The sense of smell is perceived through the medium of the nose, the channel of the breath, which alone can distinguish the odours and fragrances. The sense of hearing represents the air, and is perceived through the medium of the ears. The sense of sight represents ether, and is perceived through the medium of the eyes, which in this material body are the substitute of the soul.

Each sense has its dual aspect, Jelal and Jemal, the strong and the gentle aspects of life, which are represented by the right and left side, their action being expressive and responsive. Therefore, although the sense of sight is one, the eyes are two; the sense of hearing is one, but the ears are two; the sense of smell is one, and the nostrils two. So it is with every sense. It is this dual aspect in nature which has caused the distinction of sex, for in spirit the human is human, but as it approaches the surface it becomes either male or female. The myth of Adam and Eve expresses this to those who know: Eve coming out of Adam's rib means that two came out of the one Spirit.

In reality there is but one sense, and it is the direction of its experience which is perceived through a particular channel. This being so, each experience is different from the other. Therefore we may call this sense the five senses, although in reality it is one.

Whichever element predominates in a person's nature, the sense relative to that element in him is the most active. And as breath changes so many times throughout the day and night, its element acts in accordance with the senses. This is the cause of every demand of the senses. He who indulges in any one of the senses makes that sense dull, just as attar, kept all the time near oneself, dulls in time the sense of smell, although it enslaves one to the smell of attar. The same is the case with all senses. The Sufi, therefore, experiences life through the senses for the sake of experience and not for indulgence, the former being mastery and the latter slavery.

iv

The Source of Bodily Desires

The source of our bodily desires is one: the breath. When the breath leaves the body all desires leave it also; and as the breath changes its elements, and the elements—earth, water, fire, air, and ether—predominate in the breath by turns, this being caused by the different grades of activity in the breath, so the desires change. Therefore in a certain climate one feels hungry, and in certain weather one feels thirsty, because the influence of weather on the breath kindles in the breath more of a certain element.

The constitution of a person has a great deal to do with his bodily desires. Naturally a healthy person is often hungry and thirsty; and the unhealthy person, under the garb of piety, may say, 'How material he is!'

All bodily desires show in the physiognomy of a person; and there is no desire without the influence of a particular element behind it. Besides, everybody has a certain element predominant in his physical being, and other elements in a greater or lesser degree. Upon this each person's habits and desires depend.

The following elements and desires correspond:

Elements in the breath	*Desires*
Earth	motion
Water	urination
Fire	thirst
Air	appetite
Ether	passion

There is always a possibility of confusing desire with avidity, which is not a bodily desire, but the desire of the mind that has experienced its joy through the bodily desire. Even in the absence of the bodily desire, the mind demands and forces the body to desire. In this aspect every bodily desire is out of place and undesirable, and enslaves one.

The soul, during the satisfaction of every bodily desire, descends to earth from above. That is what the myth of Adam and Eve explains, when they were driven out from the heavens and sent down to earth. This tells the seer that heaven is the plane where the soul dwells freely in its own essence and is self-sufficient, and that the earth is the plane where the soul experiences the passing joys through the satisfaction of bodily desires depending upon external objects.

The soul becomes captive in this physical body, which is subject to death and decay, and forgets the freedom and peace of its original abode. That is why at times Sufis experience the satisfaction of desires, and at times abstain by the power of will, to allow the soul to experience its original joy, being in its own essence, independent of mind and body. By doing so the soul knows its first and last dwelling-place, and it uses the body, its earthly abode, to experience life on earth. It is as undesirable, according to the Sufi's point of view, to kill the bodily desires by absolute or partial renunciation, as to over-indulge them and enslave one's life to them. The Sufi means to possess the desires, not to be possessed by them.

V

The Source of Emotions

The source of our emotions is our breath, whose impurity brings confusion, and whose purity produces radiance. As the breath changes from one to the other element it produces in us an inclination towards a certain emotion; but according to the power of our will we control or give in to its unruly expression.

Every emotion has its colour and its savour. One emotion develops into the other, since the proportion of activity of mind, in its increase and decrease, produces emotions. No emotion is undesirable so long as it is under the power of the will, but when uncontrolled even the least effect of it is a sin. Fear has the influence of the earth element; affection has the effect of the water element; anger has the effect of the fire element; humour has the effect of the air element; and sadness has the effect of the ether element.

The nature of the elements is like colours; light in the colour makes it pale and darkness in the colour makes it deep. So is it with the emotions: the light of intelligence makes them faded, and the lack of intelligence makes them deeply felt. With light, the influence of the earth element produces caution; the influence of water with light produces benevolence; the fire element with light produces ardour; the influence of air with light produces joy; and ether with light produces peace.

If you give in to an emotion, even only once in a while, remember that the other emotions, to which you may never wish to give in, will also overpower you; because it is one energy which assumes, by the influence of different elements, the garb of different emotions. In fact it is one emotion. By controlling ourselves we control all things in the world.

VI

The Constitution of the Mind

The mind is composed of five faculties. Even as our hand has five fingers, the physical world has five chief elements which constitute it. As ether is an element separate from earth, water, fire, and air, and yet contains all these elements, so is the faculty which we call heart a faculty separate from the remaining four; and yet it contains the four faculties within itself.

The special work of the heart is to feel and to produce emotions out of itself. The second faculty is mind; its work is to think and to produce thoughts. The third faculty is memory; its work is to collect and to supply impressions. The fourth is reason; its work is to discriminate and to decide things. The fifth faculty is the ego, which makes one think of one's own person, and all else as a separate entity.

The word 'heart' in metaphysics denotes the main centre of the mental plane. The piece of flesh which we term heart is the sensitive part in us which feels the effect of all joy and pain before any other organ; and from this centre the breath carries on the work of spreading all energy throughout the physical body. That is why the Sufi works through this centre in the physical body when he wishes to impress his absolute self with a certain thought; but high development lies in purifying the five faculties before mentioned by the mystical process and in mastering them.

vii

The Influence of the Mind upon the Body, and of the Body upon the Mind

It is difficult at the first thought to say whether it is the impression of the external part of ourselves which forms the mind, or if it is the impression of the inner part which forms the body. In reality both do their work: body makes mind and mind makes body. The mind makes a stronger impression upon the body, and the body makes a clearer impression upon the mind. The thought of illness brings illness to the body; the thought of youth and beauty develops these qualities; at the same time cleanliness of body helps to bring purity to the mind; strength of body gives courage to the mind.

Every change in the muscles and features takes place under the influence of the mind. In other words the mind 'points' the picture of the body, its vehicle in life. Wrath, hatred, jealousy, prejudice, bitterness, and all evil thoughts work upon one's physical self even before manifesting themselves. In the muscles of the features, in his face, every person shows his follies, which can never be veiled from the eyes of the seer. So it is with love, kindness, appreciation, sympathy, and all good thoughts and feelings. All show in one's face and form, and give evidence of one's goodness against a thousand accusations.

Sin and virtue would have no effect upon a person if the mind did not take impressions; nor would good and evil thoughts work on the external body if impressions were erased from the mind immediately. The sages in the East have, therefore, mastered concentration, that by its help they might be able to wipe off all that is undesirable, since it is human to err. But one arrives at this power by collecting all the good one can in the mind, so that evil may be naturally repulsed. By constantly doing so one acquires mastery.

viii

The Soul in Itself Alone

The soul in itself alone is no other than consciousness, which is all-pervading. But when the same consciousness is caught in a limitation through being surrounded by elements, in that state of captivity it is called soul.

The Chinese use the simile of a bee when describing the soul. It is symbolical, and really denotes the eye, the pupil of which is like a bee; in other words the nature of the soul may be studied in the nature of the eye. All things exposed to the eye are reflected in it for the moment, and when the eye is turned away the reflection is in it no more. It had received it for the moment only.

Such is the nature of the soul. Youth, age, beauty, ugliness, sin, or virtue, all these are before the soul when they are exposed to it during the physical or mental existence; and the soul, interested in the reflection, may be for the time attracted and bound by the object reflected; but as soon as the soul turns away it is free from it. Amir Minai, the Hindustani poet, says, 'However fast I am bound by earthly ties, it will not take a moment to break them. I shall break them by changing sides.'

Every experience on the physical or astral plane is just a dream before the soul. It is ignorance when it takes this experience to be real. It does so because it cannot see itself; as the eye sees all things, but not itself. Therefore the soul identifies itself with all things that it sees, and changes its own identity with the change of its constantly changing vision.

The soul has no birth, no death, no beginning, no end. Sin cannot touch it, nor can virtue exalt it. Wisdom cannot open it up, nor can ignorance darken it. It has been always and always it will be. This is the very being of man, and all else is its cover, like a globe on the light. The soul's unfoldment comes from its own power, which ends in its breaking through the ties of the lower planes. It is free by nature, and looks for freedom during its captivity. All the holy beings of the world have become so by freeing the soul, its freedom being the only object there is in life.

IX

The Soul with Mind

The soul with mind is as water with salt. Mind comes from soul as salt from water; and there comes a time when mind is absorbed in soul, as salt dissolves in water. Mind is the outcome of soul, as salt is the outcome of water. Soul can exist without mind, but mind cannot exist without soul. But the soul is purer without mind, and is covered by the mind.

The mind covering the soul is as a globe: a sinful mind makes the soul sinful, a virtuous mind makes the soul virtuous, not in nature but in effect, as a red globe on the light makes the light red, and a green globe makes it look green, though in reality the light is neither green nor red; it is void of colour, colour being only its garb.

The soul becomes happy when there is happiness in the heart; it becomes miserable when there is misery in thought. The soul rises high with the height of imagination; the soul probes the depths with the depth of thought. The soul is restless with the restlessness of the mind, and it attains peace when the mind is peaceful. None of the above conditions of mind changes the soul in its real nature, but for the time being it seems to be so. The soul is a bird of paradise, a free dweller in the heavens. Its first prison is the mind, then the body. In these it becomes not only limited, but captive. The whole endeavour of a Sufi in life is to liberate the soul from its captivity, which he does by conquering both mind and body.

X

The Soul with Mind and Body

The body is the vehicle of the mind, formed by the mind; as the mind, which is the vehicle of the soul, is formed by the soul. The body, in other words, may be called a vehicle of the vehicle. The soul is the life and personality in both. The mind seems alive, not by its own life, but by the life of the soul. So it is with the body, which appears alive by the contact of the mind and the soul; when both are separated from it, it becomes a corpse.

The question whether the mind works upon the body or the body works upon the mind may be answered thus: it is natural that the mind should work upon the body, but usually the body works upon the mind. This happens when a person is drunk or when he is delirious with fever. In the same way the relation of the soul and the mind may be understood: it is natural that the soul must work on the mind, but usually the mind works upon the soul.

The mind cannot do more than create an illusion of joy or sorrow or knowledge or ignorance before the soul; and what the body can do to the mind is only to cause a slight confusion for the moment, to accomplish its own desire without the control of the mind. Therefore all sin, evil, and wrong is what is forced from the body on the mind and from the mind on the soul; and all that is virtuous, good, and right is that which comes from the soul to the mind and from the mind to the body. This is the real meaning of the words in Christ's prayer, 'Thy will be done, on earth as it is in heaven'. It means in other words, 'What Thou thinkest in the soul the mind should obey, and what Thou thinkest in the mind the body should obey'; so that the body may not become the commander of the mind, and the mind may not become the leader of the soul.

The soul is our real being, through which we realize and are conscious of our life. When the body, owing to loss of strength and magnetism, has lost its grip upon the mind, the seeming death comes; that which everybody calls death. Then the soul's experience of life remains only with one vehicle, that is the mind, which contains within itself a world of its own, photographed from one's experience on earth on the physical plane. This is heaven if it is full of joy, and it is hell if it is filled with sorrow. Feebleness of mind, when it loses its grip on the soul, is purgatory. When the mind has lost its grip, that is the end of the world for that soul. But the soul is alive; it is the spirit of the eternal Being, and it has no death. It is everlasting.

CHAPTER II

THE EXPERIENCE OF THE SOUL

i

The Experience of the Soul through the Body

THE SOUL experiences life through both mind and body. Without the mediation of the mind the body would be incapable of acting as a proper vehicle of the soul. To put it plainly, the mind is the vehicle of the soul and the body is the vehicle of the mind. Many believe that the brain thinks and the heart feels; but in reality the brain enables the mind to think concretely, and the physical heart enables the heart, the factor of feeling, to feel clearly.

The soul stands aloof as a mirror in which every activity of the mind and the body is reflected. The soul accomplishes its purpose through these vehicles, the purpose that it has set before itself from the beginning of its manifestation. As great as is the purpose, so great is the strength that the soul applies to its fulfilment; and as fine as is the purpose, so fine does the intelligence become for its accomplishment. This is very well said by Sa'di, 'Every soul is born for a certain purpose, and the light of that purpose has been kindled in this soul.'

ii

The Experience of the Soul through Other Beings

In this subject the first thing that we must understand is that the soul is an undivided portion of the all-pervading consciousness. It is undivided because it is the absolute Being; it is completely filled with the whole Existence. The portion of it that is reflected by a certain name or form, becomes comparatively more conscious of the object reflected in it than of all other objects. Our mind and body, being reflected upon a portion of the all-pervading consciousness, make that part of consciousness an individual soul, which in reality is a universal spirit. This individual soul experiences the external world through the medium of the bodies reflected in it, namely our mind and body.

If we think of another thing or being, forgetting our self, that thing or being becomes reflected in our soul. We ourselves become that thing or being which is reflected at that moment in our soul, and we know all about the thing or being reflected in our soul; more than we know about our self, which is in reality not our self.

It is this mystery which accounts for telepathy, thought-reading, spirit obsession, and spirit communication. By focusing our soul with responsive mind on the mind of another we read his thought; by focusing our soul with expressive mind we send a telepathic message. When a spirit focuses his soul with expressive mind upon the mind of another, it obsesses another. When we focus our soul with expressive mind, we communicate with and help the spirit on the other side; when we focus our soul with responsive mind to a spirit, we get spirit messages.

We can learn from our murshid, be inspired by a prophet, or become illuminated by the light of God without study, practice, or any effort on our part, if we only know how to focus our soul rightly in any direction desired.

iii

The Experience of the Soul through Other Things

So long as the soul has not awakened to its majesty, it is full of poverty, which is caused by its limitations. The things upon which man depends in life, and the things that man admires and wishes to possess, seem so far from his reach; not because his soul has short arms which cannot reach, but because his soul is captive in the physical body and only knows how to work with the material arms, which cannot reach further than one yard's length.

The other reason for the soul's disappointment through life is that it disconnects itself from the things and beings around it, concentrating upon the limited vehicles, the mind and body which are focused on it, and through which it experiences life. It calls these 'my individual self', thus limiting its far-reaching power and intelligence.

When the soul awakens, then no being, no thing is far from its reach, and as it becomes more capable of seeing through man, so it becomes capable of seeing through things also. In this way the soul sees through all things and knows their use, their purpose in life, and uses them for their best purpose in life.

The soul not only knows things and the secret of their nature, but it can attract things, it can construct and it can destroy things; its power is much greater than words can ever explain.

Those who cannot see, but believe by the external evidences, to them the soul is as if dead, and they are as limited as their limited body. Those who realize God, the all-knowing and almighty, and realize His intelligence and power in their soul, they, according to their evolution and power in life, inherit the power and intelligence of the heavenly Father. Rumi says, 'Earth, water, fire, and air seem things to men, but to the seer they seem living beings, waiting every moment to carry out the command of their Lord, the God of the universe.'

iv

The Experience of the Soul through the Mind

The mind has five faculties: the faculty of feeling (heart), the faculty of thinking (mind), the faculty of reasoning (consciousness), the faculty of remembering (memory), the faculty of identifying (ego).

The soul is like a light in this five-cornered room, for the soul perceives feeling, thought, memory, reason, and identity, and identifies itself with them. In reality it is aloof from them; change of feeling or thought does not change the soul. But as the soul cannot see itself, it thinks, by the help of the ego: I am sad, or I am glad, or I remember, or I have forgotten. The soul does none of these things; they are all the workings of the mind; but as the soul does not see itself, it identifies itself with what it sees at this time.

It is a fact that the light of the soul keeps the mind in working order. When its light is covered all confusion in life comes; and all intuitions and inspirations come as the soul discloses its light. When the mind is not in order the soul cannot perceive things rightly, the mind is like a telescope before the soul. Therefore both things are necessary: the mind in order, and the soul in perfect focus on the mind.

V

The Experience of the Soul through Other Beings

The mind is like a mirror, and every thought coming into the mind is reflected in this mirror. If a mirror with a reflection in it is focused on another mirror, the same reflection will be found in that mirror.

So it is with the mind. For the mystic who has developed enough to do it rightly, it is a simple task to take the reflection of the mind of another, or to throw the reflection of his own mind on the mind of another. The former is called thought-reading, the latter is called mental suggestion; and by developing this power a person can communicate not only with the living, but even with spirits. The question is who should do so and who should not do so. If it is not advisable for a little child to go in a crowd, that does not mean that the same should be applied to a grown-up person. Therefore the unselfish and wise may learn this in order to make the best use of this attainment.

VI

The Experience of the Soul through the Heart

The heart is as a globe covering the light of the soul, and its different emotions are different colours of this globe. Every emotion is produced by a certain element. While experiencing life through the heart, the soul at that moment thinks: I am sad, or glad, or afraid, or humorous. In fact it is its momentary experience. When the influence of a particular element is changed the emotion has expired and the soul is as pure as it was before. Nothing touches it. It is pure by nature and it always remains pure. If ten people in turn look in a mirror, the mirror shows everyone his face reflected in it and it is clear enough to take every other reflection. In the end the mirror is as clear as before; no face that has ever been reflected in it has left an impression on it.

There are nine different emotions which the soul experiences through the heart, and these are influenced by corresponding elements, thus:

Emotions	*Elements*
Humour	air
Joy	ether
Sorrow	earth
Fear	ether and air
Pity	water
Courage	fire and air
Indifference	ether, fire, and earth
Passion	fire
Anger	fire and air

vii

The Experience of the Soul through the Heart of Another

The soul sometimes experiences life through the heart of another. In the case of a living person it is only done when he is master of harmony and concentration. But a spirit that has left its body on earth and passed away to the other side becomes master, for it has one vehicle less of the many vehicles that keep the spirit captive.

The secret of experiencing through another person's heart is to focus one's own heart on the heart of the other. This is easily done by love, and sometimes by concentration, but concentration and love combined give mastery over it. The heart is pictured by the mystics as a mirror, and as the reflections of one mirror can be reflected in another mirror, so it is with hearts. The heart which perceives reflection from the other heart should be without any reflections in it, by which is meant it should be pure from any other thought or feeling at the time. But the heart which throws the reflection has a much more difficult part to play. It has to force its own reflection through a heart which may perhaps be full of reflections.

Therefore reading the thoughts of another, or knowing the feeling of another, is not so difficult as sending a thought to another or expressing one's feeling to another. It requires strength of will, good concentration, and the right way of directing the reflection, with fineness or purity of thought and feeling.

viii

The Experience of the Soul through the Spirit

The soul has two different sides and two different experiences. One side is the experience with the mind and body, the other side is the experience of the spirit. The former is called the outer experience, the latter the inner experience. The nature of the soul is like glass, transparent; and when one side of the glass is covered it becomes a mirror. So the soul becomes a mirror in which the outer experiences are reflected when the other side is covered.

That is why, however greatly blessed a person may be with outer knowledge, he is not necessarily gifted with inner knowledge. In order to attain to inner knowledge the Sufi covers the other side of the soul, so that its mirror part may face the spirit instead of the outer world. As soon as he is able to accomplish this he receives inspirations and revelations.

There are people who are by nature intuitive; they are sometimes called psychic or clairvoyant. It is accounted for by the other side of their soul naturally facing the spirit within. One may call them extraordinary or exceptional, but not mystical; for the mystic does not desire that position. By concentration and meditation he gains such a mastery that he can cover the soul from without to take the reflection within, and he can cover the soul from within when he requires the reflection from the outer world to its full extent. Balance is desirable, and mastery is the goal to be attained.

ix

The Experience of the Soul through the Spirit of Another

The soul experiences life through one's own spirit and also through the spirit of another, sometimes consciously, but mostly unconsciously.

It is not only in obsession that the soul experiences through the spirit of another; on the contrary it is the spirit of another that experiences through one's own spirit in obsession. Thought-reading, knowing the feeling of another, receiving sympathetic impressions upon oneself, all these things are the experiences of our soul through the spirit of another.

Then there are dreams of strange character, thoughts that do not belong to us, and different feelings that come for no reason. These are nothing but the experiences of our soul through the spirit of another. It is difficult to achieve such an experience consciously, though one often has it unconsciously. The man who can experience consciously through another person's spirit has solved one of life's great problems, for to do this he must have been able to efface his limited individuality from his soul. He is already on the journey to perfection, for in time his soul becomes the soul of all.

X

The Experience of the Soul through the Abstract

All things that manifest before the mind, such as thoughts and feelings, are in time born on the surface in the world of action, where they are called deeds. And those who cannot see them are sometimes quite unaware of the totally different form they take in their outward manifestation.

Sometimes they come before a person's eyes, and sometimes they manifest far from his notice. Those who dive deep within themselves can, when they touch the plane of the abstract, perceive things that are preparing to manifest through the mind on to the surface. But the primitive state of these things is so indistinct even to the seer, that unless he knows the language of that sphere he cannot understand what his experiences convey, though they are undoubtedly true in their effect. It is just as difficult as to read a line of fate.

In Sufi terms such experiences are called *Anvar* and *Ansar*. In them lies the secret of prophecy. The first experience is perceived by the ears of the soul, so to speak, for the first experience is audible, while the second experience is visible. And yet it is not audible to the ears nor is it visible to the eyes. The audible experience is called clairaudience, and the visible clairvoyance, although these words are misused by those who falsely claim these experiences.

CHAPTER III

THE DESTINY OF THE SOUL

i

THE JOURNEY TO THE GOAL

PEOPLE have different motives for attaining knowledge. Some attain it to gain power, occult or psychic, some for inspiration, and some out of curiosity, to see if there is really something behind the wall that stands between human perception and the life unseen.

In reality, none of these motives are true ones to have for spiritual attainment. Life in the world may be likened to a journey, and the real desire of the soul is to reach the goal. The soul is the point whence life starts and where it ends; and all religions at different times have taught man the way that seemed most desirable, the way to make his journey easy and joyful. One person goes to Mecca on horseback, the other riding on a camel, another travelling on foot. The experience and joy of each is different, though all journey to the same goal. So it is with us. All the virtuous and wicked and wise and foolish among us tread the same path and reach the same goal in the end; the difference being that some go with closed eyes and some with open, some on the back of an elephant, and some, weary and worn, journey on foot.

The mystics, therefore, try by the study and practice of the deeper side of life to make this path of life's journey smooth. Amir says, 'Beware, O travellers, the path has many charms; men and robbers and thieves are all along this path'. The real robbers and thieves are our attachments and temptations that rob us of our life, every moment of which is an invaluable privilege, thus bringing to us all disappointments and sorrows, which are not natural and do not belong to us. The path of this journey is within ourselves; just like the wide space beheld by the eyes, which do not seem more than an inch wide, yet miles of horizon can be reflected in them.

So is the true nature of the soul. It is so wide, and there is a path that runs from the body to the soul, from man to God. A person sitting at the gate will perhaps sit there for a thousand years, and never get to the goal, but he who leaves the gate behind and proceeds further will arrive at the goal by contemplation and meditation.

The Sufi's aim is not power or inspiration, though both come as he proceeds. His only aim is to tread the path until he can arrive at the end. He does not fear how long it may take, he does not worry about what sacrifice he will have to make. He desires one thing alone, be it God or goal, the attainment of which is his perfection.

ii

The Journey to the Goal (*continued*)

Though one sees different desires in different people, yet when one studies them keenly one finds they are all different paths leading to one common goal. When one realizes this one's accusations, complaints, and grudges cease at once. However, there is also a natural tendency in man to find the easiest and quickest path to reach the desired goal, and there is also the tendency to share his pleasure, happiness, or comfort with others, and it is this that prompted the prophets and reformers to help mankind on its journey to the goal. Those that follow in their footsteps, forgetting that moral, drag people by the neck to make them follow them, and this has brought about the degeneration of religions.

Christ said, 'In my Father's house are many mansions'; the Prophet has said, 'Every soul has its peculiar religion'; and there is a Sanskrit saying, which perhaps deludes those who do not understand it, but which yet means the same thing: 'As many souls as there are, so many gods are there'.

The Sufi, therefore, never troubles which path anybody takes, Islam or Kafir; nor does he worry which way anyone journeys, the way of evil or of righteousness. For every way to him seems leading to the goal, one sooner and one later, one with difficulty, one with ease. But those who walk with him willingly, trusting in his comradeship, are his mureeds and call him Murshid, and he guides them, not necessarily through the same path he has chosen for himself, but through the path best suited to them.

In reality the goal is already there where the journey begins. It is a journey in name; it is a goal in the beginning and in the end. It is absurd to say, 'How wicked I am . . .' or 'How undeveloped I am for reaching the destination!' or to think, 'How many lives will it take, before I shall be ready to arrive at the goal?' The Sufi says, 'If you have courage and if you have sense, come forward. If now you are on earth, your next step will be heaven.' The Sufi thinks, 'From mortality to immortality I will turn as quickly and as easily as I change sides in sleep.'

iii

The Purpose of Life

A deep study of anything shows the seer that there is a purpose beneath it all. Yet, if one could look beyond every purpose, there would seem to be no purpose. This boundary is called the Wall of Smiles, which means that all purposes of life, which seem at the moment to be so important, fade away as soon as one looks at them from that height called the Wall of Smiles.

But as deeply as the purpose of life can be traced, there seems to be one ultimate purpose working through all planes of life and showing itself through all planes of existence; that is as if the Knower, with His knowing faculty, had been in darkness, desiring to know something; and in order to know something He created all things. Again, it is the desire of the Creator that has been the power which created; and, too, it is the materialized substance of the spirit, a part of Himself, that has been turned into a creation, yet leaving the Creator behind as the absolute Spirit, contantly knowing and experiencing life through all different channels, some developed, some undeveloped for the purpose.

This Knower, through His final creation, man, realizes and knows more than through any other channel of knowledge, such as bird, beast, worm, germ, plant, or rock. This one Spirit, experiencing through various channels, deludes Himself with the delusion of various beings; and it is this delusion which is the individual ego. He experiences, therefore, two things in His delusion: pain and pleasure; pleasure by the experience of a little perfection, and pain by the lack of it. As long as the cover of this delusion keeps His eyes veiled He knows, yet does not know; it is an illusion; He experiences all things, and yet everything is confusion. But as time goes, when this veil becomes thinner and He begins to see through it, the first thing that comes to Him is bewilderment; but the next is knowledge, culminating in vanity, which is the purpose of life.

iv

Self-realization

Life, which is omnipresent and all-pervading, divides itself as it proceeds towards manifestation in the same way that light divides itself when it projects its rays; and although there is originally no purpose in it, every activity and all activities when summed up make a purpose or purposes. In other words, it can be said that purpose comes after the activity, not before; and when it seems to come before, it is the result of previous activity. For instance, it is true that the eyes are made to see, but in reality it is because the eyes can see that seeing is the purpose of the eyes. It is of course a poor example, for nothingness of purpose cannot be traced in objects visible and intelligible; it can only be traced in the origin of things.

The outcome of the whole of manifestation seems to be its knowledge; therefore it is knowledge alone that can be called the purpose of the whole creation. It is not the knowledge of *why* and *where* that can be the purpose of life; it is the knowledge that gives complete satisfaction. There remains no part of one's being that is hungry. There is a feeling of everlasting satisfaction in knowing something that the knower can never put into words.

It is this knowledge that mystics call self-realization, and that is recognized by some religious-minded people as God-consciousness, and by philosophical minds as cosmic consciousness. It is a knowledge which is self-sufficient; and in the moments that a soul holds this knowledge before its view no pain, or suffering, or weakness, or sorrow, or death can touch it. For this knowledge the whole world was created, and with this knowledge the soul's purpose on earth is fulfilled.

V

The Divine Light

The mystical conception that all life is the divine light and the whole creation is made of that light, which is the light of God, has its evidence in all forms of creation. In the mountains and rocks there are not necessarily separate and detached rocks. This shows that in the mineral kingdom life evolves collectively. Evolution may show singleness in the vegetable kingdom, and as every tree may be called single, so every leaf, flower, and fruit may be called single. A flower may be called single, trees and plants attached together may be called single, such as reeds and grass. The development is collective, and yet it shows singleness.

Singleness can be noticed among animals and birds, but individuality is found among men. All this shows the nature of the light: that at the source from which the rays of light start they do not start singly, separate from each other; but it is a collective light; at every step forward it separates, until at its end it takes the form of a separate ray.

Light has two tendencies: to open itself, and to withdraw, which may be likened to birth and death. Also, it has a tendency to narrow itself and to expand. This is like the first tendency, only in a different direction. The former is in the perpendicular direction and the latter activity takes the horizontal direction; and it is this idea which is symbolized in the cross.

These tendencies can be seen in every form, in its length and breadth. There is a certain time in life during which youth grows tall; after that limit, growth will spread in another direction. Therefore the soul is that point of the collective light which stands separate and aloof from other points; but the withdrawal of each ray within naturally enables it to merge into that collective light and life.

vi
THE SOUL

The word 'soul' is used by different people in different senses, but the manner of its connection with the body proves it to be divine. Therefore the Sufi conception of the soul is that it is the divine part in man. The fire that comes from coal or wood is in reality the part of the sun that is in them; and when the soul qualities arise in the heart of a man and show themselves, this proves that it is the divine part in him that rises, like the flame in the fire.

Soul is in all objects, both things and beings, but when it is recognized as soul, then it becomes a soul. It is of the soul that a Persian Sufi has said, 'God slept in the mineral kingdom, dreamed in the vegetable kingdom, awoke in the animal kingdom, and became self-conscious in man.' It is the description of the soul, starting in manifestation as one and manifested in variety.

The reason why one cannot see the soul is that it is the soul that sees all things, and the soul has to become two in order to see itself, and this can never be. As consciousness is realized by being conscious of something, and as intelligence is realized by the knowledge of things, so the existence of the soul can be proved by one's very existence. That part which exists in one, or which makes one existent, that part which sees, conceives, perceives, and is conscious of all things and yet above all things is the soul.

vii
THE DESTINY OF THE SOUL

The destiny of the soul with the mind and the body is a momentary experience when compared with the everlasting life of the soul. The soul with the mind and the body are like three persons travelling together. The difference between them is that one depends for his life upon the other two—that is the body; and one depends upon one for its life—that is the mind; and one does not depend upon either for its life—that is the soul. That is why the spiritual person, who realizes being not as body and mind alone, but as soul independent of body and mind, attains to everlasting life. But for the experience of the external life the soul depends upon the mind, and the mind depends upon the body.

There is no object or being that has no soul, but the word 'soul' is used in ordinary language only for that entity which is conscious of its individual being. The soul is the light, the mind is the furniture, and the body is the room. The furniture could be anywhere, and the room is a fitting place for it; but without light, neither room nor furniture is of any use, nor would life exist without soul.

The mind is created by the soul, yet the soul is independent of the mind; just as the body is created by the mind, but the mind is independent of the body for its life. It is the life of the body which we call life on earth, and it is the life of the mind which we call the hereafter, and it is the life of the soul which we call the life everlasting. Who lives with the body dies with the body; who lives with the mind will live long with the mind, and will die with the death of the mind; but who lives with the soul will live and live for ever. Who lives with his individual self will live so long as his individual self lives, here and hereafter, and who lives with God will live the everlasting life of God. There is a saying of Nanak that, as grain is saved from being ground in the mill by being in the centre, so the worshipper who lives with God is saved from mortality.

viii

The Connection of the Soul with the Mind and the Body

The soul is the originator and producer of the mind, and the mind is also the originator and producer of the body. The soul produces the mind out of its own self; and yet the mind is constructed fully after the formation of the body, and the soul becomes a spirit after the formation of the mind. The soul holds the mind and the mind clings to the soul, as the mind holds the body and the body clings to the mind. The soul holds the mind as long as its activity is constructive, in other words, the soul holds the mind as long as it is engaged in the creative purpose.

When the activity of the soul takes another direction, it withdraws itself from the mind; and as long as the mind has power it still clings to it, though it becomes exhausted as there is no hold on the part of the soul. This can be seen when the aged and ill begin to lose their memory and become uninterested in thinking, speaking, or hearing.

In the same way the mind works with the body. When the mind for some reason or other withdraws its activity, the body becomes disconnected from it, for it loses its hold of the mind. But if the body is still strong and healthy it clings to the mind; soon however it becomes exhausted and this causes death and disease.

Death is mostly caused by the withdrawing of the soul and the mind; it seldom happens that it is caused by the body, its weakness or disorder. When the activity of the soul and the mind is constructive and drawn within, the body with a disease or a disorder continues to live; and the cases where people live for years with disease and pain are the proof of this.

IX

The Radiance of the Soul

The phenomena of the radiance of the soul are apparent to the student of the human body. The body with its perfect mechanism loses power, magnetism, beauty, and brightness, when the soul departs from the body. This shows that the power, magnetism, beauty, and brightness belong to the soul; but since they are expressed through the body, man attributes all this to the physical body.

When we consider power, we see that the hand is not so powerful in weight and strength compared with the weight it can lift. This itself shows that it is not the hand that lifts the weight; it is something behind it. And one can notice that physical power is not the only power, but real power is something else.

As to magnetism, there is no object nor any living creature

that has as much magnetism as man. The magnetism of objects attracts man, but a keen study of life would show that objects are more attracted to man than man is to the objects. If they had only intelligence to show their attraction this fact would be clear to everybody.

There is a superstition in India that some people can light fires better than others, in other words, that fire responds to some more than to others. With plants and flowers one can see the truth of this even more. The touch of some people's hand will make them fade sooner than that of others, and certain people's touch, or even glance, would make them die. Certainly no living creature can feel man's magnetism as much as man, and yet even animals and birds are attracted to man sometimes more than to their own element. This magnetism of man is not necessarily of his physical body; it is his soul.

It is the same with what we call radiance or brightness. It is a light, something which is quite apart from the physical body; and no illness, weakness, or age can take away this brightness, although it must be understood that illness is always caused by the withdrawal of the soul to a certain extent from the body, or by the incapacity of the body to a certain extent to hold the light of the soul.

Sometimes by stretching one's hands and body one feels renewed strength, and brightness come to one's mind and body; sometimes without reason one feels depression and pain in general, and laziness besides, for which no one can suggest a cause, except that the light of the soul closes and discloses itself. When disclosed, brightness, freshness, and strength come; but when closed, depression, darkness, and weakness come. By knowing this we can realize that those who have sacrificed every pleasure, wealth, comfort, or power in life in their pursuit after the soul are justified; for a loss in pursuit of a greater gain is not necessarily a loss. Those who become independent of the physical body by meditation no doubt experience the state of the highest bliss and attain the everlasting life.

X

THE RADIANCE OF THE SOUL (*continued*)

The heart of man is like a globe over the light of the soul. When the globe is dusty, naturally the light is dim; when it is cleaned, the light increases. In fact the light is always the same; it is the fault of the globe when it is not clear. When this radiance shines out, it shows itself not only through the countenance and expression of a man, but even in the man's atmosphere. The soul-power, so to speak, freely projects outward, and the surroundings feel it. The radiance of the soul is not only a power, but it is an inspiration too. A man understands better; there is less confusion; and if he is absorbed in the contemplation of something, be it art, science, music, poetry, or philosophy, he can get inspirations clearly, and the secret of life and nature is revealed to him.

Love is the best means of making the heart capable of reflecting the soul-power—love in the sense of pain rather than as pleasure. Every blow, it seems, opens a door in the heart whence the soul-power comes forth. The concrete manifestations of the soul-power can be witnessed in the depth of the voice, in the choice of words, in the form of a sentence or a phrase, in every movement, pose, gesture, and especially in the expression of the man; even the atmosphere speaks, though it is difficult for everyone to hear it.

The heart may be likened to soil. Soil may be fertile or a barren desert, but the soil which is fertile is that which bears fruit. It is that which is chosen by living beings to dwell in, although many are lost in the soil of the desert, and lead in it a life of grief and loneliness. Man has both in him, for he is the final manifestation. He may let his heart be a desert, where everyone abides hungry and thirsty, or he may make it a fertile and fruitful land, where food is provided for hungry souls, the children of the earth, strong or weak, rich or poor, who always hunger for love and sympathy.